Native Americans of New England

Native Americans of New England

Christoph Strobel

PRAEGER®

An Imprint of ABC-CLIO, LLC
Santa Barbara, California • Denver, Colorado

Library of Congress Cataloging-in-Publication Data

Names: Strobel, Christoph, author.
Title: Native Americans of New England / Christoph Strobel.
Description: Santa Barbara, California : Praeger, 2020. | Includes bibliographical
    references and index.
Identifiers: LCCN 2019057379 (print) | LCCN 2019057380 (ebook) |
    ISBN 9781440866104 (cloth) | ISBN 9781440866111 (ebook)
Subjects: LCSH: Indians of North America—New England—History.
Classification: LCC E78.N5 S77 2020 (print) | LCC E78.N5 (ebook) |
    DDC 974.004/97—dc23
LC record available at https://lccn.loc.gov/2019057379
LC ebook record available at https://lccn.loc.gov/2019057380

ISBN: 978-1-4408-6610-4 (print)
        978-1-4408-6611-1 (ebook)

24 23 22 21 20   1 2 3 4 5

This book is also available as an eBook.

Praeger
An Imprint of ABC-CLIO, LLC

ABC-CLIO, LLC
147 Castilian Drive
Santa Barbara, California 93117
www.abc-clio.com

This book is printed on acid-free paper ∞

Manufactured in the United States of America

For Kristin, Lora, and Anne

Contents

Introduction

Beyond the Mayflower—*Indigenous Peoples in New England*

In early September 1620 an aging and relatively typical 17th-century merchant ship with square-rigged sails and three masts, looking a bit like a floating castle, left the English harbor of Plymouth to sail across the Atlantic. Early in November after an arduous and turbulent journey, the vessel, called the *Mayflower*, arrived on the tip of Cape Cod. Finding this location not satisfactory to start a colony—or, in the parlance of the day, a "plantation"—the passengers and crew of the *Mayflower* looked farther west in Cape Cod Bay. A few weeks after their arrival in the region, they ultimately chose a place that the colonists called Plymouth (located about 40 miles south of the modern city of Boston). The 102 people who had survived the Atlantic crossing faced a new challenge—a New England winter. Their prior life in England had not prepared them for the harshness of this experience. A number of colonists and sailors suffered from disease, and 45 died. Yet despite the tribulations, the colony survived.

The story of the *Mayflower* and the creation of "Plymouth Plantation" maintains a strong hold on the American imagination and popular culture, which in the United States is commemorated every fourth Thursday in November during the Thanksgiving holiday. The celebratory meal that many families all over the United States hold, at times without knowing its origins, supposedly commemorates a feast of thanksgiving for the harvest that the colonists had in the fall of 1621. The actual celebration, whatever its reasons, included the Puritans of Plymouth Colony and some of their Wampanoag neighbors, several of whom had taught the English how to farm and survive in the new land. In later years, the tradition of the meal continued among some New English families and spread beyond the region. It was Abraham Lincoln, however, who turned Thanksgiving into a public holiday during the American Civil War, hoping that this celebration would help to create unity among Americans in divisive times. Through this political maneuver, Thanksgiving gradually became part of the country's historic memory and patriotic imagination. To this day in many preschools and primary schools throughout New England and the United States, children dress up as Pilgrims and sometimes still as Indians, often learning a message about sharing and getting along, which is a simplified and partial lesson about the history of the founding of Plymouth Colony, to say the least. Many Americans see the establishment of a Puritan colony, celebrated at Thanksgiving, as the founding event of America.[1] This narrative is not only highly suspect but also ignores the creation of Jamestown as the first permanent English colony in North America in 1607 in what is today the state of Virginia, not to speak of the various Spanish, French, and Dutch North American colonies that had been established before Plymouth.

The indigenous peoples on whose lands the English moved are too often a marginal or neglected part of the national Thanksgiving story and the founding myth of America, even though their history, as this book explores, is ancient and complex and continues into the present. The Puritans did not move into a "wilderness," as the conventional accounts often maintain. In fact, when the English colonists founded Plymouth they moved right onto the site of a former Native American town called Patuxet. When the founder of the colony of New France (today's Quebec region of Canada), Samuel de Champlain, traveled in coastal New England in 1604, he described Patuxet as a prosperous and vibrant community. Yet, the inhabitants of Patuxet were likely impacted by the epidemics that distressed the indigenous populations of New England and abandoned the settlement. Perhaps they left because of the association of Patuxet with massive mortality or because they needed to find others to establish a new community that was large enough to be viable. Whatever the reason, the Patuxets who survived must have joined towns and communities some distance from their original settlement. The Puritans, like the Patuxet Indians before, understood the value of the settlement site at Plymouth, and the Native Americans had even performed the arduous task of clearing the forest for farm fields. When the passengers arrived at the place now known as Plymouth, they noted evidence of *wetus* (the style of houses built by Native Americans in southern coastal New England), slightly overgrown farm fields, and human remains such as bones and skulls.

Native Americans of New England tells an interpretive history of the peoples who were here before the *Mayflower* and those who have continued to survive in the place that many Native Americans in the region called and continue to call "Dawnland," or "Land of the Dawn." This volume provides a region-wide history of the indigenous peoples of the northeastern corner of the present United States, a region we today call New England that includes the modern states of Connecticut, Maine, Massachusetts, New Hampshire, Rhode Island, and Vermont. *Native Americans of New England* studies the history of the indigenous peoples in a long-term perspective, attempting to reconstruct this past from the earliest available archaeological evidence to the present. The text examines how historic processes shaped and reshaped the lives of indigenous peoples, using case studies, historic sketches, and biographies to tell these stories. Thus, the book does not claim to be a comprehensive history. There are many important events in New England's indigenous history or in the past of individual Native American communities in the region that this book does not discuss or only briefly covers, decisions and choices I had to make to fit this story into one volume. I hope that readers will forgive me these oversights and cases of intellectual neglect. Moreover, while this volume will not turn a blind eye to the horrendous impact that colonization, dispossession, and racism had on the lives of indigenous peoples in New England, it will emphasize Native American resistance, adaptation, and survival under often harsh and unfavorable circumstances.

As the discussion above alludes to, the term "New England" and the region that carries that name is very much a result of the history of colonization in the Americas. Why, then, should this region matter to Native American history? In many ways it should not, as indigenous patterns, lifeways, and cultures predated New England. This is why, necessarily at times, this study incorporates into its analysis the region's connection with its neighboring areas, places we today call New York, the mid-Atlantic, and southeastern Canada. Especially in the precolonial and colonial periods, this culture area, often referred to by researchers as the northern Eastern Woodlands or the Atlantic Northeast, witnessed frequent interactions between and conflicts among its indigenous peoples. That said, because Native Americans in the region have been exposed to European and especially New English colonization, New England as a region has also gained special relevance in the lives of indigenous peoples there. As a result of this history, there exist many commonalities and connections among the Native Americans of the region. Thus, despite differences in the last five centuries, New England's indigenous peoples faced many similar historic challenges, trends, and tendencies.[2]

Native Americans also significantly contributed to New England, U.S., and global culture. Many rivers, lakes, ponds, brooks, mountains, hills, states, towns, and businesses in the region have names that are indigenous in origin. This includes names such as Connecticut, Massachusetts, Niantic, Mystic, Housatonic, Wachusett, and Pawtucket, to just give a few examples. Native Americans of the Eastern Woodlands also introduced Euro-Americans and the world to corn, gourds, beans, pumpkins, sunflowers, and squash as well as such foods as maple syrup, popcorn, and hominy. Tobacco and pipes also have indigenous origins. Moreover, Native Americans had an impact on New

England's transportation culture. Canoes, snowshoes, and toboggans are indigenous inventions, and many of New England's highways, roads, and railroad lines are built on top of Native American pathways.[3]

Native Americans of New England maintains that we cannot understand the history of New England unless we understand Native American contributions to this past. We cannot ignore the central role that indigenous peoples played in shaping the development of the region. It is impossible to understand the precolonial past, the survival of Plymouth Colony, the history of slavery, wars over competition for empire as well as indigenous lands, and the development of the New England economy in such areas as whaling, tourism, canoe building, and logging without understanding the contributions that Native Americans made in these areas. Indigenous people helped to shape New England's past, just as they did the history of the United States. If we write them out of this history, we can only gain a limited and distorted understanding of the past.[4]

There is extensive academic literature on the history of indigenous peoples in New England, much of which focuses on specialized topics especially during the colonial period.[5] Multiple books discuss the individual histories of tribal communities as well as the Native American histories of several of the New England states.[6] While extremely valuable contributions, no single-authored or comprehensive study addresses the complex and diverse histories of the indigenous peoples of New England from the pre-Columbian period to the present.

Native Americans of New England thus disputes the still too widely held myth that Native Americans vanished in New England or that vast swaths of New England, such as Vermont, were empty. How did these myths emerge and gain such popularity? Several historians argue that New English colonists and later generations of New Englanders had to come to terms with the brutal violence against and murder, enslavement, dispossession, removal, and marginalization of the region's indigenous populations. Thus, New Englanders from the 17th century on began to invent convenient narratives of the "vanished Indian." In the minds of many white New Englanders, reflected in much of the literature, writings, and art, Native Americans had simply "disappeared" from New England. Indigenous peoples, the mainstream cultural consent maintained, had been pushed out and replaced by the New English. There is an irony in all of this, of course, as there always was an indigenous presence in New England despite such claims.[7] Historians have formulated several explanations to describe this intellectual process in mainstream New English society. Thomas Doughton, for instance, describes the "forgetting" and the imagined "vanishing" of Native Americans in New England as a "disappearance model."[8] Jean O'Brien, in a detailed study of local New England histories of various towns and cities published in the 19th and early 20th centuries, argues that by "writing Native Americans out of existence in New England," these accounts performed a crucial role in influencing American popular culture and imagination.[9] These archetypal local histories argued that indigenous peoples had "disappeared," even if there remained a Native American presence within many of these towns and in the region. Doughton's and O'Brien's work encapsulates and demonstrates the intellectual hold that such popular views about Native Americans hold on New English mainstream society.

Native Americans of New England is an interpretive history structured into six chapters that examine the continuous presence of indigenous peoples in the region. Chapter 1 examines the archaeological or deep history of the region before 1400 CE. The text demonstrates how the Pleistocene era helped to shape New England's natural landscape and environment, which helped to influence the lifeways that emerged among the native peoples in the region. This chapter also examines the indigenous past of the Paleo, Archaic, and Early Woodland periods. Chapter 2 provides a discussion of the lifeways of indigenous peoples in the 15th century, right on the eve of European colonization. Chapter 3 covers the period from around 1500 to the eve of King Philip's War in the 1670s. Early contacts between various Native American groups and Europeans led to exchange and trade throughout the 16th century. This chapter also examines how English colonization in the 17th century impacted many indigenous societies such as those of the Wampanoag, Pequot, and Massachusetts peoples of southern New England. The European presence aided in the escalation of brutal warfare, the spread of deadly disease, Native American servitude, religious conversion, and the dispossession of indigenous lands. Chapter 4 examines the history of Native Americans of New England from King Philip's War through the American Revolution. King Philip's War had a devastating impact on the Native American communities in southern New England, but it was only the first of a series of destructive wars that shaped the indigenous history of the region for more than 100 years. This chapter scrutinizes, for instance, the role that indigenous peoples such as the various Wabanaki communities played in the wars for empire in New England and New France. Moreover, the chapter surveys the history of Native Americans who lived "behind the frontier" in southern New England. The chapter concludes by examining the role that indigenous people in the region played in the American Revolution. Chapter 5 covers the period following the American Revolution through the mid-20th century. In this era, Native Americans participated in the New England economy in a variety of ways. They also experienced an assault on their remaining landholdings and communities. White New Englanders used arguments about race and identity as a justification for these policies, and Native Americans attempted to resist these developments through political and cultural activism. Chapter 6 surveys the period from the aftermath of World War II to the present. The text considers the political resurgence and activism, the struggle for homelands and federal recognition, the pursuit of economic and cultural revitalization, and the continuous challenges that indigenous peoples in New England face today. Thus, the book emphasizes the ongoing presence of indigenous peoples and their efforts to preserve the integrity and viability of their dynamic and self-directed societies and cultures in New England.

Native Americans of New England is intended to speak to a general audience. I began teaching Native American history in the 1990s, and through the decades many of my students in my Native American history survey courses as well as in my seminars on Native Americans of the northern Eastern Woodland and war and Native Americans in colonial New England asked numerous questions and shared their puzzlements about Native American history in general—and that of New England in particular. Given my 20 years of teaching, there are too many students to be thanked here individually for providing inspiration through their hard work and thoughtful discussions. These experiences continue to inspire me. In conversations with friends, acquaintances, and even the occasional stranger who asked me what I was working on, I learned that many had points of confusion and questions similar to those of my students. These discussions inspired me to write this book. Hopefully, this work will provide some answers to those curious about the subject matter, as it tackles the unique features of New England's indigenous past while attempting to integrate this story into a larger North American and Atlantic world perspective. At the same time, I hope that scholars and teachers of indigenous studies will find this project and its interpretive long-term and interdisciplinary analytical approach of some use as well.

Native Americans of New England would have never seen the light of day if not for the efforts, help, encouragement, and probing of many people. To begin with, this book could not have been written without the work of a large community of researchers who examine New England's indigenous past. Their work established many paths pursued in this book, and the extent of my intellectual debt to them and their influences are acknowledged in the endnotes and the bibliography. Colleagues and mentors have more directly influenced the conceptualization of this study. For three decades now, my teacher and mentor Neal Salisbury has been an inspiration and influence in my pursuits of Native American and global history. I have been blessed with many other mentors and colleagues. These individuals served as role models and inspirations and provided useful suggestions, feedback, and support over many years. I want to especially thank, in alphabetical order, David and Sigrid Anderson, Al Andrea, Kevin Boyle, Joye Bowman, Peter d'Errico, Andrew Frank, John Higginson, Paul Jentz, David Kalivas, Dane Morrison, Alice Nash, Carl Nightingale, David Northrup, and Christine Skwiot. Moreover, my editors at Praeger, Kim Kennedy-White and Michael Millman, provided valuable suggestions, feedback, and support. Of course, all the book's intellectual shortcomings are my fault alone.

The support and curiosity of loved ones deserves a special recognition, as our family lived with this project for many years. As always, my partner Kristin was my first sounding board and critic as she worked her way through the early draft of each chapter. I also owe thanks to my daughters Lora and Anne for providing me with time to work on this project but also for accompanying me to several sites of New England's indigenous past (mostly without too much complaining).

Notes

1. For a recent history that makes this argument, see Nathaniel Philbrick, *The Mayflower: A Story of Courage, Community, and War* (New York: Viking, 2006).

2. Christoph Strobel, "Conquest and Colonization," in *The Routledge Handbook to the History and Society of the Americas*, ed. Olaf Kaltmeier et al., 75–83 (New York: Routledge, 2019).

3. Lucianne Lavin, *Connecticut's Indigenous Peoples: What Archaeology, History, and Oral Traditions Teach Us about Their Communities and Cultures* (New Haven, CT: Yale University Press, 2013), 304–305.

4. On this issue see, e.g., Susan Sleeper Smith et al., eds., *Why You Can't Teach United States History without Native Americans* (Chapel Hill: University of North Carolina Press, 2015); Daniel Richter, *Facing East from Indian Country: A Native History of Early America* (Cambridge, MA: Harvard University Press, 2003).

5. The literature is too vast to be cited here. But for some influential studies see, e.g., Francis Jennings, *The Invasion of America: Indians, Colonialism, and the Cant of Conquest* (Chapel Hill: University of North Carolina Press, 1975); Neal Salisbury, *Manitou and Providence: Indians, Europeans, and the Making of New England, 1500–1643* (New York: Oxford University Press, 1982); Alden T. Vaughan, *New England Frontier: Puritans and Indians, 1620–1675*, 3rd ed. (Norman: University of Oklahoma Press, 1995); William Cronon, *Changes in the Land: Indians, Colonists, and the Ecology of New England* (New York: Hill and Wang, 1983); Daniel R. Mandell, *Behind the Frontier: Indians in Eighteenth Century Eastern Massachusetts* (Lincoln: University Nebraska Press, 1996); Daniel R. Mandell, *Tribe, Race, History: Native Americans in Southern New England, 1780–1880* (Baltimore: Johns Hopkins University Press, 2008); Margaret Ellen Newell, *Brethren by Nature: New England Indians, Colonists, and the Origins of American Slavery* (Ithaca, NY: Cornell University Press, 2015); Andrew Lipman, *The Saltwater Frontier: Indians and the Contest for the American Coast* (New Haven, CT: Yale University Press, 2015).

6. For tribal and community histories see, e.g., Frederick Matthew Wiseman, *The Voice of the Dawn: An Autohistory of the Abenaki Nation* (Hanover, NH: University Press of New England, 2001); Pauleena MacDougall, *The Penobscot Dance of Resistance: Tradition in the History of a People* (Hanover, NH: University of New Hampshire Press, 2004); Laurence M. Hauptman and James D. Wherry, eds., *The Pequots in Southern New England: The Fall and Rise of an American Indian Nation* (Norman: University of Oklahoma Press, 1990); Jean M. O'Brien, *Dispossession by*

Degrees: Indian Land and Identity in Natick, Massachusetts, 1650–1790 (Lincoln: University of Nebraska Press, 1997). See also the collection of essays by Laurie Weinstein, ed., *Enduring Traditions: The Native Peoples of New England* (Westport, CT: Bergin and Garvey, 1994). There are several Native American histories of New England states. However, the studies cited below focus on the pre-Columbian and colonial history and do not have a strong emphasis on either the colonial period or the 19th and 20th centuries. Bruce J. Bourque, *Twelve Thousand Years: American Indians in Maine* (Lincoln: University of Nebraska Press, 2001); Michael Caduto, *A Time before New Hampshire: The Story of a Land and Native Peoples* (Hanover, NH: University of New England Press, 2003); Thaddeus Piotrowski, ed., *The Indian Heritage of New Hampshire and Northern New England* (Jefferson, NC: McFarland, 2002); Lavin, *Connecticut's Indigenous Peoples*; William A. Haviland and Marjory W. Power, *The Original Vermonters: Native Inhabitants, Past and Present*, revised and expanded ed. (Hanover, NH: University Press of New England, 1994).

7. See, e.g., Christine DeLucia, "The Memory Frontier: Uncommon Puritans of Past and Place in the Northeast after King Philip's War," *Journal of American History* 98, no. 4 (March 2012): 975–997; Jill Lepore, *The Name of War: King Philip's War and the Origins of American Identity* (New York: Knopf, 1998).

8. Thomas Doughton, "Unseen Neighbors: Native Americans of Central Massachusetts, a People Who Had 'Vanished,'" in *After King Philip's War: Presence and Persistence in Indian New England*, ed. Colin Calloway, 207–230 (Hanover, NH: University Press of New England, 1997).

9. Jean O'Brien, *Firsting and Lasting: Writing Indians Out of Existence in New England* (Minneapolis: University of Minnesota Press, 2010), xii–xiii.

CHAPTER ONE

A Time before New England

A History of Early Dawnland

This chapter examines the history of the indigenous peoples who lived in the area we today call New England from roughly about 13,000 years ago to around 1000 CE. The New England of today is part of a culture area that archaeologists, anthropologists, and Native American studies scholars refer to as the "northern Eastern Woodlands" as well as the "Atlantic Northeast," two terms that help us to discuss a diverse array of indigenous peoples and places in a regional context. The Native American groups who lived in this region had different ceremonials, languages, and ways of living, but at the same time they also shared many cultural similarities. Categories such as the northern Eastern Woodlands and the Atlantic Northeast help us to gain a better understanding of the Native American past and the trends and tendencies that shaped it. Geographically speaking, these culture areas encompass what are today New England, the mid-Atlantic region, and southeastern Canada and, in the case of the northern Eastern Woodlands, also the Great Lakes region and the Midwest.[1]

Some of the Wabanaki peoples who live in northern New England, a grouping of indigenous nations that includes today's Penobscot, Passamaquoddy, and Maliseet nations as well as several other Native American groups in the northeastern United States, refer to the region we today call New England as "Dawnland," or "Land of the Dawn." This chapter adopts this indigenous nomenclature as a place-name for New England. The name "Dawnland" stems from the region's easterly geographic location on "Turtle Island" (a name used by several indigenous peoples to describe the Americas) because the sun rises there in the morning. Thus, in the minds of many Native Americans in the region, it is one of the first places on Turtle

Island to experience dawn, a fact that earned the region its designation. As a geographic location, Dawnland has various different definitions in regard to the diverse Native American peoples of New England and is not a neatly defined place. For some native groups this space includes, for instance, not only present-day New England but also Long Island and the Hudson River Valley system of present-day New York. To others, Dawnland extends up to the St. Lawrence River Valley in modern-day Canada. All this depends on the kinship, cultural, and exchange networks of a particular group. It is important to remember that for much of their history, the regional, colonial, state, and national borders of today had no relevance to Native Americans, and the peoples of Dawnland defined their space as often reaching beyond the borders of contemporary New England. Moreover, the peoples of Dawnland interacted and had connections with groups from outside of their homelands.

The narrative below also examines what many archaeologists and some historians describe as the "deep history" of Dawnland and explores how Native Americans had lived in the region for thousands of years before European colonization. The chapter sets out by analyzing the archaeological and historical methodologies used to shed light on the Native American past of New England and discusses several indigenous narratives of the creation and the shaping of their worlds. The chapter also examines how the Pleistocene era helped to shape Dawnland's natural landscape, environment, and human history. In addition, this chapter surveys Native American life in the Paleo, Archaic, and Early Woodland periods and how researchers learn about this history.

It is important to emphasize from the outset that the available evidence to reconstruct this history is limited, which makes this an especially difficult story to tell. While limited sources are a common issue faced by those who are trying to uncover the Native American past, it is especially a challenge for those trying to understand the history of the indigenous peoples of Dawnland before 1492. We lack European writings on Native Americans (which despite limitations are so often the main available source to historians of the indigenous past), and the surviving oral historical and archaeological record is limited. Thus, we have only bits and pieces that provide us a glimpse into this world, and it is likely that New England's Native American past of this period will never be fully reconstructed. Thus, much of what is discussed below is based on interpretations of incomplete evidence.

Ethnohistory, Archaeology, and Dawnland

Archaeologists, anthropologists, and other researchers of the Native American past have undertaken many efforts to shed more light on the precolonial history of Dawnland. In their pursuit to gain a better understanding of how the indigenous peoples of Dawnland lived and what their worlds looked like in the past, researchers often use archaeological and historical methods. The critical examination below of the tools that archaeologists and historical researchers use provides us a glimpse into what each disciplinary approach can add to our understanding but also considers some of the limitations of these methodologies. This discussion hopefully underscores how challenging it is to reconstruct the precolonial history of the indigenous people of Dawnland.

Both archaeologists and historians aim to get a better understanding of the past, but they use different forms of evidence. Historians traditionally rely on written texts in their work. They scour archives for letters, documents, land titles, birth and death certificates, and other materials that provide them insights into the past. Furthermore, especially in the context of Native American history, scholars often study accounts that provide them ethnographic information on indigenous peoples. These are often written by European traders, missionaries, colonial officials, soldiers, travelers, and colonists and can provide some insights into Native American cultures and lifeways. These written texts are often drawn upon when scholars try to gain a deeper understanding of the early and precolonial indigenous societies of Dawnland. Many of these narratives were produced in the 16th century and the first half of the 17th century. The passage below underscores some of the issues that relying on European sources can pose. William Bradford, the man who would become the first governor of the earliest successful and permanent New English colony at Plymouth, wrote in 1620 about North America and its indigenous peoples:

Vast & unpeopled countries of America . . . are fruitful & fitt for habitation, being devoyd of all civill inhabitants, where there are only savage & brutish men, which range up and downe, little otherwise than the wild beasts of the same. . . . And also those which should escape or overcome difficulties, should yet be in continual danger of the savage people who are cruell, barbarous, & most treacherous, being contente only to kill, & take away life, but delight to tormente men in the most bloodie maner that may be; fleaing some alive with the shells of fishes, cutting of the members & joynts of others by peesmeale, and grilling on the coles, eate the collop of their flesh in their sight whilst they live; with other cruelties most horrible to be related.[2]

As this quote illustrates, European views and descriptions of Native Americans could be biased, ignorant, and based on fear and could reveal prejudices that were centered on sentiments of chauvinism, cultural superiority, or racism. Moreover, those Europeans who interacted and even lived among Native Americans and were respectful and alert observers were still outsiders and therefore not always completely familiar with Native American customs, traditions, languages, and cultures. Thus, they were not trained ethnographers or archaeologists and often did not fully grasp or misunderstood what they saw or were told by Native Americans. Government documents and missionary writings are rich sources that are also often analyzed by scholars who want to learn about the past. But these sources have limitations as well. They often reveal the same biases mentioned above but, moreover, can also reflect certain self-interests as well as colonial or proselytizing agendas of a state, colony, church, or some other institution. Historians and researchers of Native American history need to be cognizant of these issues in their work. When tackling written Euro-American sources, they need to be critical, judicious, and open-minded and read against the grain.

From an indigenous perspective the reliance on written sources can be problematic, since many Native American peoples of Dawnland for much of their history relied on oral traditions, art, and ceremonies to preserve—and to live—their culture, traditions, and past. Thus, in the last 40 or so years a number of researchers interested in the Native American past have embraced methodologies from different academic fields such as anthropology and archaeology. They not only study written sources but also consult Native American informers and historians who preserve and remember past events and customs, and they collect and study oral traditions and indigenous stories. Of course, as with written documents, one has to be judicious with such sources. Self-interest or blurred memories of events that occurred generations in the past can be misleading. In addition, indigenous studies scholars and historians research indigenous artifacts and material culture and learn about the archaeological methods discussed below. Academics who combine these interdisciplinary approaches are sometimes called ethnohistorians. The field that combines the above-discussed methodologies is called ethnohistory.[3]

Among the indigenous peoples of Dawnland, especially the Native Americans of southern New England, a vibrant literary culture began to gradually emerge by the middle of the 17th century. Writing in the language of the New English colonizers, Native Americans used the written word to provide criticisms of New English colonization and provided alternative views, narratives, and windows into their worlds and the events and forces that shaped their lives. As an increasing number of these indigenous sources are being uncovered, they provide us a much more sophisticated and nuanced perspective of the history of the native peoples in New England.[4]

While written sources have been quite limited in shining a light on ancient Native American history, archaeologists' efforts have been far more productive in this field. In their search to reconstruct the distant past, they examine soil samples, residue, human trash, and other material evidence, often in the form of artifacts (objects made by people) such as tools and pottery or ecofacts (natural objects such as wood, shells, bones, and antlers that human beings adopted in their daily life). Archaeologists also look for evidence of human-made structures such as buildings, hearths, and burial grounds. The diverse archaeological data that researchers uncover in New England is most often in an incomplete or damaged state. Still, a thorough examination of such evidence grants us insights into how the Native Americans of Dawnland lived prior to the colonization of their lands by Europeans, providing a glimpse into their way of life and how their societies adapted and changed but also helping us to appreciate the continuities among the cultures of the indigenous peoples of New England.

Scientific approaches guide and assist archaeologists in their search, description, and interpretation of material evidence. Archaeologists, like scientists in general, do not claim that they uncover an absolute truth in their research. Rather, they operate with degrees of probability and try to reconstruct the most probable scenario or representation of how things were at a certain point in time based on the material evidence they examine. Thus, as an academic discipline, archaeology produces detailed descriptions and analyses of material objects such as spear points, stone tools, and potsherds, which is an important part of the work. There is also a broader purpose to this methodology. In their scholarly analysis archaeologists are especially interested in uncovering patterns of human behavior. This and the next chapter focus less on the descriptive detail provided in much of the archaeological research of Dawnland and instead observe what this evidence tells us about the New England environment, the region's Native American history, and how it changed over time. Readers who want to learn in more detail about the indigenous peoples of Dawnland's archaeological past are encouraged to consult the works cited in the endnotes of this chapter.

Archaeologists, with the interdisciplinary help of academic fields such as geology, geography, and biology, have done much to enhance our understanding of what New England looked like, how the environment and landscape of the region changed over the millennia, and how Native Americans lived in this space. Researchers are able to map the location of long-gone or rerouted bodies of water by studying the landscape for evidence of former shorelines or the existence of river and lake beds that are now dried up. Using various scientific tools, they can also determine the ocean levels at certain points in the history of the region. By studying the geological formation of natural features such as hills, mountains, and plains as well as the distribution of sediment and the location of granite boulders, scientists can get clues about how the New England landscape was formed and how it changed over time. Studying the underwater coastline, researchers can gain an understanding of what those looked like during the late Ice Age and the Paleo Indian period. The now-submerged areas that used to be inland could likely provide further insights into Dawnland's ancient indigenous past. For instance, in the 1970s during a routine dredging operation about 900 feet off Hammonasset Beach in Madison, Connecticut, a work crew came across a material object that turned out to be a fluted spear point from the Paleo Indian period. The fields of archaeobotany or paleoethnobotany, which is the archaeological analysis of plant remains recovered from digs, and palynology (the study of pollen, spores, and microscopic plant and animal structures) also provide a unique glimpse into the ancient history of Dawnland. Through these interdisciplinary methods, which mix archaeological and biological sciences, archaeologists are able to identify plant life (trees, grasses, and other flora) and thus can get a window into what the natural environment looked like throughout the past.

In order to understand how people lived in the past, archaeologists study locations, which they call "sites." These are places where Native Americans of Dawnland left evidence that provides us special insights into their way of life. Sites are often places of former human settlements where archaeologists look for the above-discussed evidence. They can also be places that Native Americans used for the extraction of resources, such as quarries with desirable stones for tool and weapon making, or other places such as desirable hunting and fishing sites.

Archaeologists use several methods to obtain and examine material evidence. The process begins with an excavation of a chosen site, where researchers dig the location in one or many squares that are set up in a grid pattern. The soil is carefully removed and sifted through a very fine screen as the crew searches for organic materials and artifacts, proceeding layer by layer. Found items are cataloged and noted on a map of the dig to show the exact location where they have been found in the site. This careful approach helps archaeologists with the dating of materials but also with figuring out the relationship between different material items, which can provide researchers insights into the former occupants' daily life. Much of this work occurs after the dig in a laboratory when archaeologists apply various techniques of investigation to find out more about the data they have collected during the excavation. During field and lab analysis, as we have already discussed, researchers spend significant time and effort to describe, evaluate, and analyze the physical appearance of the evidence. Archaeologists also try to determine the age of objects pulled out of a site (or ages, as certain locations had continuous or long-term on-and-off occupation for centuries or even millennia). Carbon dating is an important tool for calibrating dates of organic materials pulled out of digs, as scientists can approximate an item's age by measuring the disintegration of carbon 14. Moreover, dendrochronology (a technique of dating that uses tree rings) and thermoluminescence (a process to assess the age of artifacts that have been burned, such as pottery) are additional methods to help in the dating of recovered materials.

Archaeologists also examine how Native Americans in Dawnland maintained contacts with communities outside of their region. Researchers are able to trace to at least some degree that Native Americans traveled and traded by using pathways, roadways, rivers, portages, and coastal waterways. Native Americans followed these corridors in pursuit of food but also to obtain goods, such as workable stones, desirable teeth, shells, animal skins, and many other materials. Material objects can also help archaeologists prove long-distance connections when their style, or the substance they are made out of, indicate a faraway origin. For instance, by using geological techniques, geoarchaeologists can trace the approximate origin of a stone, jasper, or chert that was used by the indigenous inhabitants of Dawnland in their tool making. Furthermore, indigenous communities in New England adapted the pottery-making and tool-making styles of neighboring regions, which again supports the theory that there existed faraway contacts. Thus, the Native Americans of Dawnland, just like Native Americans from all over the Americas, were tied into regional and long-distance exchange networks.

Archaeology has done much to enhance our understanding of the history of Dawnland prior to 1492, but it is not a perfect vehicle to uncover the past. As we will discuss in more detail below, just as there are shortcomings when we use historical methodologies, archaeological evidence and analysis has limitations as well.[5]

The Creation and Shaping of Dawnland

Native peoples in New England have additional ways to make sense of their past, and we continue our exploration in this chapter about the early history of Dawnland by examining the stories that indigenous peoples tell about the creation of their world. The indigenous oral traditions enhance our understanding about the creation and shaping of Dawnland and provide a unique window into the culture, values, and traditions of the Native Americans of New England. The indigenous peoples of Dawnland had divergent accounts about the creation and the shaping of their world as well as their place in it. These stories differ from the explanation of the New English colonizers, who have created different narratives in their own efforts to reconstruct and understand the history before New England. For instance, New English colonists of the 17th century often tried to find biblical explanations to explain the Native American presence and, conveniently, why the English were entitled to Native American lands. In contrast, the indigenous origin stories, while some have been altered over time and many more have been lost, speak of the permanent presence of Native Americans as well as their belonging to the region. These stories provide a deep sense of being embedded in the land—and a sense of home.

The indigenous peoples of Dawnland, today consisting of nations such as the Narrangansett, Pequot, Mohegan, Schaghticoke, Nipmuc, Pennacook, Sokoki, Abenaki, Penobscot, Passamaquoddy, Micmac, and Maliseet, have many stories about the creation and shaping of their world. These stories were handed down from earlier generations and they provide a window into the worlds of their ancestors. Archaeologists, anthropologists, and Native American studies scholars at times refer to the above-mentioned nations as well as several other indigenous groups of the northern parts of the Eastern Woodlands as "Algonquian speakers." Examining linguistic evidence, scholars argue that the languages spoken by these groups are related and that they share a distant origin in a proto-Algonquian language from which all the others emerged. Still, Algonquian speakers hardly thought of themselves as being members of a singular nation. Throughout much of their history the peoples of Dawnland fought conflicts and competed over land and resources, but they also created systems of alliance and kinship and traded and cooperated with each other. Nevertheless, in terms of their cultures, worldviews, and lifeways, the peoples of Dawnland share many commonalities.

The stories that the various peoples of Dawnland tell about the origins of their world vary widely in detail regarding how these processes came about, yet they share certain common features. These narratives usually tell us that the world is created by a powerful supernatural being generally described as a "Great Spirit," a "Creator," or "Manitou" (an Algonquian word that is often translated as "spirit"), which is at the top of a spiritual continuum that is filled with beings that have spirits of varying powers.

After the world is created, the indigenous stories become dominated by culture heroes who helped to shape Dawnland. Some of these characters are wise, while others are foolish. As the examples below underscore, these stories help to explain, for instance, the characteristics of animals, why certain places have certain geographic features, and how individuals should behave toward others. Thus, the purpose of these stories is not just to attempt to explain the world; at the same time, they also teach about moral behavior and perseverance and help to make sense of a world that is often cruel, unfair, and unpredictable.

One such example is the Wampanoag story about how the tribe's culture hero, a giant called Moshup, helped to shape the Aquinnah cliffs, a sacred place for the Wampanoags on the island of Noepe, a place that Americans today call Martha's Vineyard. The cliffs are an important place for the Wampanoags. Moshup was a sachem (the name for a chief in several southern New England communities) who was a leader on the island a long time ago. He loved to eat whale. The stories tell that he could eat an entire creature in one sitting. In order to satisfy his enormous appetite, Moshup would enter the ocean, grab a whale, and throw the large animal against the cliffs to kill it fast so it would not have to suffer. Then he would pick up the animal and broil it for a meal, either for himself or to feed his Wampanoag people. The Wampanoag legends maintain that the reddish colorations that are part of the cliff formations were left by the animals' blood. The Wampanoags also believe that Moshup created many other shapes and features on the island of Noepe and credit him with teaching them how to be respectful and charitable. The importance of Moshup is underscored by the tribal logo of the modern Aquinnahs (also known as the Wampanoag Tribe of Gay Head) on Martha's Vineyard, which shows Moshup holding a whale as he stands on the cliffs.[6]

Klose-kur-beh, Gluskabe, or Glooscap, to just list a few spellings of his name, is a culture hero of the Wabanaki peoples of northern New England and is another insightful example about how stories can provide us a glimpse into the world of the peoples of Dawnland. While there are many variations on the stories about Klose-kur-beh, they generally speak of his creative forces and his kindness. The Penobscot Joseph Nicolar, who we will learn more about in Chapter 5, wrote about Klose-kur-beh in his cultural history of the Penobscots, *The Life and Traditions of the Red Man*, published in 1893. Nicolar depicts a culture hero who has transformational powers. Klose-kur-beh commits errors—some funny, others dangerous—but eventually learns about his powers, an endeavor in which he is tremendously helped by his grandmother. This life journey of learning eventually enables him to help others and pass on his knowledge.[7]

In the stories of the Abenaki people of Vermont and New Hampshire, the figures of Tabaldak and Odziozo play an important role in the history of the creation and shaping of Dawnland. Tabaldak is the creator of all living things, including the ancestors of the Abenaki people whom he created out of wood after an earlier failed attempt to create people out of stone, an experiment with which Tabaldak had been unhappy because these creatures' hearts had been too cold. Thus, Tabaldak destroys these humans. The only thing he did not create is the giant Odziozo, known as the "Transformer," who slowly emerges into existence by creating himself. Once corporeal, the Abenaki stories tell us, Odziozo creates Lake Champlain and many of the region's rivers, mountains, and islands. The story of Tabaldak and Odziozo explains to the Abenakis how their world came into being and how it took shape. But the story also reminds the Abenakis about the importance of maintaining a balance of power among all living creatures, appreciating the beauty of the creation, and performing rituals.[8]

The late 18th- and early 19th-century Native American leader and diplomat Hendrick Aupaumut, who was born in the indigenous Stockbridge community in western Massachusetts and became a leader in the Mahican community, provides a very different origin story:

The etymology of the word *Muhheakunnuk* [Mahican], according to original signifying, is great waters or sea, which are constantly in motion, either flowing or ebbing. Our forefathers asserted that their ancestors were emigrated from west by north of another country; they passed over the great waters, where this and the other country is nearly connected, called *Ukhkokpeck*; it signifies snake water, or water where snakes abounded; and that they lived by [the] side of [a] greater water or sea, from whence they derive the name of *Muhheakunnuk* nation.[9]

This testimony suggests that at least some Native Americans in New England believed that they had migrated to the region via an ocean or a water route, which corresponds with the theories of many archaeologists and anthropologists about the peopling of the Americas by the continent's indigenous peoples.

Many of the stories about the origins and shaping of Dawnland have been lost, and even those that have survived, such as the examples above, have been changed and likely only survive in fragmentary form. The crux of the account is still being presented, but many of the details are missing. Thus, much of this earlier knowledge and wisdom that could help us flesh out our understanding about indigenous cultures has been lost, leaving huge gaps in the record and our understanding. In the last 500 years these developments were brought about by processes of colonization, which had a devastating impact on Native American oral traditions and cultures. Years of warfare, competition for land, servitude, dispossession, removal, diaspora, disease, poverty, social destitution, and the cultural impact of New English missionaries, reformers, and schools have eradicated vital elements of Native American cultures and beliefs. Yet despite this destructive impact, indigenous peoples in New England were able to preserve and maintain much of their culture and knowledge and creatively adapted to the changing circumstances in the last five centuries.[10]

A Buried Past: Toward a Deep History of Dawnland

Just like the descendants of the indigenous peoples who have lived in Dawnland for thousands of years and have shed light on the creation and shaping of their world through stories, archaeologists aim to gain a better understanding of New England's pre-Columbian history through the analysis of archaeological sites and material objects. In this pursuit, scholars and the general public still too often refer to the Native American past before 1492 as "prehistory." This is in many ways a misleading term, as it suggests that there was no history among indigenous societies prior to European colonization. Using "early history" could be a potentially more elegant and accurate alternative that would not carry the same negative connotations, but at the same time this is an imprecise and potentially confusing term, since historians call "early America" the period of U.S. history from roughly 1500 to around 1800. Some archaeologists use the term "deep history" as an academic organizing principle to describe the period before 1492. They argue that deep history reaches back for millennia and played a crucial role in shaping the world's geography, the environment, and human history.[11]

Deep history is a helpful notion that refers to a past that is buried and needs to be unearthed. The uncovering of the deep history of Dawnland, however, becomes complicated by the fact that in the last few centuries a lot of archaeological evidence has been destroyed, largely as a result of development. There is an unintended and added meaning that makes deep history a useful concept for the study of the Native American past of New England. Dawnland's deep history is buried in more than one way. As will emerge throughout the book, from the 17th century on many members of New English society propagated that the region's indigenous peoples had "vanished" or "disappeared," a conviction that remains pervasive despite the continuous indigenous presence in contemporary society. Thus, Native American culture—past and present—is buried not only deep in the ground but also in the popular historic myths and memory of dominant New English society. This is a past that is often forgotten or ignored.

The use of archaeological evidence is a contentious topic among many Native Americans who favor the return of indigenous cultural items and especially human remains found in archaeological digs, held by private collectors, and displayed in museums. Hence, the archaeological pursuit of the indigenous past raises several ethical issues and is accompanied by a debate about who owns the past. Darrell Newell, a Passamaquoddy from Maine, expresses the frustration of many New England Native Americans about this issue. His observation helps us to bring an indigenous perspective to this subject matter. Speaking on the issue of human and funerary remains from a local burial site held by the Peabody Museum of Archaeology and Ethnology at Harvard University, Newell says that "the most valuable spiritual thing I do is bringing back the bones of our old ones and putting them back in their proper place."[12] Speaking of museums such as the Peabody, he argues that

> they hold sacred burial belongings and human remains that date back 65,000 years. . . . We don't have an archaeological background. They're the educated people, so it's real difficult to be at odds with them and be effective. Their position is that [the remains] are not culturally affiliated to the Passamaquoddy or any present-day living tribe, so technically they're culturally unidentifiable.[13]

Indigenous people contest such cases not only in New England but also all over North America and around the world.

It is hard to convey to a nonnative audience the emotional and spiritual pain that the disturbance of an ancestral burial site means to many indigenous people and communities in the northeastern United States. The indigenous peoples of Dawnland see their world and how they interact with it in very different ways than the New English newcomers. In the context of burial grounds, the violation and total destruction of one's place of worship and cemetery in Western cultural beliefs would be somewhat of an approximation but by no means an equivalent. To Westerners, it is morally reprehensible to destroy such places, and it is important not to violate a sacred space. But many indigenous people in the Northeast do not see a clear separation between the "sacred" and the "profane" world (to use inappropriate terminology to illustrate a point to a non–Native American audience), as is the case in contemporary mainstream North American and European societies. In the cosmology of indigenous New Englanders, the spiritual and the current reality are closely connected and constantly interact with a life-giving force. The human corpse needs to return to its natural environment, or its home, so that the deceased's energy can help later generations prosper. Thus, the violation or destruction of a burial site is seen not just as a despicable act; even more importantly, it is seen as a disruption to the natural order of things and the world. Many indigenous people in Dawnland believe that the disruption of ancestral burial grounds threatens the existence of present and future generations. This is why Native Americans throughout the Northeast have such a strong desire to protect existing burial grounds and restore excavated human remains to their original resting place.[14]

To create greater awareness about this and many other issues among the next generation of archaeologists, several tribes in Connecticut have sponsored institutions such as the Mohegan Archaeological Field School and the Eastern Pequot Archaeological Field School, which in collaboration with archaeology programs at the University of Connecticut, Eastern Connecticut State University, and the University of Massachusetts–Boston have investigated archaeological sites on reservation lands. The hope is that such initiatives are more inclusive, community-based, and collaborative and that this kind of research will lead to better practices among academics. Maybe such cooperative archaeological digs among tribal governments, Native American descendant groups, and archaeologists will, at least in part, encourage more trust and responsible behavior.[15]

Despite the occasionally contentious and incomplete archaeological record that leaves many questions unanswered, there is convincing evidence that suggests the long-standing and significant presence of Native Americans in Dawnland. A study of the Merrimack River Valley that was published in the early 1930s, for instance, provides some insights into these issues. This survey was intended to be a preliminary study of this New England river valley system but remains the most complete and thorough examination to this date. The study noted many indigenous settlement sites and provides us a limited glimpse into the deep history of the region. There was an abundance of communities that existed throughout the long precolonial history, and they could be found all over the river valley in many places. In fact, the locations of many indigenous settlements were right in the same places as many New England towns and the now postindustrial cities such as Manchester in today's New Hampshire and Lowell in modern-day Massachusetts. Evidence of precolonial sites also indicates that the indigenous peoples of Dawnland occupied settlements for extended periods and farmed the region's most productive agricultural lands; one such site that archaeologists explored is at Shattuck Farm in Andover, Massachusetts. Evidence from all over the region reminds us that indigenous peoples occupied these archaeological sites for hundreds and thousands of years, suggesting not only their deep historical presence but also that the indigenous peoples of Dawnland knew the best sites for residential occupation and the most productive farmlands.[16]

Anyone who has wandered the New England woods, where remnants of old farm walls are scattered widely, can get a sense of the power of nature to claim back evidence of an earlier human presence. The walls are signifiers of former farm fields and pastures that were abandoned starting at the end of the 19th century, when farming played an ever less central role in the New England economy. Since then New England saw massive reforestation efforts, and over time the walls and other evidence of human settlement have been increasingly overtaken by vegetation and eroded.

With the passage of time archaeological evidence deteriorates, more so the older the evidence or the archaeological site is that is being examined. The uncovered materials are often piecemeal, with crucial parts that are either lost or destroyed. In a sense it as much like trying to build a puzzle with many missing pieces. Moreover, New England's acidic soil provides an extremely destructive burial ground for archaeological evidence. Thus, stone tools, especially the more ancient a discovered site is, are the most commonly found artifacts. Yet, archaeological sites of Dawnland also can reveal evidence of tools and weapons that were made of bones and wood as well as ceramics, residue of structural construction, burial grounds, artistic production that can provide a rare glimpse into indigenous cosmology and culture, and remnants of refuse heaps that teach us about what plants and animals indigenous peoples were eating and about their material culture.

English colonization of the 17th and 18th centuries, industrial and urban development in the 19th and 20th centuries, post–World War II suburban and exurban construction, and all the accompanying efforts at development that were part of these specific episodes in New England history also had a damaging effect on the precolonial indigenous human record and destroyed many Native American sites.[17] As pointed out above, the Native Americans of Dawnland knew the most opportune locations to create communities, and New English development since the 17th century has happened right on top of many former indigenous village and town sites. Since the 1600s, European-style plows and the construction of New English villages, towns, cities, and suburban and exurban communities have been destructive. Development has been accompanied by its share of construction of factories, office parks, mall landscapes, housing, and infrastructure, which likely destroyed and continues to destroy a lot of the evidence that could provide us additional information into the indigenous history of Dawnland before European colonization. It is this limited evidence that can only provide imperfect answers. The further back in time we try to explore, the harder it becomes to reconstruct this story.

Though the damage to the archaeological record complicates the reconstruction of the pre-Columbian history of Dawnland, there are additional dynamics that confound this task. An undamaged site only provides a narrow glimpse, and like historians, archaeologists constantly reinterpret the existing evidence. These explorations aid our understanding of the indigenous precolonial past, but they also help us to gain insights into the intellectual debates that occur among archaeologists. Archaeology, anthropology, and history have often carried the mantle of being "scientific" or "objective" in their pursuit of "the truth," but many scholars in these fields are now far more critical about their disciplines' pasts in this regard and acknowledge that as part of their intellectual heritage archaeology, anthropology, and history have played a role in advancing, justifying, and reinforcing colonial narratives and biased depictions of Native Americans. This intellectual history is further complicated, as indigenous voices, which are scant in the European and Euro-American records, are even harder to locate in the precolonial past. Hence, a growing number of archaeologists work with indigenous informers, historians, and scholars to gain a better understanding. These Native American perspectives provide us a glimpse into indigenous cosmology, values, and culture and further our understanding in many other areas.[18]

The history of Dawnland and New England is in part influenced by the region's geology, which began to take shape in its current form toward the end of the Pleistocene era at the end of the last Ice Age, roughly 20,000 to 15,000 years ago. Certainly, key topographies such as the region's mountain ranges and the earlier mentioned cliff of Aquinnah predated this last Ice Age. Nevertheless, many other important natural features emerged during this period. For instance, the deep freeze in the last Ice Age captured considerable amounts of the globe's water, thereby significantly lowering the coastlines. Today's coastlines only slowly emerged as a result of warming trends and a northward receding ice sheet. In New England, just as in other parts of the world, the diminishing ice layer aided in the development of large lakes, many of which have either disappeared today or are much smaller. These bodies of water often had an outflow that might again connect to another lake or move toward the ocean, which helped to create the riverbeds for the waterways we now call the Connecticut River and the Merrimack River. The melting glacier, by depositing erosional debris and by creating streams of melting water, formed many of the valleys in the region. The granite boulders that can be found all over New England's landscape are also remnants from this period. The awesome power of the receding ice, imprinted on these large rocks by scrapes, dragged them for often hundreds of miles from their points of origin and left them scattered all over the region. The elliptical hill formations, known as drumlins, are another notable feature of the New England landscape and were formed as a result of moving ice and glacial drift. Many other features that have come to define New England's landscape emerged during this time. Massive buried ice masses, for instance, eventually aided in the formation of water-filled depressions. Today we know these bodies of water as kettle ponds. They can be found all over New England. One such example is Walden Pond, a body of water where the antebellum American writer and thinker Henry David Thoreau resided for some time and was inspired to write his book *Walden*. Moreover, Cape Cod and Maine's magnificent coastlines as well as many other of the region's geological and topographical features emerged during this period.

There is ample proof that suggests an extensive and long-term indigenous presence in the region. For the last few centuries, professional and amateur archaeologists in official and unofficial digs, builders, construction workers, farmers, gardeners, and hikers have unearthed or stumbled upon Native American artifacts, material objects, and the occasional skeletal remain. Especially in the days before state building regulations and the Native American Graves Protection and Repatriation Act of 1990 (NAGPRA), archaeological discoveries could be quickly dispensed with, ignored, or obliterated out of ignorance, disinterest, or to guarantee the quick execution of a construction project. While federal and state laws are far from perfect and many points of conflict and contestation remain, such regulations provide at least some protection and, especially with NAGPRA, have led to wider discussions about who owns the past. Many an archaeological find has ended up in private homes and unofficial collections. Likely, some priceless artifacts and entire such collections have been discarded after the collector died and her or his next of kin had little appreciation of or knowledge about the materials their deceased relative had assembled. Despite all this, sufficient materials have been assembled, preserved, and studied that provide us a glimpse into the deep history of Dawnland.

As earlier alluded to, the archaeological record suggests a long human presence in Dawnland. Some archaeologists argue that there is some evidence that hints at a presence of Paleo Indians during the Late Pleistocene era more than 10,000 years ago. The data is more conclusive for the Archaic (roughly 10,000 to 3,000 years ago) and Woodland (about 3,000 to 1,500 years ago) periods. Material objects and skeletal remains indicate that there was a permanent Native American occupation of the region. This evidence, often in partial form, includes celts, cooking stones, mortars, gouges, stone tools, plummets, pestles, pipes, soapstone containers, ceramics, ornaments, bones, and skeletal remains as well as stone weapons such as knife-shaped implements, axes, spear points, throwing spears points (atlatls), and other projectile points. Archaeological digs and refuse heaps found in various places, discussed in more detail below, suggest that the indigenous peoples of Dawnland consumed fish and shellfish from the region's ocean, rivers, lakes, ponds, and streams. Native peoples gathered and hunted but in later years also developed agriculture to procure food.

Compared to the precolonial indigenous cultures often referred to as Mound Builders, located in what is today the Midwest and the South of the United States, the Native American societies of the northern Eastern Woodlands were smaller. Farther west and south one could find large cities such as Cahokia, close to modern-day St. Louis, which at the height of its power in the 11th and 12th centuries was the home of a population of at least 10,000 to 20,000 inhabitants. Such an urban center could compete in size with Europe's largest cities of that period. The agrarian mound-building societies called the Mississippians (800 to 1600 CE) constructed large earthworks and urban centers throughout the Midwest and the South. Moreover, archaeological evidence suggests that the mound-building societies of the Eastern Woodlands participated in a continent spanning exchange and trade network. Thus, from a continental precolonial perspective, several archaeologists argue, the Native American societies of Dawnland lived in the peripheral parts of North America and lacked the larger agrarian state structures that emerged in the Midwest and the South.[19]

How useful is this characterization given the complexity of the pre-Columbian Native American societies of New England? As we will see throughout this chapter and in the next chapter, indigenous communities in Dawnland had developed sustainable, complex, and sophisticated lifeways and societies. They had developed agriculture. They also practiced forest efficiency, a way to manage the wooded landscape to increase the animal population that could be hunted. Moreover, Native Americans exploited the resources of the region's waterways. Finally, Native Americans in Dawnland participated in complex and fluid long-distance exchange networks (including with the above-discussed Mound Builders) and had developed complex systems of social and cultural organization.

A Time before New England

Native American life in Dawnland was sustained by the region's river valleys, abundant coastal areas, ponds and lakes, seasonally varying climates, and natural resources. Nonetheless, compared to other regions of the pre-Columbian Western Hemisphere such as the ancient civilizations of Central and South America or the Mound Builders, archaeologists have neglected to study the region. One expert on New England archaeology, Elizabeth Chilton, writes that "archaeology" treats the precolonial history of the region as a "backwater of cultural evolution." She argues that many of the "social evolutionary models" that archaeologists generally use, such as "hunter gatherers," "horticulturalist," and "complex," really leave no room to encapsulate the "mobile farmer" way of life that emerged among New England's Native Americans on the eve of colonization.[20] The precolonial history discussed in this chapter and the next are of great importance. As Chilton argues, "New England Algonquians offer us an important historical example of great social and ecological stability—as well as social complexity—over more than 10 millennia." Dawnland's Native Americans had subsisted, farmed, and lived in the region in a sustainable way and adapted well to their environment. They provide us an "alternative pathway in human history."[21]

The remainder of this chapter briefly explores what little we know about the lifeways of Native Americans of New England from roughly 13,000 or so years ago to around 1000 CE. Archaeologists frequently divide this long span of time into what they describe as three distinct periods: Paleo Indian, Archaic, and Woodland. A few decades ago, archaeologists of North America connected the Paleo Indian period to big-game hunting lifeways and saw the Archaic as a transitionary period in which Native American lifeways became defined by hunting and gathering. These conventional narratives connected the Woodland period of Native American history with the adoption of pottery, the use of the bow and arrow, and the development of horticulture. Most archaeologists today would suggest that these characterizations of each period are too simplistic. For instance, evidence that connects Paleo Indians in New England to big-game hunting is tenuous. Moreover, in some ways, as the discussion below points out, recent research and analysis suggests that the distinctions between these three periods might not be as dramatic as terminology might indicate. Many Archaic lifeways, patterns, and technologies continued into the Woodland periods, just as they persisted from the Paleo Indian into the Archaic periods. Thus, while this chapter adopts the organizing principles (or labels) of "Paleo Indian," "Archaic," and "Woodland," it also raises some questions about the assumptions that are often associated with these terms. However, the main point this section emphasizes is that the Native Americans who lived in Dawnland for the millennia before the coming of Europeans demonstrated a great ability to adapt to a changing world and created a variety of tools and strategies to enable their survival in the region.

Paleo Indians and Dawnland

Archaeologists classify the period from approximately 13,000 to about 9,000 years ago in New England history as the Paleo Indian period. Archaeologists believe that Native Americans at the time lived in small communities and were mobile, flexible, and adaptable in a world with a changing climate and environment. Researchers have uncovered and continue to uncover evidence of Paleo Indians in Dawnland, which indicates that there was a Native American presence in the region during this period. Many archaeologists have suggested that during the Paleo Indian era there was abundant food in North America, which in turn led to an increase in the human population across the continent. It was this demographic expansion, they argue, that might have brought the first Paleo Indians to Dawnland. Archaeological evidence from sites, which usually comes in the form of stone spear points and tools, suggests that there was an indigenous presence some 10,000 to 11,000 years ago. However, this does not mean that this is the exact time when the first Paleo Indians arrived in the region. It just means that these are the earliest materials that archaeologists have found and were able to date with at least some approximate certainty. There are sites such as the Bull Brook site in Ipswich, Massachusetts, that several archaeologists have approximated to be older. Some researchers have argued that Bull Brook was settled more than 12,000 years ago, but an exact date could not be verified during work on this site. New finds in the future might provide more conclusive evidence for an earlier indigenous presence in the region.

At the end of the last Ice Age, approximately 13,000 years ago, New England was a very different and much more barren place. This environment only gradually filled with the plant life that we are accustomed to today, but it is important to remember that the contemporary woodlands of New England are the product of 20th-century reforestation efforts. It took several thousand years for the woodland environment of southern New England, which is dominated by deciduous woodlands and predominated in large parts of Dawnland at the time of European conquest and colonization, to emerge. About 13,000 years ago the climate was significantly colder and unstable and fluctuated to larger degrees. The retreating glaciers had left a treeless arctic tundra-like landscape, dominated by mosses, grasses, and low-growing shrubs. As mentioned earlier, the coastlines of New England were also significantly lower, which gave the region a much different outline than it has today, as much more of the North American continental landmass was exposed. This was also an era when larger inland lakes existed. These bodies of water were fed by glacial melt and in turn sustained rivers, which aided the rapidly rising ocean level. Archaeobotanical evidence suggests that starting about 12,000 years ago in southern New England, spruce, pine, fir, and larch began to gradually grow in the tundra environment. As the number of trees increased over time, the tundra landscape was transformed into mixed conifer woodlands. In much of New England, these evergreen forests were eventually replaced by deciduous woodlands. However, modern adaptations of the conifer timberlands can still be found in the mountainous regions of northern New England, such as in the White Mountains of New Hampshire and in the boreal forests that we can find today in the northern portions of Dawnland.

During the Paleo Indian period, the environment supported a diverse group of megafauna (large animals). The megafauna of New England likely included the famous wooly mammoth—a fur-covered species related to modern elephants—with tusks and a strong trunk that was the approximate size of the African elephant and was perfectly adapted to living in a cold climate. At least in parts of the southwestern portions of New England, some archaeological digs suggest, mastodons, another relative of modern elephants, seemed to have had a presence. Giant beavers also were likely part of the New England environment. This genus could easily reach over 6 feet in length (about 180 centimeters) at full maturity and would weigh at least about 200 pounds (over 90 kilograms) at maturity. Another impressive representative of North America's megafauna was the giant ground sloth. North America and Dawnland also was home to animals such as caribou, moose, and likely musk ox. The *bison latifron*, also known as the giant North American bison, might have also had a presence in the region. This animal was around more than 3 feet (or 1 meter) higher at the shoulder than the modern bison (buffalo), and the distance from its horn could reach over 84 inches (or more than 2 meters), compared to today's genus at 26 inches. Horses, though significantly smaller than their modern relatives, were part of North America's megafauna, and these species also went extinct. The wild horses of North America today would only be introduced by the Spanish in the 16th century.

Evidence suggests that Paleo Indians hunted these large animals in North America, meaning that associations in archaeological sites can be drawn that connect these animals (i.e., through bones, antlers, teeth, a spear head found with animal bones, etc.) to human beings. Several archaeologists argue that Paleo Indians might have hunted the megafauna to extinction. We have no proof that would help us to support these claims in Dawnland, at least at this point. Future finds might shed light on these questions. But at the same time, it is important to underscore that finding this kind of evidence in New England, given the region's natural environment, soils and history of development, is difficult.[22]

There is limited evidence that connects the Native Americans of New England to the hunt of megafauna such as the famous mammoth and mastodon, an image that is often embedded in the general popular perceptions of Paleo Indians. Archaeological evidence discovered in New England, at least, does not seem to support this notion. Archaeological specimens from the Whipple site in Swanzey in the modern state of New Hampshire and, less conclusively, from the earlier-mentioned Bull Brook site, however, point to some associations between a human presence and caribou and beaver. Given the fairly uniform and cooler climate in North America, the assumption among many archaeologists was that the lifeways of the indigenous peoples who lived in Dawnland were similar to those of other Native Americans who lived across Turtle Island in regions where there is evidence that suggests that Paleo Indians hunted megafauna. But in the context of the history of Native Americans in New England, the theory of the big-game hunter cannot be conclusively proven. Is it possible that the indigenous peoples in the region adopted divergent ways of life from other Paleo Indian groups in North America? Might a different environment have led the Paleo Indians of Dawnland to settle and subsist in different ways? This would still mean that Paleo Indians hunted animals (large as well as small ones), subsisted on wild foods that they gathered, and lived mobile lives in their efforts to subsist but that large-game hunting could have played a less important role in the region than it might have done in other parts of Turtle Island. Based on the evidence we cannot conclusively know, but these are certainly central questions that archaeologists raise and debate.[23]

Significant portions of the evidence uncovered at archaeological sites from the Paleo Indian period suggests that hunting occurred in these societies. Many of the spear points and stone tools found in several Paleo Indian sites throughout Dawnland were likely used for the hunting and processing of killed animals. The shrewdly manufactured spear heads often have notice-able indentations, grooves, or flutes on their nonpointed end, likely to attach it to a wooden spear handle (organic evidence by now disappeared). Archae-ologists call this type of artifact "fluted points," a name that is descriptive of the shape of the spear points. Sometimes these fluted projectile points are also called Folsom points, named after a village in New Mexico and the site where the first spear point of this kind was found.

Does this mean that the Paleo Indian communities that lived in Dawn-land consumed mainly meat and that their lifeways were dominated by the hunt? We do not know for sure, but we do understand that it is stone spear points and other stone tools that are the material culture items most likely to survive the millennia underground in the acidic soil of Dawnland, as opposed to, say, evidence connected to gathering of food such as plant resi-due that is likely to have perished or decayed. Thus, it is the context of the surviving evidence that is left to archaeologists to interpret, which influences our perceptions and understandings of the Paleo Indian lifeways.

Archaeologists who specialize in New England's Paleo Indian era organize the discovered fluted points from the region into different types. Researchers have used three distinct categories to identify these spear heads and use the name of the first Paleo Indian site where they were originally discovered to name fluted points of similar styles discovered at other sites. It needs to be underscored, though, that even though some archaeologists have used these three distinct classifications of styles, there exists a high degree of variability in what the points from each category actually look like. The earliest Paleo

Indian fluted points are named after the Bull Brook site in Ipswich, Massa-chusetts. These fluted points tend to be longer (six to eight centimeters), are the most parallel sided, and look the bulkiest. The second style of fluted point is named after the Neponset site in Canton, Massachusetts. These points are called Middle Paleo Indian fluted points. These tend to be the pointiest spear heads among the Paleo Indian varieties in New England, averaging about six centimeters in length, and they tend to have the longest fluting that covers about half of the object from the lower wide end up. The third category of spear head, also described as Late Paleo Indian fluted points, is the Nicholas style, which is named after a site in Oxford, Maine. These tend to be the smallest among the points, with minimal fluting at the bottom end and a slightly narrowing pointed form. By examining the differ-ent styles and how the fluted points transformed over time, archaeologists try to gain a glimpse into how Paleo Indian cultures in Dawnland changed over time.[24]

The fluted points and stone tools found at archaeological sites can also provide a glimpse into the expansive migratory patterns of Paleo Indian cul-tures in New England or indicate the existence of long-distance exchange networks among Paleo Indians. The tools found at the early Paleo Indian Bull Brook site, for instance, indicate that the stones used to make these artifacts had distant origins. They are believed to have originated from northern New Hampshire, Maine, Vermont, Pennsylvania, and New York. Archaeologists believe that Paleo Indian groups did not exchange the tools or the stones to make the artifacts; rather, as indicated at Bull Brooks, Paleo Indians obtained them from these varied places themselves. Chips, flakes, and incomplete artifacts at sites indicate that Paleo Indians, such as the ones at Bull Brook, likely produced the material objects at the sites where they found the stones. Thus, if this hypothesis holds true, it suggests that early Paleo Indian people who occupied Bull Brook knew Dawnland and its resources very well. Of course, this does not necessarily mean that each and every item used was gathered up by one group. Some archaeologists suggest that Bull Brook might have served as a meeting point for various groups that gathered to hunt as a community.[25] Thus, in a way, various groups might have not only gathered to meet to hunt but similarly, in such instances, also might have exchanged various desired material objects from other groups, which might support the theory of the existence of informal long-distance exchange networks among Paleo Indian cultures. Much of this is, of course, based on an interpretation of very limited evidence. Archaeological work is often as valuable in raising elucidating questions as it is in providing answers.

The situation seems a bit different at the Middle Paleo Indian period site of Neponset, located in Canton, Massachusetts. The site's occupants seemed to have actively worked on spear points. However, they seemed to have worked not with local stones but rather, as excavated evidence suggests, with materials from a place we call today Mt. Jasper, located in Berlin, New Hampshire. Evidence suggests that throughout the precontact period, indigenous peoples of Dawnland went to Mt. Jasper to mine for stone. They seem to have valued the rhyolite stone they extracted there as a highly prized raw material for tool making. There is evidence that indigenous people worked the stone at Mt. Jasper, turning it into artifacts right on site. The Native Americans who occupied the site at Neponset, though, seemed to have worked the stone at their campsite in Canton. Some archaeologists have suggested that Neponset's residents must have gathered or mined the stones at Mt. Jaspar during the warmer months in the summer, when they pursued caribou farther north, but then brought the raw material in manageable smaller chunks onto a 200-mile (320-kilometer) trip back south to the Canton site. These researchers argue that Neponset served as a winter camp and that the inhabitants must have spent the cold months, at least in part, making fluted spear points, as several broken and discarded objects as well as chips and clippings that were found at the site seem to indicate.

Researchers also discovered miniature fluted points at Neponset that are of interest to archaeologists. This was not an unusual discovery, as these small spear heads have been found in other Paleo Indian digs. But what were these smaller fluted points used for? Again, as so often, we can only speculate. Some researchers argue that some of the smaller points might have been used by children to learn how to hunt or maybe as miniature sets to look like adult sets, possibly to be used as toys to play-hunt. Other scholars have proposed that the fluted points, or at least some of them, might have been used for decorative purposes or had cultural meanings; maybe they were imbued with spiritual or supernatural significance, which we cannot understand today with the limited evidence that is available to us.[26]

Given New England's acidic soil and the destructive impact this has on organic evidence, in terms of material culture we know disproportionately more about the Paleo Indian hunting culture than many other aspects. Several archaeologists believe that Paleo Indians likely used various types of spears to hunt. They likely used larger lances, thrusting spears, and, many archaeologists believe, throwing spears launched with a throwing device today called by its Mexica name, atlatl. The atlatl was basically a wooden tool, or launcher, with a grip on one end and a launching hook on the other. This technological device enabled a trained hunter to throw a spear farther, harder, and with better aim. Native Americans of early Dawnland most likely also hunted small game, fish, and birds. In their pursuit of food, the region's early hunters likely used several of the hunting devices discussed above as well as clubs, nets, harpoons, and leisters for spear fishing. Various other surviving tools found in Paleo Indian sites were likely used to process meat but likely also to make clothing, build housing, and turn bones, antlers, wood, and other naturally occurring materials into useful tools and other material objects. Archaeologists have uncovered a range of knives, scrappers, and drills likely used to perform these tasks. Yet, much of the material culture of Dawnland has been destroyed by the passage of time, and much of what is presented here is based on archaeological interpretations of incomplete evidence.[27]

Judging from other Paleo sites in North America, Paleo Indians had sophisticated material culture that we still do not understand today given our limited knowledge of these societies. Moreover, in other parts of the United States at least, some evidence suggests that Paleo Indians built complex and labor-intensive housing, which was likely for longer-term occupation. Such observations raise some questions and could complicate our understanding about the mobility among at least some of the Paleo Indian societies. Thus, given the complexity of the subject and the limited available information, there remain many unanswered questions and points of confusion.

When it comes to the Paleo Indians of New England, there are many other areas that we know little or next to nothing about. Many of the questions raised here about Paleo Indians can be equally applied to the indigenous people who lived in the Archaic and Woodland periods. For instance, what role did women and men play in these societies? Was there a gendered division of labor, and if so, what tasks did women fulfill, and which ones did men do? Or did women and men take care of many similar tasks, and could members of the community perform and be trained to be competent in chores that were key in the survival and prosperity of their societies? What kind of clothing did they wear? What languages did they speak? What beliefs did they hold in terms of spirituality, cosmology, life, death, values, and cultural norms? What place and what role did they think they held in their world? What was their social and political organization? What cultural systems emerged in these societies? Did they have music, creation stories, and other cultural traditions, and if so, what were they? For these and for many other questions, we have no reliable answers. Hence, it remains difficult to uncover Paleo Indians and the pre-Columbian past on the imperfect archaeological record. The absence, as much as the presence, of evidence defines work in the field.[28]

Dawnland during the Archaic Period

The global warming trends that occurred throughout the Paleo Indian period continued into the millennia that followed and led to dramatic changes but also saw some continuity in the lifeways of Native Americans of New England. The changes in climate and environment likely aided in the gradual waning and morphing of Paleo Indian ways of life into what archaeologists have called "Archaic Indian" lifeways. The warming climate and the changes in the environment they caused led to a gradual alteration of the ways of life among the indigenous peoples of Dawnland and Turtle Island more generally. The indigenous peoples of New England, as with the Native Americans in other parts of North America, adapted to these changing realities in order to survive. Over the millennia of the Archaic period, the indigenous people of Dawnland developed new ways of subsistence based on changing food supplies. They learned about novel building materials to build new types of housing. They created new kinds of clothing, tools, weapons, and other material culture items. Yet despite these changes, there also seem to be continuities in the lifeways of the indigenous peoples of Dawnland. While it is hard to determine this on the available evidence, Native Americans likely continued to develop unique systems of food procurement, social organization, cultural practices, spiritual beliefs, customs, traditions, and technologies.

Much of our understanding is confined to the information we can gather from archaeological sites, and this can only provide a limited glimpse. Yet the overall picture that emerges underscores that patterns of subsistence and daily life seem to defy easy characterization, making it often hard to speak of a "Paleo Indian," an "Archaic," or later a "Woodland period" in New England. As with the Paleo Indian period, there is much we do not know about the Archaic and Woodland periods. From gender roles to various aspects of daily life, cultural traditions and systems, and social and political organization, there are many issues we lack conclusive information on. Yet, we can gather from the evidence that there existed local diversity and flux in the region through time and space and that indigenous peoples lived in a complex and at times interconnected world.

A number of archaeologists and researchers who specialize in the early human history of New England argue that the Archaic period began somewhere around 10,000 to 9,000 years ago and ended approximately 2,500 years ago. This period saw an overall warming of the climate, a drying of the environment, and a continued rise of the Atlantic Ocean's water level. In southern New England, oaks and hemlocks gradually expanded their presence at the expense of fir, spruce, and larch, but there existed a variety of plant and tree species that appeared and disappeared during the many millennia that encompassed the Archaic and Paleo Indian periods. Moreover, compared to the Paleo Indian archaeological sites, the Archaic period digs suggest the presence of larger settlements, increased regional differences and diversity among Native American societies, a higher population density, projective points made in several unique styles, and a wider range of tools used by indigenous people during this period.

Native Americans in Dawnland in the Archaic period undertook many activities in their daily life. They continued to hunt, produced chipped stone tools, and participated in either long-distance migratory or trade systems to obtain desirable materials from faraway places. Archaic Indians, however, also expanded their tool production more widely by adopting the grounding of stones. Indigenous peoples gathered, fished, looked for shellfish, used ornamentation and paint, practiced burials, built pole-frame lodgings, and produced a variety of other material objects during this era. Some archaeologists suggest that some of these activities might have predated the Archaic period, but we have more conclusive archaeological evidence that suggests that Native Americans were doing these activities at that time. We also have the first evidence of the production of canoes from this time.[29]

Similar to Paleo Indian sites, Archaic period digs in New England tend to have material culture items that are related to the hunt. Archaeological sites reveal evidence in the form of spear heads as well as stone knives and other tools likely used to hunt and process animals. Throughout the Archaic period, the indigenous peoples of Dawnland developed a variety of styles and processes to make points and other tools. Styles and production processes not only changed over time; evidence also suggests that relative contemporary societies would use different technologies and tool-making techniques. To archaeologists, this underscores the cultural diversity that must have existed among the indigenous peoples in the region. Native Americans during this period hunted an animal population that would be a lot more familiar to us than the megafauna of the Paleo Indian period. Roughly 6,000 years ago, just as now, Dawnland's forests and other landscapes were home to white-tailed deer, turkeys, lynxes, red foxes, water fowl and other birds, beavers, rabbits, squirrels, turtles, snakes, and other reptiles. Thus, there was a rich diversity of animal life that could be hunted. Native Americans continued to hunt using the atlatl and developed new hunting strategies and technologies such as, maybe by the end of the Archaic period, the bow and arrow.

The evidence at Early Archaic period sites such as Dill Hill Farm, located in today's East Haddam in Connecticut, and at several other sites also indicates the presence of hazelnut and walnut shells and other plant foods. Such pieces of evidence help us to assume that Native Americans also gathered food as a subsistence strategy. Thus, on the evidence we have a link to the gathering of food in the Archaic period, whereas during the Paleo Indian era in New England, given the paucity of evidence, many archaeologists today can mostly infer that this mode of subsistence existed.[30]

It is quite likely that gathering as a source of food procurement played a central role in the lives of the indigenous peoples of Dawnland during the Archaic period. Native American communities gathered nuts, seeds, likely berries, and other edible wild plant foods. Evidence also suggests that plants were used to make paints likely for ornamentation and decoration. Anthropologists often point out that in so-called hunter-gatherer societies, gathered food often contributes more calories to the community than hunted food could provide. Some argue that the nomenclature "gatherer-hunter" society would be a more accurate label. Also, the lifeways of gathering and hunting in certain fertile locales at various points in time, some archaeologists suggest, was able to sustain relatively large societies. This evidence challenges the often-held conventional wisdom that maintains that hunter-gatherers lived in small and egalitarian societies.[31]

In many hunter-gatherer societies, much of the ethnographic literature maintains, it is the women who gather and the men who hunt. We of course do not know about the gendered division of labor in the indigenous societies that lived in the Archaic period throughout New England. There is little evidence that directly links women to gathering and men to hunting in those communities. However, given the gendered division of labor noted by European observers in the early contact period, in which indigenous women farmed and gathered while men hunted, it is possible that this could have been a continuation from precolonial times that might have taken shape in the Archaic period, though it might be equally possible that in those days a more shared system of tasks and labor existed. In fact, even in the post-Columbian period, while European observers often spoke of the labor division along gender lines, there were certainly also tasks that could involve the entire community. The Puritan minister and founder of Rhode Island Roger Williams, for instance, observed that

> When a field is to be broken up, they have a very loving sociable speedy way to dispatch it: All the neighbours men and women forty, fifty, a hundred etc. joyne, and come in to help freely. With friendly joining they breake up their fields, build their Forts, hunt the Woods, stop and kill fish in the Rivers, it being true with them as in all the World in the Affaires of Earth or Heaven: by concord little things grow great, by discord the greatest come to nothing.[32]

Thus, while gendered division of labor might have been long established in the indigenous societies of Dawnland, Native American women and men often bridged these gaps and worked together for the benefit of their communities.

Archaeological evidence from Dawnland also suggests that the gathering and hunting of food, at least during specific times and for certain societies, became tied to specific locations. Some evidence suggests that Native Americans tended to regularly revisit places during specific seasons where desired foods could be found—either to gather or to hunt. For instance, indigenous groups might have returned to the same camps during hunting season, as archaeological sites suggest multiple recurring occupations. Moreover, in their seasonal subsistence and migratory patterns, it is likely that the same communities returned to the same spaces to gather desirable plant foods, likely managing the land to aid the expansion of the plants they harvested.

That Native American daily life might have been, at least for some groups, more settled and regular in its migratory patterns during the Archaic period seems to be supported by the evidence found at several archaeological sites. At the Sandy Hill site at Mashantucket in Connecticut, evidence suggests the presence of semisubterranean and timber-framed housing structures. Evidence of pole-framed houses and involved food storage exists at other digs as well. The effort that it would take to construct such houses and the presence of food storage suggests that people would at least spend some time in these settlements. The Sandy Hill site also supports the thesis that indigenous peoples made wide use of plants in their construction of housing and in their diet.[33]

Many New England Archaic population settlements were often located next to and likely took advantage of the region's waterways. Settlements around Dawnland's many waterways indicate that during the spawning season, many Native American groups migrated to the rivers to catch fish. Archaeological evidence also suggests settlements around rivers during other seasons. The Neville site at Amoskeag Falls on the Merrimack River in today's Manchester, New Hampshire, for instance, is a site that seems to have been occupied for much of the last 8,000 years. Several river valleys also proved to be rich agricultural lands when Native Americans adopted farming. Similarly, archaeologists have uncovered sites at the many lakes and ponds of Dawnland. These locations indicate at various times short-term, seasonal, and long-term occupation. Atlantic Ocean communities are also likely to have fished and gathered shellfish. As we will discuss in more detail later in the book, using various ways of fishing as a strategy of subsistence continued into the Woodland and post-Columbian periods. Native Americans also used waterways for transportation and travel. Moreover, there is evidence of the first use of dugout canoes during the Archaic period.[34]

However, archaeological evidence from the Archaic period also suggests that not all Native American populations in Dawnland caught fish or gathered shellfish. In archaeological sites connected to Broad Spear settlements, so named after the shape of the points found at the sites affiliated with these groups, there seems to be no evidence of fish or shellfish refuse as well as no evidence of equipment used for fishing. This fact seems additionally curious, since several Broad Spear sites were found in the vicinities of rivers. Thus, it is likely that these groups lived on foods they hunted on land. To some archaeologists, this fact is another example that underscores the diversity that must have existed among the indigenous peoples of the Archaic Dawnland.[35]

As during the Paleo Indian period, the Native Americans of New England in the Archaic period seemed to have either traveled far distances to obtain stones or participated in long-distance exchange to obtain these and other raw materials. Cherts and rhyolites uncovered at various sites that frequently came from distant locations seem to support this theory. The Dill Farm site in Connecticut serves again as an elucidating example. Various material culture objects found there dating from the Early Archaic period were made from stones that were obtained from some distance away. The site is located in the Uplands region of Connecticut. Yet, the closest supply of rhyolite can be found in the coastal basin where today Boston is located or, alternatively, in present-day central New Hampshire. The nearest chert supply, on the other hand, is located in the Hudson River Valley. Thus, the Early Archaic period occupants of the Dill Farm site, just like many other communities at the time, obtained at least a portion of the materials they used in their daily life from some distance away. But again, we have to be careful with overgeneraliza-tions. For example, at the Sandy Hill site at Mashantucket, over 95 percent of the stone tools and other material objects are made from local sources.[36]

The limited evidence from the Archaic period suggests that there existed tremendous diversity in the lifeways of the indigenous peoples of Dawnland. Indigenous communities seem to have varied in size and used different tech-nologies, and they had diverse modes of subsistence and likely differed in how widely they migrated. This makes it hard to generalize about Archaic Indians.

Dawnland and the Woodland Period to 1000 CE

According to several archaeologists, the Woodland period in Dawnland lasted from roughly 2,500 years ago to the 1600s CE. The end of the period was a time when Europeans established the first permanent colonies in the northern parts of the Eastern Woodlands, such as when Samuel de Cham-plain and his crew founded Quebec in 1608 in today's Canada and a group of English Puritans started Plymouth Colony in what is now Massachusetts. However, as we will explore in more detail in Chapter 3, Native American societies in New England had already experienced dramatic changes to their lifeways long before these colonial beachheads were established. Native Americans of Dawnland had felt the European presence for many decades before. Thus, in this book we will use the 1490s as the cut off mark for the Woodland period in Dawnland.

The Woodland period, according to archaeologists, is defined by the introduction of maize horticulture, the making of ceramics, and use of the bow and arrow. In fact, underscoring the importance of these newly acquired skills, archaeologist Dean R. Snow refers to the Woodland period as the "Horticultural Period" and archaeologist Bruce Bourque calls it the "Ceramic Period." It is important to underscore, as limited archaeological evidence suggests, that some indigenous peoples in various parts of Dawnland seemed to have used bow and arrows, ceramics, and early forms of horticulture already by the Terminal Archaic period (about 3,800 to 2,700 years ago).

This serves as an important reminder that periodization is by no means an exact science.[37]

This section of the chapter briefly explores the broader outlines of the Native American history of the Woodland period to 1000 CE. The lifeways of the indigenous peoples of Dawnland during this era will be discussed in more detail in Chapter 2. There the discussion predominantly focuses on the period from roughly 1000 CE to 1500 CE, an era that archaeologists often call the Late Woodland period.

There seem to be fewer Early Woodland period sites in southern New England (from about 2,700 to 1,650 years ago), compared with the Late Terminal or Middle Woodland period (roughly from 1,650 years ago to ca. 1000 CE). This data has led some archaeologists of southern New England to conclude that there might have been a population decline during this period, a development that might have been spurred by a cooling of the climate. Other researchers suggest, however, that Dawnland instead experienced an alteration of settlement patterns during the Early Woodland period, meaning that indigenous communities now settled in areas that were most conducive to their patterns of subsistence. Other scholars maintain that likely a combination of population decline and a change in settlement patterns occurred at the time.[38]

By the Late Woodland period, roughly from around 1000 CE through the 15th century, the lifeways of peoples of Dawnland that prevailed during the contact period with Europeans had taken shape. As populations expanded, some distinct patterns emerged in the region. Inland groups subsisted predominantly on agriculture supplemented by some foraging and hunting. Coastal groups also farmed, but in addition they took advantage of the rich sources of the ocean, consuming fish and shellfish, which made them less dependent on agriculture. North of a line that roughly runs through the middle of the modern states of Maine, New Hampshire, and Vermont, farming became trickier and less reliable, since the growing season is much shorter. Thus, the Native American groups living in this area relied more heavily on the resources of the woodlands that could be hunted and gathered. The forests had plenty of animals that provided meat, fur, and animal skins. Using long-established trade routes, northern groups sent their thicker furs south, often in exchange for corn. However, this general impression should not be oversimplified. Even to the north of this agricultural line, Native American farmers worked fields in several river valleys and on the plains of lakes. In the early 17th century, for instance, the French explorer and first governor of New France, Samuel de Champlain, observed a rich and sophisticated agricultural economy on the shores of the large northern New England lake that bears his name today.

By the 1400s, indigenous people farmed, foraged, and hunted to subsist throughout Dawnland. In the spring, Native Americans tapped maple trees for their sap. Many Native American groups also adopted maize agriculture, likely introduced to the region through long-distance exchange networks with peoples farther to the west and south. These ways of subsistence led to a gradual increase of the Native American population in the region. By the 15th century, indigenous peoples lived all over New England. They lived semisedentary lives, moving their farm fields when they were exhausted. This guaranteed fertile planting grounds but also meant that village sites were moved every several years. Moreover, especially in New England's interior, many indigenous peoples pursued a seasonal cycle, settling in their villages in the spring and summer and moving to hunting camps in the winter. The bow and arrow became a widely used tool in the hunt. Native people developed various technologies to store food. During the Late Archaic period and into the Woodland period, we also increasingly have evidence that Native American populations of Dawnland made and used soapstone containers and decorative items and especially ceramics. Native American homeland territories were defined by fluid and complex kinship and trade connections. As we will explore in more detail in the next chapter, in the Woodland period Native Americans participated in sophisticated long-distance exchange networks that connected much of the North American continent. Native Americans of Dawnland grew beans, tobacco (for ceremonial purposes), squash, and sunflowers. Maize (corn) became the main agricultural staple in the region. Native Americans used animal furs and hides to make clothing. They used wood, bark, and plant fibers to build their houses and canoes.

The next chapter will expand on this important story and will focus on the lifeways of the native peoples of Dawnland in the Late Woodland period, right on the eve of European colonization. Chapter 2 aims to provide a glimpse into indigenous cultures, histories, and societies—underscoring the complexity of the precolonial past. These pre-Columbian histories play a vital role in our understanding of the New England past. Moreover, a glimpse into the Native American world before 1492 helps us to gain a sense about how dramatic and often destructive the impact of European colonization was on the Native Americans of New England.

Notes

1. "Eastern Woodland" is a widely used category by archaeologists, anthropologists, and ethnohistorians to describe the region of what is today the United States east of the Mississippi River and of southeastern Canada. AltaMira Press, for instance, publishes the series Issues in Eastern Woodland Archaeology, and there are a number of books that examine various aspects of the history of this culture area. For an introduction into the archaeology of the region, see Dean R. Snow, *Archaeology of New England* (New York: Academic Press, 1980). Snow's book is the most recent comprehensive study of New England archaeology.

While still a fine book, at 40 years of age (and out of print) it is understandably not up to date with many important recent archaeological finds. Of further interest is the collection of essays by Mary Ann Levine, Kenneth E. Sassaman, and Michael S. Nassaney, eds., *The Archaeological Northeast* (Westport, CT: Bergin and Garvey, 1999). Some of the studies that survey the Native American archaeological past of some of the states might also be of some use to readers. For an excellent example, see Lucianne Lavin, *Connecticut's Indigenous Peoples: What Archaeology, History, and Oral Traditions Teach Us about Their Communities and Cultures* (New Haven, CT: Yale University Press, 2013). For an interesting perspective of the early history of the Wabanakis, see Frederick Matthew Wiseman, *Reclaiming the Ancestors: Decolonizing a Taken Prehistory of the Far Northeast* (Hanover, NH: University Press of New England, 2005). For a discussion of the academic organizing principle of the Native Atlantic Northeast, see Neal Salisbury, "The Atlantic Northeast," in *The Oxford Handbook of American Indian History*, ed. Frederick E. Hoxie, 352–355 (New York: Oxford University Press, 2016).

2. Stacy Kowtko, *Nature and Environment in Pre-Columbian American Life* (Westport, CT: Greenwood, 2006), 2.

3. James Axtell, "Ethnohistory: A Historian's Viewpoint," *Ethnohistory* 26 (Winter 1979): 1–13.

4. On this issue see, e.g., Kristina Bross and Hilary E. Wyss, eds., *Early Native Literacies in New England: A Documentary and Critical Anthology* (Amherst: University of Massachusetts Press, 2008); Hilary Wyss, *Writing Indians: Literacy, Christianity, and Native Community in Early America* (Amherst: University of Massachusetts Press, 2000).

5. My discussion of archaeological methodology draws from James W. Bradley, *Origins and Ancestors: Investigating New England's Paleo Indians* (Andover, MA: Robert S. Peabody Museum of Archaeology, 1998), 6–10; William A. Haviland and Marjory W. Power, *The Original Vermonters: Native Inhabitants, Past and Present*, revised and expanded ed. (Hanover, NH: University of New England Press, 1994), chap. 1; Lavin, *Connecticut's Indigenous Peoples*, 25–34, 38. For good general surveys of the archaeology of North America, see Timothy R. Pauketat, ed., *The Oxford Handbook of North American Archaeology* (New York: Oxford University Press, 2012); Brian M. Fagan, *Ancient North America: The Archaeology of a Continent*, 4th ed. (New York: Thames and Hudson, 2005).

6. This section draws from Alice Nash and Christoph Strobel, *Daily Life of Native Americans from Post-Columbian through Nineteenth Century America* (Westport, CT: Greenwood, 2006), 4–6.

7. Joseph Nicolar, *The Life and Traditions of the Red Man*, ed. Annette Kolodny (Durham, NC: Duke University Press, 2007), chap. 1. For some of the stories on this culture hero from the Micmac tradition, see Michael B. Runningwolf and Patricia Clark Smith, *On the Trail of the Elder Brother: Glous'gap Stories of the Micmac Indians* (New York: Persea, 2000).

8. See Nash and Strobel, *Daily Life of Native Americans from Post-Columbian through Nineteenth Century America,* 5; Gordon M. Day, "The Western Abenaki Transformer," *Journal of the Folklore Institute* 13 (1976): 77–84.

9. Lavin, *Connecticut's Indigenous Peoples,* 35.

10. Nash and Strobel, *Daily Life of Native Americans from Post-Columbian through Nineteenth Century America,* 6.

11. See, e.g., Alice Beck Kehoe, *The Land of Prehistory: A Critical History of American Archaeology* (New York: Routledge 1998). For an introduction to the field of deep history, see Andrew Shryock and Daniel Lord Smail, eds., *Deep History: The Architecture of Past and Present* (Berkeley: University of California Press, 2011).

12. Darrell Newell (Passamaquoddy), "A Man of the Dawn," in *Indian Voices: Listening to Native Americans,* ed. Alison Ownings (New Brunswick, NJ: Rutgers, 2017), 15.

13. Ibid. See also Susan Sleeper-Smith, ed., *Contesting Knowledge: Museums and Indigenous Perspectives* (Lincoln: University of Nebraska Press, 2009); Chip Colwell, *Plundered Skulls and Stolen Spirits: Inside the Fight to Reclaim Native America's Culture* (Chicago: University of Chicago Press, 2017).

14. A radio documentary on the Shinnecock Nation's struggle with development is illustrative of these issues. While on Long Island and thus technically outside of New England, the Shinnecocks had long-established exchange networks and kinship relations with several Native American groups in southern New England and are culturally closely related. See Becka Wurmfeld, "Neighbourhood: At Conscience Point," BBC World Service, August 15, 2018, https://www.bbc.co.uk/programmes/w3csxh4h (accessed August 27, 2018).

15. Lavin, *Connecticut's Indigenous Peoples,* 24.

16. See Warren King Moorehead, *The Merrimack Archaeological Survey: A Preliminary Paper* (Salem, MA: Peabody Museum, 1931). While this discussion focuses on areas in Massachusetts and New Hampshire, my observations certainly also apply to other parts of New England. See, e.g., Haviland and Power, *The Original Vermonters*; Bruce J. Bourque, *Twelve Thousand Years: American Indians in Maine* (Lincoln: University of Nebraska Press, 2001); Michael Caduto, *A Time before New Hampshire: The Story of a Land and Native Peoples* (Hanover, NH: University of New England Press, 2003); Lavin, *Connecticut's Indigenous Peoples.*

17. For a useful overview of the history of the New England economy, see Peter Temin, ed., *Engines of Enterprise: An Economic History of New England* (Cambridge, MA: Harvard University Press, 2000).

18. On this issue see, e.g., Douglas Hunter, *The Place of Stone: Dighton Rock and the Erasure of America's Indigenous Past* (Chapel Hill: University of North Carolina Press, 2017); Charlotte Damm, "Archaeology, Ethnohistory and Oral Traditions: Approaches to the Indigenous Past," *Norwegian Archaeological Review* 38, no. 2 (2005): 73–87.

19. On this subject see, e.g., Timothy R. Pauketat, *Cahokia: Ancient America's Great City on the Mississippi* (New York: Viking, 2009); Lynda Norene Shaffer, *Native Americans before 1492: The Moundbuilding Centers of the Eastern Woodlands* (Armonk, NY: M. E. Sharpe, 1992).

20. Elizabeth S. Chilton, "New England Algonquians: Navigating 'Backwaters' and Typological Boundaries" in *The Oxford Handbook of North American Archaeology,* 262.

21. Ibid., 262–263; Neal Salisbury, "The Indians' Old World: Native Americans and the Coming of Europeans," *William and Mary Quarterly* 53 (July 1996): 435–458. See also Christoph Strobel, *The Global Atlantic 1400–1900* (New York: Routledge, 2015), 13, 34–35.

22. This section draws from Caduto, *A Time before New Hampshire,* chap. 4; Haviland and Power, *The Original Vermonters,* chap. 2; Lavin, *Connecticut's Indigenous Peoples,* chap. 1; Bourque, *Twelve Thousand Years,* chap. 1; Snow, *Archaeology of New England,* chap. 3.

23. This section draws from Lavin, *Connecticut's Indigenous Peoples,* chap. 1.

24. Bradley, *Origins and Ancestors,* 10.

25. The discussion of the Bull Brook site draws from ibid., 11–12.

26. The discussion of the Neponset site draws from ibid., 22–23.

27. Lavin, *Connecticut's Indigenous Peoples,* 41–42; Bradley, *Origins and Ancestors,* 12–13, 25.

28. Bradley, *Origins and Ancestors,* 25, 32.

29. For a general introduction to the Archaic period in New England, see Snow, *Archaeology of New England,* chaps. 4–6. For more up-to-date analysis based on individual states, see Lavin, *Connecticut's Indigenous Peoples,* chaps. 2–5; Caduto, *A Time before New Hampshire,* chap. 5; Bourque, *Twelve Thousand Years,* chap. 2; Haviland and Power, *The Original Vermonters,* chap. 3.

30. Lavin, *Connecticut's Indigenous Peoples,* chap. 2; Caduto, *A Time before New Hampshire,* chap. 5.

31. Lavin, *Connecticut's Indigenous Peoples,* chaps, 2–5.

32. Roger Williams, *A Key into the Language of America,* eds. John J. Teunissen and Evelyn J. Hinz (Detroit: Wayne State University Press, 1973), 170.

33. Lavin, *Connecticut's Indigenous Peoples,* 61–62.

34. Caduto, *A Time before New Hampshire,* 104–109, 111–112. On the Neville site, see Dena Ferran, *The Neville Site: 8,000 Years at Amoskeag, Manchester, New Hampshire* (Cambridge, MA: Peabody Museum of Archaeology and Ethnology Press, 1976); Moorehead, *The Merrimack Archaeological Survey: A Preliminary Paper,* 61–64. On the importance of rivers to Native Americans in the colonial northern Eastern Woodlands, see Lisa Brooks, *The Common Pot: The Recovery of Native Space in the Northeast* (Minneapolis: University of Minnesota Press, 2008), introduction and chap. 1.

35. Lavin, *Connecticut's Indigenous Peoples,* 134.

36. Ibid., 60–61.

37. For a general introduction to the Woodland period in New England, see Snow, *Archaeology of New England,* chaps. 7–8. For more up-to-date analysis based on individual states, see Lavin, *Connecticut's Indigenous Peoples,* chaps. 6–10; Caduto, *A Time before New Hampshire,* chap. 6; Bourque, *Twelve Thousand Years,* chap. 3; Haviland and Power, *The Original Vermonters,* chaps. 4 and 5.

38. Lavin, *Connecticut's Indigenous Peoples,* 150–151.

CHAPTER TWO

Dawnland on the Eve of Colonization

During the period of 1000–1500 CE, an era that archaeologists often call the "Late Woodland," the lifeways of the indigenous societies in Dawnland had been well established and had ancient roots that went back many thousands of years. Native Americans of the region that would later be called New England had well-established ways of subsistence as well as cultural, political, social, and diplomatic systems. While there were differences between the cultures, ceremonials, and lifeways, there existed also some regional similarities in terms of food production and procurement, culture, politics, and diplomacy. Moreover, and though these communities speak and spoke different languages, linguists believe that their languages are related and group them together as "Algonquian speakers." By the 1400s and emerging out of the early history of Dawnland—in which indigenous peoples had adapted to dramatic changes throughout the millennia—the Algonquian inhabitants of the region developed complex and sophisticated lifeways and societies of tremendous regional diversity. Indigenous lifeways and social organization could vary dramatically often depending on a group's geographic location.

This chapter explores the complex cultural, social, economic, and political life of the indigenous peoples of Dawnland. The text sets out by examining demographic factors in New England and explores issues of nomenclature as well as social and political organization in Native American communities. The chapter also examines aspects of indigenous ways of subsistence, social history, and how long-distance exchange networks helped to shape the lives of native peoples on the eve of colonization. These precolonial histories provide us a glimpse into the trajectory of development and change that characterized indigenous societies and helps us to get a better grasp of their ways of life.[1]

The methodological limitations discussed in Chapter 1 regarding archaeo-logical evidence, oral traditions, and the use of early modern European sources will become apparent below and remain an issue, but nonetheless a study of the precolonial past on the eve of colonization is an essential part in our pursuit to better understand the history of Native Americans of New England. Their earlier experiences and social and cultural developments influenced the choices that Native Americans made as societies, groups, and individuals when they had to face European colonization.[2] These histories would shape later interactions in several ways. For one, Native Americans of Dawnland participated in transregional exchange networks, which affected their material culture, patterns of consumption, and daily life and shaped the protocols of their later trade interactions with Europeans. Second, estab-lished precolonial political and diplomatic patterns would have some influ-ence in the postcontact world and would shape how Native Americans and Europeans interacted. Third, the ways of indigenous agriculture and other modes of subsistence would have an impact on the way New English colo-nists would grow and procure food, especially during the early decades of their colonies. Moreover, and while there is a lot we do not know, the preco-lonial history of Native Americans of New England is a fascinating subject worthy of pursuit and exploration in its own right. To gain a better under-standing of the diversity of this earlier past, this chapter examines the ways of life and the cultural, social, and political patterns and organization of the indigenous peoples of Dawnland on the eve of European colonization.

Thus, this chapter runs counter to the many accounts that have long shaped mainstream society's popular perceptions of New England's Native American history. Writers throughout the colonial period and then in the 19th and early 20th centuries, amateur historians who wrote a multitude of local histories of New English towns, created narratives about Native Ameri-cans that were based on stereotypical descriptions. These narratives have a strong legacy because they still influence and shape the way many New En-glanders think about Native Americans today. Many of these authors described Native Americans as "savages" who were "uncivilized" and argued that they were "vanishing Indians." One such writer, reflecting the often racist tenor of the late 19th and early 20th centuries against people of color, wrote that "but a brief account of the Indian inhabitants" was needed. The same author referred to New England's indigenous peoples as "polytheists and polyga-mists, untruthful and fond of gambling" and added pejorative labels such as "hospitable and fond of extravagant dancing and reveling" but also stated that the Native American showed "kindness" to animals and that their forms of "government possessed some noble traits." This writer also argued that Native Americans "can hardly be said to have had proprietary right to the land. They were nomadic, occupying certain territory as long as it afforded them a livelihood." Native Americans were a "wild" and "vanishing race," which "cleared the land" for a more "advanced" and "deserving" New English "civilization." Yet, while these depictions were largely historically inaccurate, these stereotypical representations nonetheless had a powerful impact on popular culture. Their intellectual legacy still shapes the way that many people in mainstream society and beyond imagine the indigenous peoples of the region. Even though Native Americans could be found all over the region, by claiming that they had "vanished" these authors wrote indigenous communities and people "out of existence in New England."[3]

As the discussion below explores, the above account is a misrepresentation of the cultures and histories of the Native Americans of New England. Indigenous peoples in Dawnland had long lived in villages and towns, built houses, practiced agriculture, managed their forests so they could efficiently hunt for meat, fished, and gathered shellfish as well as some other items of importance for them in their daily life. In addition, they used a network of Indian pathways; the rivers, often traveling on portages between different drainage systems; and the ocean for long-distance exchange.

Native Populations of Dawnland

It is impossible to determine the exact indigenous population in New England before 1492, and projections range between 60,000 to more than 200,000. Daniel Gookin, a 17th-century New English colonist and the first superintendent for Praying Indians, for instance, estimated that 126,000 to 144,000 Native Americans lived in southern New England prior to English settlement. Population numbers are based on estimates, and given the destruction of the archaeological record, we likely will never get exact numbers or even estimates. It is also important to underscore that while these population numbers might seem small from a modern perspective, the world's estimated population around 1500 CE was less than half a billion people.[4]

Indigenous voices provide an additional perspective into the density of Native American settlement in Dawnland prior to colonization. Membertou of the Micmacs, a people who lived in what is today Quebec and northern New England and was claimed to be over 100 years old, told the governor of New France, Samuel de Champlain, in 1603 that during his childhood Native Americans were "as thickly planted as the hairs on his head" but that now their numbers had become thin.[5]

As we will explore in the next chapter, the indigenous peoples of Dawnland were among the first in the Americas to experience sustained contact with Europeans, which had a horrible impact on the region's Native American population. The 16th century brought European explorers, shipwreck survivors, traders, fishermen, and slave raiders, and by the 17th century permanent colonial settlements became established in the region. Early contact and colonization also brought trade that exacerbated intergroup conflicts among Native Americans, colonial warfare, and waves of epidemics, all of which proved harmful to the indigenous peoples of Dawnland.[6]

The issue of what we should call the indigenous peoples of Dawnland is also a challenge, complicated by the history of European colonization in the Western Hemisphere. We have already discussed the obvious colonial roots of the geographic signifier "New England." "Native American," a term widely used in this and many other books and which enjoys popularity in contemporary American society to describe the indigenous inhabitants of the Western Hemisphere, also has its shortcomings. For instance, anyone born in a certain place becomes a native of that particular location. Moreover, the word "America" was introduced by the Central European mapmaker Martin Waldseemueller, who named the Western Hemisphere after the Southern European navigator Amerigo Vespucci. The label "Indian," which is an alternative name for the indigenous peoples of the Americas, was probably coined by Christopher Columbus, who in 1492 thought that he had sailed to Asia, then a place that Europeans often called the "Indies." In addition, since labels such as "Native American" and "Indian" are used to describe a wide array of peoples from Dawnland and the entire continental landmass of the Americas, they fail to encapsulate the diversity that existed among indigenous peoples.

The story of nomenclature is equally complex when studied at a more local level, as an examination of this issue among the indigenous peoples of the Merrimack River Valley and its tributaries, a drainage system located in what is today New Hampshire, the southern corner of Maine, and northeastern Massachusetts, makes clear. In the 1620s and 1630s, for instance, some New English colonists called the indigenous groups in that area "Aberginians." Experts are not sure if this name derives from some inexplicable root or from "Aborigine" or "Wabanaki." The term "Wabanaki," referring to a conglomerate of various Native American groups in northern New England and southeastern Canada, becomes further complicated as indigenous studies researchers subdivide these communities into Western, Eastern, and in some cases even a Central Wabanaki category. In addition, 17th-century New English colonial records name several indigenous groups that lived in the greater Merrimack River Valley drainage system such as the "Pawtucket," "Amoskeag," "Agawam," "Wachusett," "Nashawy," "Winnipesaukee," "Pentucket," and "Naumkeag," just to mention a few. Some scholars argue that several of the above-listed groups were part of an alliance network they call the "Pennacook," which was also the name of a Native American town that could be found on the site where today the city of Concord in New Hampshire stands.[7] However, beyond this our understanding of the indigenous peoples of the Merrimack River Valley—the organization of their alliance, their territorial reach, and ethnic makeup—is limited.

Much of what we think we know about Native Americans of Dawnland prior to contact comes from sources from the 16th and 17th centuries. Some researchers who study these primary documents argue that the indigenous peoples of New England at the time participated in flexible political alliance systems that included multiple towns and villages—formations that European colonists and later Euro-Americans would refer to as "tribes." Yet, these tribes were generally lose associations, and Native American towns and villages ran their affairs independently, acted on their own, followed different interests and goals, and were politically fluid structures.[8]

We also have to ask, especially given the devastating impact that colonization and disease had on the indigenous peoples of Dawnland, how representative are the tribes described in 17th-century European records of the political and social structures that existed before the coming of Europeans? How much had the situation changed for indigenous peoples in the contact period? Did germs and colonization result in high mortality rates, shifting alliances, conflict, and the need to take in more neighbors as a result of increased warfare, disease, or slave raiding? In other words, did political and community structures change as a result of the coming of the Europeans? Much of this discussion is ground for speculation, but it is likely that the indigenous populations and social structures prior to colonization looked different from the ones described by European sources in the 17th century.

Thus, as much as possible this chapter attempts to avoid the use of contemporary or historic names of Native Americans groups from Dawnland to describe the indigenous populations before 1492. There is a problem of imposing historic and contemporary indigenous groups on the precolonial past, about which we know so little. While this will make the discussion of Native American groups at times vague, it is a more honest way of discussing this history. This is an exercise–it must be emphasized–about nomenclature, as there are clear links between contemporary indigenous nations and Native American groups of the precolonial past. Yet, these links, as we will see in the chapters below, were dramatically changed, interrupted, and destroyed, which required indigenous people to nurture, repair, and rebuild their communities and lives in order to survive. There is much we still do not understand about the massively disruptive impact that colonization had on the indigenous peoples of New England and the Western Hemisphere. However, it is clear that European colonization not only dramatically altered the lives of Native Americans, often in a destructive manner, but also likely obliterated indigenous political and social structures. The indigenous world before 1492 looked quite different from that of later centuries. Still, it is important to recall that the indigenous peoples of Dawnland throughout their history adapted, changed, and survived—despite often dramatic transformations to their world and lives.[9]

Ways of Subsistence

On the eve of colonization, Native Americans of Dawnland had developed complex ways of subsistence. Many of the region's indigenous peoples farmed. Due to the absence of domestic animals in North America, Native Americans not only developed divergent ways of agriculture compared to Europeans but also had to rely on hunting and fishing as a means to procure protein for their diet. They also gathered plants for food, medicine, and other uses.

Agriculture played a central part in the subsistence of Native American communities of southern New England and was also practiced by villages farther north when microclimates and geographic circumstances allowed for farming. Towns and villages all over the region were located next to farm fields. With no indigenous North American beasts of burden, Native Americans developed an agricultural labor system that was based on the use of hoes and digging sticks rather than the use of plows pulled by draft animals, as existed in Europe. Because of the upper-body strength needed to operate a plow, males likely emerged as the primary farmers in European society. Maybe women were the primary agricultural producers in the indigenous societies of the Eastern Woodlands because the work process with hoes and digging sticks did not bias toward male operation or because of the cultural connection that the peoples of Dawnland drew between women and fertility, the fact that women were seen as the givers of life or sustenance, or maybe for other unknown reasons.

That said, men helped with the extremely time-consuming and labor-intensive task of clearing the agricultural fields. This was a job that had to be done every few years as Native American farming societies in New England moved their farm fields and settlements. This guaranteed that their agricultural fields stayed fertile and allowed abandoned lands to rejuvenate and regenerate. It was a sustainable way of farming and land use.

This was likely a major reason why in later years European observers would dismiss the existence of or belittle Native American agriculture, since this work was done by women. Due to the alternative and, to them, alien-gendered division of labor, Europeans often depicted indigenous men as "lazy" and described women as living a life of "drudgery."[10] Such observers refused to grasp that farming provided indigenous women with a degree of status, prestige, and power in their societies. This was a reality that most New English refused to acknowledge, and they instead continued to dismiss or ignore the farming work of Native American women into the 19th century, because traditional ways of farming continued to persist in many parts of New England until then.

The claim that indigenous people did not farm or that they were nomadic served an additional purpose, as it became a way to legitimize the dispossession of aboriginal lands. Developing European legal systems in the early modern period came to increasingly theorize that hunter-gatherers and pastoralists were not using the land adequately. According to this theory, European empires and colonists were entitled to take over these lands and make them theirs. By claiming that indigenous peoples in New England were nomadic, even though they were agriculturalists, Europeans came up with a "legal" justification to take over aboriginal lands. Such beliefs, alongside other "legal" arguments, justified dispossession of indigenous lands in the Americas as well as lands in Oceania, Africa, and Asia.[11]

Despite the New English colonial legal fictions of the 17th and 18th centuries, the indigenous peoples of Dawnland had long farmed corn, squash, pumpkins, and beans. They planted crops in April and May. They worked the fields in the spring with a hoe, clearing them of weeds. The hoes that women farmers used before European contact were often long sticks with a freshwater or saltwater shell or a bone attached at the end. This useful tool could be used to clear weeds, and at the beginning of the summer season women used them to hill the corn. They pushed little earth piles of a few inches around the stem of the corn. This procedure helped the plant to grow straight, strong, and tall and made it more drought resistant. The little earth mounds were also perfect for growing beans, which helped to increase the corn's fertility and provided the plant extra support, thereby increasing its stability. Women also planted pumpkins, gourds, squash, and herbs in the same field, which again increased the fertility of the soil. Throughout the growing season women and children would weed the fields and protect their crops from intruding animals.

To this day, corn plays an important role in the ceremonial and cultural life of many of the indigenous peoples of Dawnland. Many Native American stories mention the importance of corn as a life-giving force or how communities obtained this crop. Moreover, many Native American communities in contemporary New England, such as the Narragansett and the Wampanoag communities, celebrate the Green Corn Festival in the late summer and fall, right at the point when the corn is ready to be harvested. Traditionally as today, the event celebrates this essential and life-supporting crop and is a ceremony of thanksgiving for a sustaining harvest.

New English colonists quickly learned the importance of corn. In fact, colonial farmers adopted the crop once they had learned from their indigenous neighbors how to grow it. New English colonists grasped the centrality that corn played in the lives of Native Americans. During King Philip's War and during other wars in the 17th and 18th centuries, New English militias often attacked in the summer and frequently burned the cornfields of Native Americans. The militias also often targeted and destroyed the corn supplies during attacks on indigenous towns and villages. This strategy of total warfare aimed to push Native American opponents to either starve, retreat, or submit to New English authority.

A northeastern Algonquian Indian account recorded in the early 19th century provides us an insightful glimpse into the subsistence of Native Americans during the Woodland period. This is an interesting piece of evidence, found in New English documents, of Native Americans' knowledge of their ancestors' precolonial subsistence and history:

> As our ancestors had no art of manufacturing any sort of metal they had no implements of husbandry; therefor were not able to cultivate their lands but little, that of planting skommon or Indian corn, beans, and little squashes, which was chiefly under the management of women. . . . When they found that their fields will fail, they are to prepare another piece of lands [sic]; . . . they make a fire round the foot of every tree, as many trees as standing on the ground they intend to clear, until the bark of the tree is burnt through, for trees are killed very easy in this manner. They planted while trees are standing after they are killed; and as soon as trees are fell, they burnt it of such length that they might roll the logs together, and burnt them up to ashes, thus they do till they get it quite clear. An industrious woman, when great many dry logs are fallen, could burn off as many logs in one day as a smart man can chop in two or three days time with an axe. They make use of only an uthonnetmuhheakun or a stone axe, something like the shape of an axe, . . . with which they rub the coals of the burning logs.[12]

Thus, on the eve of colonization Native Americans had developed an efficient system of slash-and-burn agriculture, and by moving their farm fields and villages after several years of use, Dawnland's indigenous mobile farmers developed a sustainable system of land use.

Native Americans built an array of styles of houses in their settlements throughout Dawnland. Daniel Gookin wrote, for instance, that indigenous *wetus*, which he and other New English writers called "wigwams," the oval-shaped traditional houses of many of the Native Americans who lived in southern New England, were "built with small poles fixed in the ground, bent and fastened." *Wetus* could be easily assembled, taken down, and rebuilt. They were thus mobile dwellings that could be moved if farm fields had to be moved and were well adapted to the lifeways of mobile farming societies. "The best sort of their houses are covered very neatly tight, and warm, with bark of trees. . . . The meaner sort of wigwams are covered with mats, they make of" cattail, which grows in wetlands all over New England. Cattail was not only used in the building of walls but was also used to produce mats that would line the inside of *wetus*. These mats were then often covered with fur or deerskin for increased comfort and warmth. Native Americans built the *wetus* to be well insulated and warm in the winter. Gookin wrote that "I have often lodged in their wigwams; and have found them as warm as the best

English houses." They were heated by a varying number of fireplaces, which depended on the size of the building. According to Gookin, indigenous people in the region built the "houses" in "several sizes, according to their activity and ability; some twenty, some forty feet long, and broad. Some I have seen . . . of a hundred feet long, and thirty feet broad."[13] Thus, Native Americans built housing in various forms and sizes and out of locally available and abundant materials. Samuel de Champlain's observations further underscore the rich variety of housing that existed in Dawnland. During his exploration of the New England coast from 1604 to 1607, Champlain observed "large," "circular shape[d]" houses on what is now Cape Cod. These were covered with grass, corn husks, and reeds.[14] But there was an even greater variety of housing styles. Native Americans also built smaller hunting residences, huts, and shelters according to their needs, and regional and seasonal variations shaped the housing styles of the indigenous peoples of Dawnland.

European writers of the 17th century also mentioned that Native Americans built palisaded structures made of trees to protect their settlements or that they had such structures close by to their settlements to seek refuge in. There is debate among researchers as to whether Native Americans of New England built forts before European colonization or if these forts were only built as a result of contact with Europeans, a development that likely reinforced increased intergroup rivalries in the region.

As noted previously, the domesticated animals that played a central role in European farming were largely absent from the Americas. Short of the dog and in the Andes the lama, there were no animals in the Western Hemisphere that could be domesticated.[15] Thus, Native Americans had developed different strategies to farm but also to get meat and protein into their diet.

The Native American peoples of Dawnland relied on hunting and fishing as their means to procure animal meat. Indigenous peoples all over the Eastern Woodlands created methods to manage the woods, which made the forest more useful and productive. They burned the undergrowth and brush of the woods, thereby opening up the forest. Through such methods of forest management, the woods became more attractive to deer and other animals, as the reshaped sylvan landscape was more conducive to the growth of plants that various creatures liked to consume. Moreover, Native American men, who were generally the hunters, could more easily spot, pursue, and stalk their prey, and their arrows could more easily hit their target, as undergrowth did not impede their arrows or view. Thus, just like farmers and pastoralists in Europe, Asia, and Africa who worked their pasture land to feed and create better conditions for their domestic animals, indigenous peoples of the Eastern Woodlands manipulated their ecosystems to increase their meat supply by actively managing their forest environments.[16]

Native Americans of New England hunted a wide variety of animals. They pursued larger game such as deer, moose, and caribou. At least during the early years of European colonization, records seem to suggest that Native Americans held communal hunts of these animals in the fall after harvest and in the winter months. Hunters and hunting parties in the regions also regularly hunted bears and likely also killed the occasional catamount, lynx, coyote, or wolf. Indigenous peoples also hunted and trapped for smaller animals such as wild turkeys, rabbits, squirrels, Canada geese, ducks, other migratory water fowl, birds, beavers, otters, raccoons, turtles, snakes, and other reptiles. Smaller game was generally pursued by individual hunters rather than by hunting parties.[17]

Moreover, smaller animals were often pursued by younger boys and sometimes girls in close vicinity to their home community. These local hunts were part entertainment but also education. Moving quietly through the woods, stalking animals, learning about which areas are suitable for which wildlife and what their places of dwelling looked like, covering up body odor, and using the natural elements such as wind, sun, and rain to your advantage were all skills that young hunters would learn in their pursuits.

The account by a northeastern Algonquian Indian from the early 19th century on hunting and fishing proves again to be an insightful window into the lifeways of the indigenous peoples of Dawnland. He wrote that Native American men

> used bow and arrow to kill game, with which they were expert. They used to catch deer by ensnaring them with strings. By hunting they supplied themselves with cloathing and diet; they seldom felt much want, and they were very well contented with their condition; having food and raiment was their only aim. They were not to kill more than was necessary, for there was none to barter with them that would have tempted them to waste their animals, as they did after the Chuckopek, or white people came on this island, consequently game was never diminished. They hunted occasionally a whole year; but hunting seasons are properly divided into two part of a year. In fall, they hunt for deer, bear, beaver, otter, rakoon, fishes, marten for their cloathing and drying meat for the ensuing season; and in the beginning of March, they used to go out to hunt for moose on the green mountains, where these animals keep for winter quarters. From thence, they go again for beaver hunting as soon as the rivers, ponds, and creeks are open; but they used to take good care not to stay over two months.[18]

As this Native American observer suggests, the subsistence hunting patterns of the indigenous peoples in Dawnland were thus at least in part shaped by the changing seasonal cycles in the region. Moreover, this account alludes to great changes over time. The increasing European presence in the region altered the dynamics that the hunt played in the daily life of the Native Americans.

Comments by Nicholas Denys, a French aristocrat, colonist, and governor of New France who was also a familiar observer of the indigenous peoples of Dawnland, seem to support the earlier view that hunting changed dramatically due to the impact of European colonization in the region. He wrote in 1672 that

> The hunting by the Indians in old times was easy for them. They killed animals only in proportion as they had need of them. When they were tired of eating one sort, they killed some of another. If they did not wish to eat meat, they caught some fish. They never made accumulation of skins of Moose, Beaver, Otter, or others, but only so far as they needed them for personal use.[19]

Traditionally, hunting and fishing provided Native Americans with a source of protein, thereby enriching their diet. Yet, European colonization in Dawnland also drew Native Americans into the fur trade, thus leading to the ensuing changes in hunting behavior not only among the indigenous peoples of New England but also in many other parts of North America. By hunting beaver and other animals, Native Americans in the region participated in a transatlantic and global trade. Their furs and animal skins were sold in European and global markets and would allow Native Americans to purchase European and Asian goods. The trade, spurred by European colonization, had a disruptive influence on Native Americans in Dawnland, spurring conflict among the diverse indigenous communities around the region who competed for access to hunting grounds. This competition reinforced intergroup rivalries and led to increased warfare, conflicts during which Native Americans made wide use of firearms. At the same time, the fur trade provided indigenous peoples with economic opportunities and lasted as a way of subsistence in northern New England for a small number of Native Americans well into the 19th century.[20]

Archaeological evidence and 16th- and 17th-century writings by Europeans on Native Americans of Dawnland suggest that leather and fur, obtained through the hunt, were the major fabrics used by indigenous people to produce clothing prior to colonization and during the early contact period. The aboriginal style of dress was perfectly adapted to New England's weather of "assaulting heat of their parching summers and the piercing cold of the icy winters." Native Americans tanned deer and moose skins and turned them into leather, which they used to make clothing such as shoes, dresses, and leg coverings. This leather gear was particularly water repellent and fast drying. Men would generally wear breeches as undergarments, and in the hot months it would be their major dress, while in the colder months they wore leg and upper-body coverings. Women wore aprons as undergarments and usually wore dresses over them. In colder months Native Americans would also wear a mantle made of fur, usually put together from the skins of animals such as moose, beaver, otter, and raccoon.[21] Indigenous people also used dyes and paints made from berries and roots to decorate, color, or dye clothes. These natural dyes held color in severe weather and for long periods of time. Moreover, Native Americans of Dawnland wore accessories and jewelry, such as necklaces and earrings, and women often wore strings of beads around their necks and ankles, while men often wore tobacco bags around their necks.

Native Americans also used tattoos to decorate their bodies. Some Native Americans, observed an English colonist in the 1630s, had images of animals tattooed on their cheeks such as "bears, deer, moose, wolves, . . . eagles, hawks." They did these by making "incision, or else by raising of their skin with a small sharp instrument which makes the desired form apparent and permanent."[22] Another New English colonist observed that the indigenous peoples of Dawnland "oil their skins and hair with bear's grease." They also "paint their faces with vermilion, or other red. . . . Also they use black and white paints, and make one part of their face of one colour; and another, of another, very deformedly. The women especially do thus; some men also, especially when they are marching to their wars . . . [as] they think, [they] are [thus] more terrible to their enemies."[23]

Just as in earlier times, gathering of shellfish and fishing continued to play an important role in the subsistence of many Native Americans in the Late Woodland period. Indigenous people continued to use the Atlantic Ocean and the region's rivers, brooks, ponds, and lakes as a source for food. Like meat, fish and shellfish were a great source of protein and minerals that enriched the diet of indigenous people in Dawnland. Native Americans had rich shellfishing and fishing traditions and used many tools and strategies in their pursuit of this mode of subsistence.

Throughout the year Native Americans harvested shellfish in saltwater and freshwater. For those who had access to them, saltwater and freshwater clams provided a major food item. Like venison, a meat widely eaten by Native Americans, clams are low in calories, cholesterol, and fats but at the same time are a rich source of minerals, vitamins, and protein. Other than clams, the indigenous peoples of Dawnland gathered and pursued a rich variety of other shellfish such as oysters, quahogs, scallops, lobsters, crabs, and crayfish. In coastal areas, Native Americans gathered shellfish year-round and inland for as long as the waterways were not frozen. Archaeologists have frequently found old shellfish heaps in close vicinity to precolonial and early contact period Native American settlement sites situated around the region's waterways and extensive coastline. Moreover, researchers have uncovered sites going back to the Archaic period that are in close vicinity to spawning grounds, where waste and high mercury residue in the ground suggest that Native Americans have fished in these locations.[24]

Native Americans fished in the Atlantic as well as in the interior water-ways. In the ocean they caught fish such as sturgeon, striped bass, cunner, bluefish, blackfish, and scup. Rivers, ponds, and lakes provided rich fishing grounds for trout, eel, and other native freshwater fish species. Moreover, the region's rivers became active during spawning season, and the waterfalls became rich hunting grounds during these times. As fish such as salmon, alewife, and shad moved upstream, waterfalls became gathering places for many indigenous peoples who met up to take advantage of the abundance of fish that were trying to cross these natural barriers in their efforts to pro-create upstream. Colonial records and oral traditions suggest that this con-vergence of indigenous peoples also provided an opportunity to partake in diplomatic and political exchanges as well as to socialize. The population size of precolonial Native American towns such as Pawtucket and Amoskeag, both located in close vicinity to waterfalls on the Merrimack River, quadru-pled during those periods. Spawning season was a time in which Native American alliance systems or related groups would gather in such places to hold council. Likely spurred by a joyful mood created by the abundance of fish, this was also a period of celebration and social gatherings in which aboriginal Dawnlanders connected and reunited with friends and family who lived in communities often some distance away from their settlement.

New England's Native American populations also knew about the migra-tory behavior of other species of fish. They knew, for instance, that eel had an opposite migratory pattern compared to anadromous fish such as salmon, alewife, and shad. While these species moved upriver from the sea to pro-create, the eel populations that lived in the freshwaters of New England would return to the ocean to spawn. Other fish such as herring and Atlantic sturgeon also come into freshwater during certain seasons, while striped bass and bluefish spend time in coastal waters during certain times of the year. The indigenous peoples of Dawnland knew the migratory patterns of fish and adapted their fishing practices, techniques, and subsistence patterns accordingly.[25]

Early English colonists were especially impressed by the size and volume of fish they could catch off the coast and in the waterways. Colonial writings on the abundance of fish provides a small glimpse into the wealth of natural resources that existed in precolonial Dawnland that provided to its indige-nous peoples lavish resources for their subsistence. "The sturgeons," wrote one colonist in the early 1630s, "be all over the country, but the best catching of them is upon the shoals of Cape Cod and in the river of Merrimac, where much is taken, pickled, and brought for England. Some of these be 12, 14, 18 foot long. I set not down the price of fish there because it is so cheap."[26] Euro-pean colonization resulted in the depletion and destruction of the region's many resources, including the diverse and healthy fish population.

Native Americans of New England had developed a sophisticated material culture around fishing. Nets and lines weighed down with pebbles, harpoons, leister, bone gorges, and fishing hooks were widely used to catch fish. Indigenous peoples in the region also built and used fishing weirs (cane basket fish traps) very effectively. There is also evidence that suggests that Native Americans constructed wooden scaffolding and fishing platforms at waterfalls. These allowed indigenous fishermen to maximize their access to waterfalls and rivers, enabling them to increase their catch during spawning season. The ropes and lines that Native Americans made and used for fishing and construction, a material described by New English colonists as "Indian hemp," was recognized for its quality and durability.[27]

Whales are another likely ocean creature that Native Americans in coastal New England subsisted on, harvesting the animal for its meat, bones, and oil. Recall the earlier Aquinnah story of Mashup on the island of Noepe (Martha's Vineyard). Moshup, the giant, leader, and culture hero of the island's indigenous inhabitants, fed his people the whales that he caught in the ocean and threw on land. Evidence suggests that the indigenous peoples in coastal Dawnland ate and processed beached whales. In fact, the Aquinnahs today argue that they retain the right to any drift whale stranded on the island. The closely related and frequently interacting indigenous communities of coastal southern New England and Long Island also built sturdy and large oceangoing canoes, which they used to catch fish at sea. There is severe disagreement among those who study the history of these communities, but some suggest that the region's Native Americans also might have used their large canoes to hunt whales.[28]

Despite the importance that farming, hunting, and fishing played in the subsistence of Dawnland's indigenous societies, Native Americans also gathered edible wild plants, berries, and nuts as part of their diet. In the spring, Native Americans gathered fiddlehead fern, dandelions, Jack-in-the-pulpit, wild leek, skunk cabbage, and strawberries. During the summer, they collected plants such as wild plums, cattail, and wild grapes. In the fall, they gathered things such as acorns, goosefoot, and wild rice. During the winter months Native Americans would consume dried mushrooms, walnuts, and cattail. But this is only a small list of the many edible plants that the indigenous peoples of New England knew and ate.[29]

Likely, it was women and children who gathered bulbs, shoots, leaves, blossoms, nuts, berries, tubers, and roots, and they prepared these foods in a variety of ways by, for example, boiling, baking, steaming, or adding them to meals, stews, or mush. Native Americans also ate several edible plants, fruits, and nuts either fresh or dried. Other plant varieties, such as cattail, groundnut, Jerusalem artichoke, and nuts were pounded into flour. This flour was then used to make breads and cakes and to thicken liquid gruels. Nuts were also sometimes boiled for their oil. Native Americans in Dawnland also dried fruits and later added them to meals. The region's indigenous peoples also used plant-based foods to flavor their meals, and many of these were gathered or collected. For instance, indigenous peoples tapped maple, birch, and several other trees for naturally occurring sugars. They also used the roots of cattails as a natural sweetener. Wild varieties of parsley, garlic, leek, mint, and onion as well as black mustard, catbrier, and dried sassafras and flowers of the milkweed plant, in addition to the roots of the purple avens (which has a chocolaty flavor) and coltsfoot (which after drying and burning to ash assumes a salty flavor), were used to add spice and enhance the taste of meals. Moreover, all the above-discussed food items helped to enrich the diet. These foods helped to provide local populations with essential protein, minerals, vitamins, and fatty acid, all a strong basis for a healthy diet.[30]

Native Americans in Dawnland had significant knowledge of the medicinal and healing powers of many of the plants in their environment. Indigenous peoples used part of the sassafras plant, which can be found in the dry and open woodlands in southern New England, including its roots, bark, twigs, and leaves as medicine. The bark from the winged sumac, a tree that, like the sassafras plant, grows in dry woods as well as in clearings, was used to concoct a liquid to treat blisters. Some used the roots from this plant to make an infusion to treat dysentery. The hazelnut plant, which can be found growing in woodland thickets, not only bore nuts that can be eaten but also the source of a brewed liquid concoction from its bark that could be used to treat hives and fevers and as an ointment to dress wounds. These are just a few examples of how indigenous peoples used plants as medicine.[31]

As alluded to in the discussion above, food preparation and diet were diverse among the Native Americans of New England. Daniel Gookin provides us a glimpse into the aboriginal ways of cooking and baking—especially the making of gruel and bread:

> Their food is generally boiled maize, or Indian corn, mixed with kidney beans, or sometimes without. Also they frequently boil in this pottage fish, either new or dried, as shad, eels, alewives or a kind of herring, or any other sort of fish. . . . Also they boil in this furmentry all sorts of flesh, they take in hunting; as venison, beaver, bear's flesh, moose, otters, rackoons, or any kind that they take in hunting. Also they mix with the said pottage several sorts of roots; as Jerusalem artichokes, and ground sorts, and other roots, and pompions [pumpkin], and squashes and also several sorts of nuts or masts, as oak-acorns, chesnuts, walnuts: these husked and dried, and powdered, they thicken their pottage therewith. Also sometimes they beat their maize into meal, and sift it through a basket, made for that purpose. With this meal they make bread, baking it in the ashes, covering the dough with leaves. Sometimes they make of their meal a small sort of cakes, and boil them. They also make a certain sort of meal of parched

maize. This meal they call nokake. It is so sweet, toothsome and hearty, that an Indian will travel many days with no other food but this meal, which he eatheth as he needs, and after drinketh water. And for this end, when they travel a journey, or go hunting, they carry this nokake in a basket, or bag, for their use.[32]

While many European observers often disparaged the taste of these dishes, such meals provided a healthy, sustaining, and sustainable cuisine to those who ate it.

Early European observers and colonists often ascribed the healthy appearance of Native Americans to their diet and lifeways. William Wood, an English colonist who spent some time in Massachusetts around the early 1630s and wrote a book titled *New England's Prospect,* which focused on the region's environment and indigenous peoples, described the Native Americans of New England as "healthful," "straight bodied, strongly composed," and "tall." He observed that he had "been in many places, yet did I never see one . . . that sickness had deformed." He also noticed that "when they change their bare Indian commons for the plenty of England's fuller diet, it is so contrary to their stomachs that death or desperate sickness immediately accrues, which makes so few of them desirous to see England."[33] The early 17th-century English explorer John Brereton echoed Wood's observation. Brereton described the indigenous people he encountered in southeastern New England as "exceedingly . . . well-conditioned . . . of stature much higher than we."[34] European observers in the 17th century certainly noticed that Dawnland's indigenous people had healthier lifeways compared to Europeans, and this subject fascinated several writers including Wood and Brereton.

New English writers also often commented on the hospitality of the Native Americans of Dawnland. Daniel Gookin wrote, for instance, that "if any stranger come to their houses, they will give him the best lodgings and diet they have."[35] These rules of hospitality were likely in place before the coming of Europeans. They were probably shaped by moral codes of reciprocity and were made possible by the indigenous peoples' ability to master and maximize the region's resources for their subsistence. Yet even during the hardship years when war with and territorial encroachments by the New English had a devastating impact on the region throughout the 17th and 18th centuries, Native Americans would provide refuge to members of neighboring groups who had been pushed out or were forced to flee, a moral commitment often rationalized as needing to aid one's "kin"—relationships that were as often imagined as they were real. During these conflicts, the indigenous peoples of Dawnland would also feed and treat many of their European war captives with respect, despite the devastation that colonization and war had brought to their homelands.

Toward a Social History of the Precolonial Dawnland

The limited evidence based on the observations of 16th- and 17th-century Europeans as well as limited archaeological data and oral traditions provides us only a glimpse into the social and cultural history of the indigenous peoples of Dawnland on the eve of colonization. Our fragmentary knowledge creates analytical problems, but it is the only window through which we can gain some limited insights into issues such as conflict, social and community organization, family, and some indigenous cultural beliefs and practices.

Judging from Native American oral traditions, conflict was part of Native American life in Dawnland on the eve of colonization. Human remains found by archaeologists also suggest that Native Americans were killed or injured in skirmishes. Skeletal remains indicate that there are incidents when indigenous peoples were killed by head injuries, likely inflicted by war clubs, and there is also evidence of others being killed or mortally wounded by arrowheads and spear points. War clubs, protective armor, shields, and bows and arrows made up the diverse weaponry. Oral traditions also suggest that Native American fighters were expected to display decisiveness and bravery on the battlefield. Strategic retreats when facing undefeatable odds or finding safety in a fortification during an enemy attack, however, were frequent strategic choices. These decisions were often belittled by European writers as cowardice. Equally, underscoring the bravery of Native American fighters, it was not unusual for much smaller war parties to attack larger ones or even the settlements of enemy groups if they felt that the element of surprise could strike fear into their enemy and provide the attackers with a significant enough advantage to carry the battle. Indigenous fighters were also expected to be tough and stoic when injured in battle. One colonial writer observed in the early 1630s that the "unexpected approach of a mortal wound by a bullet, an arrow, or sword strikes no more terror, causes no more exclamation, no more complaint or winceing than if it had been shot into a tree."[36] Warfare and Native American use of technology in warfare would alter after 1500, when European colonization brought about dramatic changes in Dawnland, which also had a dramatic impact on indigenous warfare practices and technology.[37]

The social and cultural organization in precolonial Dawnland societies was also diverse and complex and was guided by leaders who spearheaded indigenous communities and alliance systems (which as we discussed earlier in the chapter usually consisted of an amalgamation of indigenous settlements). Given the diversity in size of indigenous societies in the region, there also existed various systems of social organization and leadership models. Early English observers usually called indigenous leaders by names such as "king," "sachem," "sagamore," "*bashaba*," and "chief," and several of these terms had been adopted by European colonial writers from indigenous languages. While the historic record suggests that many leaders were male, it is important to underscore that there are also examples of female authority figures, whom some communities in southeastern New England called *sunq-squaws*. In coastal Dawnland, especially in the southern parts of the region, indigenous societies on the eve of colonization were led by sachems with centralized powers and authority. The coastal communities also had an elite group of warriors and political leaders who had authority over communities in the alliance system; these individuals served as advisers to the sachem and helped to guide their nation. But while this might have been the system of governance in the coastal areas of southern New England, this was certainly not a universal arrangement of political and social organization. The limited evidence suggests that indigenous communities farther to the north and in the interior tended to be smaller, less centralized in the implementation of power, and also more egalitarian. Beyond these generalities, these communities had diverse and varied systems of leadership and social organization.[38]

Spiritual leaders, whom European sources call "medicine men," "priests," "shamans," or some variation of "*powah*," also played an important role in aboriginal Dawnland societies. Their power was based on their medicinal knowledge, but many of these leaders were also believed to have certain supernatural abilities and connections. Both men and women could hold the power and office of a spiritual leader. Gookin wrote in 1674, for instance, that "there are among them certain men and women, whom they call pow-wows: These are partly wizards and witches . . . and partly are physicians, and make use at least in show, of herbs and roots for curing the sick and diseased."[39] But it was their spiritual abilities that had the greatest healing power, Native Americans believed. "In sickness the Priest comes close to the sick person," wrote the governor of Rhode Island, Roger Williams, describing a healing ritual of a spiritual leader in 1643 who "performes many strange Actions about him, and threatens and conjures out the sickness. They conceive that there are many Gods or divine Powers within the body of a man: In his pulse, his heart, his Longs, & c." Activating these forces through supernatural connections could help a sick person to heal. In addition, spiritual leaders were not only healers but also performed diverse ceremonial functions, which varied across the many indigenous societies of Dawnland. Williams provides a glimpse into one of those ceremonials among the native groups in southeastern New England. "These doe begin and order their service and Invocation of their Gods, and all the people follow, and joyne interchangeably in a laborious service, into sweating, especially of the Priest, who spends himself." But these sources equally reveal the weaknesses, biases, and stereotypes of the colonial era records. "Beholding what their Worship was," Williams quickly left because he did not want to be a "partaker of Sathans Inventions and Worships."[40] Such biases in the documentary record and the missing links in the oral traditions on precolonial societies, which were caused by the high mortality rates from epidemics and colonization, and the limitations of the archaeological evidence to provide conclusive answers in these particular areas make it hard for us to know more about political and spiritual leadership in precontact indigenous communities specifically but also the social and cultural history of Native Americans of New England on the eve of colonization more generally.

There is also evidence from the colonial period that suggests that sometimes the power of political and spiritual leadership could be combined in one person. New English writers often cite the 17th-century Native American leader Passaconaway from the Merrimack River Valley as an example. Passaconaway was not only the *bashaba,* or leader, of an alliance of Native American communities in the region but was also reputed to have magical and supernatural powers. An early colonist in New England named Thomas Morton wrote in the early 1630s that Passaconaway could dive "under water to the further side of the" Merrimack River, a distance too wide "for any man to undertake with a breath & deluding the company with casting a mist before their eyes that see him enter in and come out." Morton also wrote that several English observers had seen Passaconaway "make Ice appeare in a bowl of faire water."[41] The Englishman William Wood, who was less of a believer in supernatural and magical powers than most of his Puritan New English contemporaries, observed that if "we believe" the Native American accounts, Passaconaway "can make the water burn, the rocks move, the trees dance, metamorphise himself into a flaming man." Passaconaway's power also reportedly enabled him to produce "a new green leaf" from the ashes of an old burned one in the middle of winter "and make of a dead snake's skin a living snake."[42]

There are gaping holes in our knowledge of the spiritual and philosophical life of pre-Columbian Native American communities in Dawnland. "Their religion is as of other gentiles," wrote Gookin. "Some of their Gods adore the sun; others the moon; some the earth; others, the fire. . . . Yet generally they acknowledge one great supreme-being doer of good; and him they call Woonand, or Mannit [Manitou]."[43] Oral traditions and early European observers suggest that the indigenous peoples in the region saw themselves as having close spiritual connections with the natural world. Moreover, they saw their world as being spiritually alive and imbued with celestial forces. The indigenous peoples in Dawnland, according to the Jesuit missionary Father Paul Le Jeune who worked among the Montagnais Indians in New France in the 1630s, "address themselves to the Earth, to Rivers, to Lakes, to dangerous Rocks, but above all, to the Sky. . . . They have recourse to the Sky in almost all their necessities and respect the great bodies [stars] in it above all creatures."[44] Sources such as the ones cited above merely provide superficial and oversimplified insights into what the spiritual life and cosmology of Native American societies must have looked like on the eve of colonization. Given the available evidence, we know next to nothing about the tremendous regional diversity as well as many specific aspects of indigenous beliefs.

Several stone monuments that can be found in various parts of New England are also a source of intellectual controversy among students of Native American studies. For instance, James Mavor and Byron Dix have argued that several of these "stone ruins" served as ritual sites for indigenous peoples and maintain that several have archaeoastronomical significance.[45] Many archaeologists and other researchers dismiss these arguments. They argue that many stone constructions were built by New English settlers in the 17th and 18th centuries and that several other sites were created by the receding Ice Age and not by humans. Certainly many of the stone walls and stone piles that can be found all over New England where built by white colonizers. Nevertheless, several of the stone ruins, marked stones, standing stones, underground chambers, and stone mounds are likely creations of Dawnland's indigenous peoples. There is much we do not understand about these sites, and they are impossible to date. Maybe they are not of astronomical importance as suggested by Mavor and Dix, but they might have served other purposes. The meaning, the purpose, and the indigenous, philosophical, or astronomical body of knowledge that might have led to the construction of such sites and would explain the marking on rocks is little understood at this point. Moreover, as with so much archaeological evidence, New English colonization has not been kind to many of the stone monuments and other indigenous sacred sites, for that matter, countless of which have been destroyed or changed dramatically.[46]

We also have limited evidence on how the indigenous peoples of Dawnland kept track of time and the seasons. Seventeenth-century European writings merely provide a glimpse into these issues. Roger Williams, for instance, wrote that "they are punctual in their promises of keeping time; and sometimes they have charged me with a lie for not punctually keeping time, though hindered."[47] Surviving indigenous religions and philosophical practices in the northern Eastern Woodlands indicate the importance of the moon cycles as well as the stars to keep track of the year and the seasons. The observations by European colonists, such as the Puritan Edward Winslow who traveled on the *Mayflower*, support the oral traditions. He wrote in 1624 that "they keep account of time by the moon and [by] winters and summers. They know divers of the stars by name. In particular they know the North Star and call it *Maske*, which is to say 'the bear.'"[48] Given the sophisticated astronomical knowledge and perception of time among many of the Native American societies throughout the Americas and the limited insights from colonial period documents and oral histories, we can assume that the indigenous peoples of Dawnland had vast knowledge in these fields.

The protection of burial sites and the human remains of their ancestors, as we discussed in the prior chapter, is an important part of Native American activism, and it is no surprise, given the contemporary importance of burial sites, that burials also played an important role in the Native American past. There was a tremendous diversity of techniques and styles in how the indigenous peoples of New England, throughout time and space, buried their dead. Moreover, some of the human remains that have been found were cremated, but many others were not. During the early period of New English colonization, the style of burial in the southern coastal parts of the region were described by Edward Winslow:

> When they bury the dead, they sweep up the corpse in a mat, and so put it in the earth. If the party be a sachem, they cover him with many curious matt and bury all his riches with him, and enclose the grave with a pale. If it be a child, the father will also put his own most special jewels and ornaments in the earth with it; [he] also will cut his hair, and disfigure himself very much, [as a] token of sorrow.[49]

Earlier generations of archaeologists were also interested in the material culture items, alluded to in the above quote, that are left in burial sites and, they argue, can provide them a glimpse into aboriginal cultures and belief systems, but this is a contested practice among Native Americans.[50]

Along with their village, town, or settlement, family played an important role in the social and daily life of the indigenous peoples of Dawnland. Oral traditions and the writings of early European observers suggest that Native Americans valued social cohesion and harmony in their communities and families. According to Roger Williams, "Their affections, especially to their children, are very strong. . . . There are no beggars amongst them, nor fatherless children unprovided for." Child-rearing as well, especially compared to their New English neighbors, was far less authoritarian and much more in line with our modern standards about how to raise children.[51]

The sexual behavior of the indigenous peoples of New England struck their Puritan observers with some shock. They frequently commented on the fact that it was not unusual for unmarried individuals to have sexual relations. They also often commented on the fact that divorce was a common feature in Native American societies. Yet, they equally acknowledged approvingly that married couples lived in committed relationship and that many of them had been together for several decades. Moreover, they liked that Native American children were respectful toward adults.[52]

Oral traditions, archaeological evidence, and 16th- and 17th-century European observers also indicate that Native Americans in New England celebrated a diverse array of rituals. Such celebrations, sometimes referred to as powwows by English observers, marked important events on the ceremonial calendar. This could be the harvest or maturing of crops (such as corn) or a particular plant (such as strawberry), spawning season, and many other occasions in the ritual, seasonal, and subsistence cycle of the various indigenous societies of Dawnland. There was regional diversity in rituals, which differed widely among the Native American societies of New England, but such celebrations were often accompanied by feasting, dancing, games, and at times even the distribution of assets. This redistribution of wealth would guarantee greater material equality in a community but also became a ritualized way for leaders to display their generosity and abilities. New English colonization had a dramatic impact on Native American life in general and on aboriginal ritual practices in particular. Starting in the 17th century, several of the New English colonies would begin to ban indigenous rituals, festivals, and gatherings, which forced many Native American groups and families to continue these traditions as lower-profile events and out of sight of mainstream society to escape the ire of colonial and later American officials.[53]

Music also likely played an important part in the life and identity of the precolonial Native American populations in New England, and according to 17th-century European observers, music was an essential part during the region's indigenous festivals, celebrations, and social gatherings. The playing of music was often accompanied by dancing, sometimes performed for ritual purposes and at other times for social purposes. Native Americans made and played instruments such as hand drums, rattles, and other hand percussion instruments. Flutes were also a popular instrument among the indigenous peoples of Dawnland. They made these musical instruments out of wood, bark, gourds, rawhide, and turtle shells. Unfortunately, as with so much of the pre-Columbian cultural and social history of the region, our knowledge in the area of music and dance is relatively limited.[54]

The indigenous peoples of Dawnland also played a number of games to gain physical and mental strength. Team sports were a common feature in Native American society, as they helped individuals work together, an essential skill that contributed to the survival and well-being of indigenous societies. Lacrosse was a popular team sport in New England. The game was extremely physical, requiring cooperation and toughness as well as endurance and dexterity. Lacrosse games were often attended by large crowds of spectators and seemed to have regularly occurred during important celebrations. While many games were played among members of a settlement, they could also be held among different Native American communities. Such games could be an extension of diplomatic overtures but could also be an opportunity to settle a dispute. Native Americans also played card- and dice-like games. They used cards made out of rush stems and stones that were thrown as dice. Native American children also played with dolls (although not all dolls were playthings, as some had important ritual roles) and kid-size weaponry, to train them in the skills to be fighters and hunters, and also played various other games.[55]

Connections: Dawnland and Long-Distance Exchange Networks

Beyond being important sources for subsistence, rivers, lakes, and the Atlantic Ocean played other significant roles in the lives of the indigenous peoples of Dawnland. The region consists of many waterways, which Native Americans used for transportation of trade goods and to travel by to conduct diplomacy as well as war. Such commercial and political exchanges likely aided in the reinforcement and maintenance of ties and relations between different groups. Moreover, by using the ocean and complex networks of pathways and canoe portages, indigenous peoples often traveled beyond their river valleys and homelands and engaged in multifaceted long-distance exchange networks that often reached beyond New England.[56]

Given the centrality of waterways, canoe making was an important part of Native American artisanal production. Gookin wrote on this issue:

> For their water passage, travels and fishing, they make boats, or canoes, either of great trees, pine or chestnut, made hollow, and artificially; which they do by burning them; and after with tools, scraping, smoothing, shaping. Of these they make greater or lesser [in size]. Some I have seen will carry twenty persons, being forty or fifty feet in length, and as broad as a tree will bear.
>
> They make another sort of canoes of birchen bark, which they close together, sewing them with some kind of bark, and then smearing the places with turpentine of the pine tree. They are strengthened in the inside with some few timbers and ribs; yet they are so light, that one man will, and doth, ordinarily carry one of them upon his back several miles, that will transport five or six people.[57]

Canoes were so useful for navigating the interior waterways of North America that European colonists quickly adopted them post-1500. The aboriginal peoples of Dawnland also invented snowshoes, which enabled them to travel long distances overland in wintertime. This was another technology that European colonists quickly adopted when they began to colonize the region.

Native Americans in Dawnland had also developed a network of Indian pathways that reached across the region and far beyond. As we explored earlier, Paleo and Archaic Indians obtained rhyolites, cherts, and flint stones often from long distances away. Recall that they did this by either traveling those distances themselves to obtain and mine these raw materials or trading them with neighboring peoples. To conduct trade, Native Americans on the eve of colonization had also developed a sophisticated path system that not only connected various parts of Dawnland but also connected the region into a continental-wide system in which indigenous peoples exchanged many desired goods over long distances. Yet it is likely that these exchanges not only brought goods but also had more far-reaching cultural and intellectual influences on Dawnland. Did these exchanges help in the development of horticulture, ceramic making, and burial practices and influence local belief systems? While much of this hypothesis is based on educated speculation, the archaeological evidence certainly suggests that this theory was likely the case, as artisanal and artistic production and burial practices indicate some potential influences by the earlier mentioned Mound Builder societies of the Midwest as well as by the cultural practices of other neighboring Native American groups from the Eastern Woodlands. There are several researchers who emphasize these links. Moreover, the legacies of these indigenous long-distance exchange networks often remain a part of our daily life, albeit one we are not conscious of. Several of New England's modern highways and routes follow in close proximity or are built on top of the ancient networks of the Native American pathways of Dawnland.[58]

Wampum, a small bead that Native American craftspeople made out of shells that could be strung into bracelets or belts or attached to clothing, was likely one of the region's most desired long-distance trade items. Wampum brought prosperity and wealth to the coastal communities of today's southern New England and Long Island. Wampum had spiritual importance in the region as a purifying and protective material, and there is archaeological evidence from burials where deceased members of communities wore wampum as jewelry or had clothes that were adorned with the material. Moreover, belts made of wampum became objects to commemorate important events or to note an important diplomatic alliance. Wampum beads were white and purple in tone, and in several northern Eastern Woodland societies, to bring a string of white or purple wampum to competitors was a way to give that group a choice between purple, which represented conflict, and white, which represented peace. White wampum was made from the North American channeled whelk shell, and the purple wampum beads were made from quahog shells. Going several thousand years back, wampum has been found in archaeological sites all over Dawnland and what is today upstate New York, which suggests that this commodity was widely traded and desired in parts of the northern Eastern Woodlands. Given the cultural significance that wampum played among the Native Americans of the northern Eastern Woodlands in the colonial period, it is very likely that its importance dated back to the precolonial era. In the colonial era, wampum could serve as a form of compensation. Gookin wrote that "if any murther, or any great wrong upon any of their relatives or kindred, be committed, all of that and consanguinity look upon themselves concerned to revenge that wrong, or murder, unless the business be taken up by the payment of wompompeague."[59] By the early 17th century, when European colonists arrived in Dawnland, they increasingly understood the value of wampum to the indigenous peoples of the region, they began to use wampum as a form of currency, and, as we shall see later in the book, they took aggressive steps to take control of the trade.[60]

Conclusion

This discussion of Native American populations, ways of subsistence, social history, and involvement in long-distance networks demonstrates that there existed sophisticated but also very divergent and diverse ways of life in New England. Regional diversity and complexity existed in the political, economic, and cultural lives of the indigenous peoples of Dawnland. As the last two chapters explored, Native Americans had lived rich and long histories in New England—a past that speaks to the ancient Native American presence in the region of over 10 millennia. The indigenous peoples of Dawnland had created a world of relative ecological and social stability as they farmed, subsisted, and lived on their land. While there is much we do not know given the limited evidence, study of the pre-Columbian past helps us to better understand the history of Native Americans of New England. These earlier experiences and developments influenced the choices that Native Americans made as societies, groups, and individuals when they came to face European colonization. This invasion, as we explore in the next two chapters, would turn the Native American world upside down.

Notes

1. Readers who are interested in learning more on the subject beyond what this chapter provides might be interested in the book-length study by Howard S. Russell, *Indian New England before the Mayflower* (Hanover, NH: University Press of New England, 1980).

2. My argument here draws from Neal Salisbury, "The Indians' Old World: Native Americans and the Coming of the Europeans," *William and Mary Quarterly* 53, no. 3 (July 1996): 435–458. See also Christoph Strobel, *The Global Atlantic, 1400–1900* (New York: Routledge, 2015), 13.

3. Wilson Waters, *History of Chelmsford, Massachusetts* (Lowell, MA: Courier Citizen Company, 1917), chap. 1. On this issue more generally, see Jean O'Brien, *Firsting and Lasting: Writing Indians Out of Existence in New England* (Minneapolis: University of Minnesota Press, 2010).

4. My discussion of population numbers draws from Alan C. Swedlund, "Contagion, Conflict, and Captivity in Interior New England: Native American and European Contacts in the Middle Connecticut River Valley of Massachusetts, 1616–2004," in *Beyond Germs: Native Depopulation in North America*, ed. Catherine

Cameron, Paul Kelton, and Alan Swedlund, 150–154 (Tucson: University of Arizona Press, 2015); Daniel Gookin, *Historical Collections of the Indians of New England of Their Several Nations, Numbers, Customs, Manners, Religions, and Government before the English Planted There* (Boston: Belknap and Hall, 1674), 8–9.

5. Reuben Gold Thwaites, *The Jesuit Relations and Allied Documents: Travels and Explorations of the Jesuit Missionaries in New France, 1610–1791*, 73 vols. (Cleveland, OH: Burrow Brothers, 1896–1901), 1:177.

6. Disease and the demographic catastrophe it might have caused among Native American populations is a widely discussed topic. Influential is Dobyns's wide-ranging work on this subject. For a good summary that pertains to the Eastern Woodlands, see Henry Dobyns, *Their Numbers Became Thinned: Native American Population Dynamics in Eastern North America* (Knoxville: University of Tennessee Press, 1983). See also Alfred Crosby, *The Columbian Exchange: Biological and Cultural Consequences of 1492* (Westport, CT: Greenwood, 1973); Alfred Crosby, *Ecological Imperialism: The Biological Expansion of Europe, 900–1900* (New York: Cambridge University Press, 1986), 209–215; Charles Mann, *1491: New Revelations of the Americas before Columbus* (New York: Vintage, 2006). For a study on the demographic legacy of disease see, e.g., Russel Thornton, *American Indian Holocaust and Survival: A Population History since 1492* (Norman: University Press of Oklahoma, 1987). The essays in Catherine Cameron, Paul Kelton, and Alan Swedlund, eds., *Beyond Germs: Native Depopulation in North America* (Tucson: University of Arizona Press, 2015) underscore that conquest, land loss, slave raiding, and removal also had a devastating impact on the indigenous peoples of the Americas. Challenging Dobyns's and Crosby's historiographic assumption on this issue, the researchers in *Beyond Germs* suggest that the impact of conquest and colonization might have been more devastating for indigenous Americans than disease.

7. On the issue of Pennacook nomenclature and history, see David Stewart-Smith, "The Pennacook Indians and the New England Frontier, circa 1604–1733" (PhD diss., Union Institute, 1998); Christoph Strobel, "Pawtucket and Wamesit: The Challenges of [Reconstructing the History of] Two New England Native Communities," in *Ethnicity in Lowell: Ethnographic Overview and Assessment*, Robert Forrant and Christoph Strobel (Boston: Northeast Region Ethnography Program, National Park Service, U.S. Department of the Interior, 2011), 9–24; Christoph Strobel and Robert Forrant, "'Into a New Canoe': Thinking and Teaching Locally and Globally about Native Americans on the Confluence of the Merrimack and the Concord Rivers," *New England Journal of History* 72, no. (2016): 62–75.

8. See, e.g., Bert Salwen, "Indians of Southern New England and Long Island: Early Period," in *Handbook of North American Indians*, Vol. 15, *Northeast*, ed. Bruce Trigger (Washington, DC: Smithsonian Institution, 1978), 168. See also Kathleen Bragdon, *Native People of Southern New England, 1500–1650* (Norman: University of Oklahoma Press, 1996), 23–25.

9. My discussion here draws from Dean R. Snow, *The Archaeology of New England* (New York: Academic Press, 1980), esp. 70–71. For a discussion of the

impact that conquest and colonization had on indigenous peoples across the Americas, see Christoph Strobel, "Conquest and Colonization," *The Routledge Handbook to the History and Society of the Americas*, ed. Olaf Kaltmeier et al. (New York: Routledge, 2019), 75–83.

10. For a typical discussion of this topic see, e.g., William Wood, *New England's Prospect*, ed. Alden T. Vaughan (Amherst: University of Massachusetts Press, 1977), 112–116. For a detailed critical analysis of this primary document, which is widely used by scholars of New England, see Christoph Strobel, "Indigenous Peoples of the Merrimack River Valley in the Early Seventeenth Century: An Atlantic Perspective on Northeastern America," *World History Connected* 16, no. 1 (2019), https://worldhistoryconnected.press.uillinois.edu/16.1/forum _strobel.html. Accessed June 4, 2019.

11. On this topic and more generally see, e.g., Robert A. Williams Jr., *The American Indian in Western Legal Thought: The Discourses of Conquest* (New York: Oxford University Press, 1992). For a global perspective on the issue of dispossession of indigenous peoples see, e.g., John C. Weaver, *The Great Land Rush and the Making of the Modern World, 1600–1900* (Montreal: McGill University Press, 2006).

12. Anonymous, "Extract from an Indian History," *Collections of the Massachusetts Historical Society,* Vol. 9 (Boston: Hall and Hiller, 1804), 100–101.

13. Gookin, *Historical Collections of the Indians of New England*, 10.

14. See Samuel de Champlain's account, originally published in 1613, *Voyages of Samuel Champlain, 1604–1616* (New York: Barnes and Noble, 1946), 95–96.

15. For a more extensive discussion of this subject, see Jared Diamond, *Guns, Germs, and Steel: The Fates of Human Societies* (New York: Norton, 1997).

16. Gordon M. Day, "The Indian as Ecological Factor in the Northeastern Forest," *Ecology* 34, no. 2 (1953): 329–346; William Cronon, *Changes in the Land: Indians, Colonists, and the Ecology of New England* (New York: Hill and Wang, 1983).

17. See, e.g., Wood, *New England's Prospect,* 106–107.

18. Anonymous, "Extract from an Indian History," 100–101.

19. James Axtell, ed., *The Indian Peoples of Eastern America: A Documentary History of the Sexes* (New York: Oxford University Press, 1981), 114.

20. On the fur trade, see Susan Sleeper Smith, ed., *Rethinking the Fur Trade: Cultures of Exchange in an Atlantic World* (Lincoln: University of Nebraska Press, 2009). On the global connections of the fur trade, see Claudio Saunt, *West of the Revolution: An Uncommon History of 1776* (New York: Norton, 2015), chaps. 1 and 5. For the role that Native Americans played in the global economy more generally, see Strobel, *The Global Atlantic, 1400–1900*, 96–99, 134–135, 144–145.

21. Wood, *New England's Prospect,* 84–85.

22. Ibid., 85.

23. Gookin, *Historical Collections of the Indians of New England*, 13.

24. Lucianne Lavin, *Connecticut's Indigenous Peoples: What Archaeology, History, and Oral Traditions Teach Us about their Communities and Cultures* (New Haven, CT: Yale University Press, 2013), 78–79, 86–90.

25. For the centrality of rivers, waterfalls, and fishing and the development of native New England settlements, see Dena Ferran, *The Neville Site: 8000 Years at Amoskeag, Manchester, New Hampshire* (Cambridge, MA: Peabody Museum of Archaeology and Ethnology Press, 1976); Warren King Moorehead, *The Merrimack Archaeological Survey: A Preliminary Paper* (Salem, MA: Peabody Museum, 1931), 61–64. See also Wood, *New England's Prospect,* 107–108.

26. Wood, *New England's Prospect,* 55.

27. On fishing see, e.g., Lavin, *Connecticut's Indigenous Peoples,* 110–113; Wood, *New England's Prospect,* chap. 16.

28. For an introduction to the precontact history of this region, see Andrew Lipman, *The Saltwater Frontier: Indians and the Contest of the American Coast* (New Haven, CT: Yale University Press, 2015), chap. 1.

29. Lavin, *Connecticut's Indigenous Peoples,* 87–88. For an introduction on New England's edible plants, see Russ Cohen with Stephanie Lettendre, *Wild Plants I Have Known . . . And Eaten* (Essex, MA: Essex Greenbelt Association, 2004).

30. Lavin, *Connecticut's Indigenous Peoples,* 86.

31. For an introduction to the folk medicine of the indigenous peoples of the northern Eastern Woodlands see, e.g., the book by the Mohegan Indian Gladys Tantaquidgeon, *Folk Medicine of the Delaware and Related Algonkian Indians* (Harrisburg: Pennsylvania Historical Museum Commission, 1977).

32. Gookin, *Historical Collections of the Indians of New England,* 10–11.

33. Wood, *New England's Prospect,* 82.

34. Brereton cited in Lavin, *Connecticut's Indigenous Peoples,* 90.

35. Gookin, *Historical Collections of the Indians of New England,* 13.

36. Wood, *New England's Prospect,* 93.

37. For an introduction to the topic of changes in Native American warfare and technology, see Patrick M. Malone, *The Skulking Way of War: Technology and Tactics among the New England Indians* (Lanham, MD: Madison Books, 1991).

38. See, e.g., Lavin, *Connecticut's Indigenous Peoples,* 244–245; and Wood, *New England's Prospect,* 97–99.

39. Gookin, *Historical Collections of the Indians of New England,* 12.

40. Roger Williams, *The Complete Writings of Roger Williams,* Vol. 1, *Introductions: Key into the Language of America; Letters Regarding John Cotton* (Eugene, OR: Wipf and Stock Publishers, 2007), 152.

41. Bragdon, *Native People of Southern New England,* 207.

42. Wood, *New England's Prospect,* 100–101.

43. Gookin, *Historical Collections of the Indians of New England,* 14.

44. James W. Mavor Jr. and Byron E. Dix, *Manitou: The Sacred Landscape, New England's Native Civilization* (Rochester, VT: Inner Traditions, 1989), 2.

45. Ibid.

46. Lavin, *Connecticut's Indigenous Peoples,* 286–296.

47. Mary Emery Hall, *Roger Williams* (Boston: Pilgrim, 1917), 87.

48. Edward Winslow, "Winslow Relation," in *Chronicles of the Pilgrim Fathers of the Colony of Plymouth from 1602 to 1625,* 2nd ed., ed. Alexander Young (Boston: Charles C. Little and James Brown, 1844), 366.

49. Bragdon, *Native People of Southern New England*, 234.

50. On this issue, see also Lavin, *Connecticut's Indigenous Peoples*, 101, 116–117, 282–286.

51. Lavin, *Connecticut's Indigenous Peoples*, 308.

52. See Wood, *New England's Prospect*, 99–100; Gookin, *Historical Collections of the Indians of New England*, 9.

53. Bragdon, *Native People of Southern New England*, 226–230.

54. Lavin, *Connecticut's Indigenous Peoples*, 235–240.

55. Ibid., 241–242.

56. On the importance of rivers to Native Americans, see Lisa Brooks, *The Common Pot: The Recovery of Native Space in the Northeast* (Minneapolis: University of Minnesota Press, 2008), introduction and chap. 1.

57. Gookin, *Historical Collections of the Indians of New England*, 12–13.

58. Lavin, *Connecticut's Indigenous Peoples*, 115–116, 151–165.

59. Gookin, *Historical Collections of the Indians of New England*, 9.

60. On wampum, see Lavin, *Connecticut's Indigenous Peoples*, 155–156, 300–302.

CHAPTER THREE

Indigenous Peoples, European Colonization, and the Making of New England

European colonization dramatically changed the lifeways of Native Americans from all over the Western Hemisphere. Indigenous experiences with colonization varied widely. How the colonial processes influenced Native American societies depended on where indigenous peoples lived and at what time they experienced colonization. Still, overall, colonization had a disruptive impact on the life of Native Americans and forced many into marginal positions in societies across the Americas. In North America, New England was among the first regions to experience colonization, a phenomenon that has shaped the history of the indigenous peoples there for the last 500 or so years.

Colonization followed certain patterns that could be observed in other areas of the Americas, but in New England regionally distinct patterns were also evident. Between the late 15th century and the early 1600s, numerous European ships explored and exploited the fishing grounds off the Atlantic northeastern seaboard. European intruders also traded with the indigenous populations and raided the area for human captives. By the early 17th century, the French, Dutch, and English were able to establish permanent colonies in the Atlantic Northeast after earlier failed attempts to establish beachheads in the region.

Europeans legitimized colonization in a variety of ways. Some of them claimed that they obtained indigenous lands by "right of discovery" or due to divine intervention by God. Others argued that they needed to Christianize or help indigenous peoples. Over the years, Europeans also came to justify indigenous dispossession by claiming that they had won "just wars" against Native Americans. Others argued that they were merely claiming "wilderness" or advocated that they had a right to trade and explore.[1]

In the Atlantic Northeast, European colonization began to gradually reshape the world of Native Americans starting in the late 15th century and continuing throughout the 16th century. Thus, Native Americans had already long felt the impact of Europe's global expansion before the English established a permanent settlement in 1620 at a place they called Plymouth Plantation, which became the first permanent colony in what is today New England.

European colonization had a dramatic impact on the indigenous peoples of New England from the 1500s to the 1780s, a period that American historians either often call "Early American" or "colonial" history, both intellectual organizing principles that raise issues of conceptualization when discussing them in the context of Native American history. As we explored earlier and even though historians are becoming more aware of this issue, when using the nomenclature of "Early American" history for this period, many still too often tend to neglect that there was a long and complicated indigenous past before 1492 in the Western Hemisphere. This area of the past is generally left to archaeologists. Yet, it is important to underscore that it was these precolonial histories that shaped the way indigenous groups interacted with European colonizers. Using the term "colonial" for this period also has its shortcomings, as it suggests that colonization came to an end after the American Revolution. From an indigenous perspective, however, New English colonization never really ended. Thus, conventional periodization does not always capture the experience of indigenous peoples and often brushes aside the importance of the history before 1492 or the continual challenges that Native Americans face.

The period from the 1500s to the 1780s led to complex cultural interactions between Native Americans and colonists. In the 16th and early 17th centuries, the European presence was accompanied by captive taking, and in the 17th and 18th centuries the English created systems of native servitude, bondage, and labor arrangements that integrated indigenous peoples into the colonial economy. The European presence also led to the outbreak of devastating epidemics, as it tied Native Americans to networks of global commerce. Moreover, English colonization caused the indigenous communities to suffer from dramatic land losses.

This chapter covers the period from around the 1490s to the eve of King Philip's War in the 1670s. The text examines early contacts between various Algonquian-speaking Native American groups and Europeans that resulted in exchanges and trade throughout the 16th century. The chapter also investigates how English colonization in the 17th century impacted many of the

Native American communities in the region. From the 1620s through the 1670s, English colonists created various colonial societies. In addition, English colonization had a complex impact on the Native Americans of Dawnland, leading to destruction and cultural re-creation as indigenous peoples were forced to adapt and change in order to survive in the emerging New English societies.

Early Contacts between Indigenous Peoples and Europeans

While coastal Dawnland was far from the Caribbean where Christopher Columbus had arrived in 1492, indigenous peoples in the Atlantic Northeast likely noticed a European presence from the late 15th century on. Archaeologists and anthropologists sometimes refer to the period between 1492 and before Europeans established permanent settlements in New England in the early 17th century, as the "Final Woodland period."[2] But as we will explore below, there was already sustained and frequent interaction between Native Americans and Europeans during this time. Hence, this chapter refers to this period as a time of "early contacts." Conventionally, history textbooks and timelines list the expedition led by Giovanni Caboto (John Cabot), a Venetian mariner who sailed under the English flag and explored the eastern coast of North America, reaching from today's Nova Scotia down to the coastal Carolinas from 1497 to 1498, as the first European presence in the region. It was likely at this point already, however, that the Native Americans of coastal Dawnland were used to the presence of European boats, or "floating islands" as indigenous witnesses often called these vessels in their testimonials of their first encounters with Europeans. The occasional fishing, reconnaissance, trading, or slave-raiding vessel was present in the region throughout this period. It is also likely that during this time some shipwreck survivors ended up on Native American land. Moreover, Europeans launched a few failed efforts at creating colonies in the region.

We know about these early encounters from the 1490s to the early 17th century through a variety of sources. For one, early Native American voices describing these contacts are preserved in some of the oral traditions of Native American communities of New England or have been written down by European writers who recorded a likely often skewed representation of the indigenous perspectives of these encounters. Europeans also left records in diaries, logs, journals, and travel accounts describing early European–Native American contacts. Moreover, the work of archaeologists has provided interesting insights into the early contacts between indigenous peoples and Europeans.

In the late 15th century and throughout the 16th century, European fishermen as well as other mariners had a presence in the coastal waters of Dawnland, and their visits led to exchanges and ever more complex interactions with indigenous peoples. Basque and Portuguese fisherman from the Iberian Peninsula and fisherman from various other corners of Europe exploited the rich grounds of the region. In the early 17th century, Samuel Argall was sent by Jamestown Colony to explore the New England waters from Penobscot Bay to Cape Cod. As a result of this mission, Jamestown Colony sent several fishing missions to the region. These endeavors helped to feed the struggling early English settlement in Virginia. Thus, it is important to note that the exploitation of New England's fishing grounds by Europeans was based on informal expeditions launched by various European coastal communities in search of richer waters. At the same time, as demonstrated by Argall's mission, these fishing excursions could also be part of the nascent European efforts at empire building in the Americas.

The coastal regions of Dawnland were busy places of interaction. Recall that the coastal waters served as an important indigenous space. Native Americans harvested ocean waters for fish and traveled and traded over long distances in their large oceangoing canoes. Thus, in the 16th century and the first decades of the 17th century, the New England seacoast had become a zone of contact between Native Americans and Europeans—a space that the historian Andrew Lipman calls "the saltwater frontier."[3]

Fishing the waters off coastal Dawnland, European mariners also tended to spend at least some time on land processing and salting their fish harvest, and during these stays a number of fisherman also interacted and traded with Native Americans. Sixteenth-century European fishermen, maritime explorers, and merchants were especially interested in fur and animal skins, as they fetched a high price in Europe. For some fishermen as well as other European mariners, the fur trade developed into a lucrative side business. In return, Native Americans received a wide array of desirable goods in these exchanges: metal tools and utensils, beads made out of glass and metal, cloth, blankets, and, especially of growing importance by the 17th century, firearms and ammunition. While trade could often be cordial and mutually beneficial, at times it also led to misunderstandings, discord, and conflict.

Some coastal encounters between Native Americans and Europeans underscore these tensions. In 1524 during his exploration of the North American Atlantic coast, the Italian-speaking mariner Giovanni da Verrazano, on a mission under the French flag, recorded his interaction with coastal Native Americans around Casco Bay in today's Maine. Verrazano was annoyed at the cool reception given by the indigenous peoples there, as he had experienced friendlier interactions with Native Americans farther to the south. Verrazano complained "that we could never make any communication with them, however many signs we made to them."[4] The reaction of the area's indigenous peoples seemed to indicate that they had experienced prior negative experiences with Europeans:

If we wanted to trade with them . . . they would come to the seashore on some rocks where the breakers were most violent while we remained on the little boat, and they sent us what they wanted to give on rope, continually shouting to us not to approach the land; they gave us the barter quickly, and would take in exchange only knives, hooks for fishing, and sharp metal.[5]

Verrazano continued to complain that "when we had nothing more to exchange and left them, the men made all the signs of scorn and shame."[6]

The Native Americans' vigilance seemed well founded, as European territorial encroachments and raids for human captives was a common occurrence in the region. Maybe showing some truer colors further into his account, Verrazano and 20 men "disembarked on the shore" even though this was against the wishes of the local Native American population. A Native American war party responded by shooting at the European intruders "with their bows and uttered loud cries before fleeing into the woods."[7] Historic records also indicate, for instance, that sailors from France had captured several Native Americans in what is today Newfoundland. Moreover, in 1525 the Portuguese captain Estevao Gomez and his crew returned to Europe with several Algonquian-speaking Native American captives, taken during a voyage to the Atlantic Northeast. These were likely only two of several reported kidnappings in the first decades of the 16th century. It is hard to estimate how many Native Americans in the 16th and 17th centuries were abducted and enslaved in such a manner. As the discussion here and below makes clear, the taking of Native Americans happened frequently. For many of those whose capture was noted in the written record, it is likely that many others were taken without a trace of written evidence. For others, the documented evidence has likely long been lost. Thus, we probably will never obtain exact numbers or even approximations of how many Native Americans from Dawnland perished in the 16th- and 17th-century world of Atlantic slavery. Moreover, it is likely that news of such abductions, territorial encroachments, and attacks by Europeans spread throughout Dawnland and beyond, and it was such raids and aggressive behavior that led to the defensive responses by Native Americans.

The encounter between the coastal peoples at Casco Bay and Verrazano and his crew stands in clear contrast to the meeting that the French mariner Jacques Cartier and his men had about 10 years later. Farther to the north in the place today known as the Bay of Chaleur, this expedition came across a group of about 300 Native Americans. Cartier said that the local indigenous population appeared friendly and made "signs to us that they had come to barter with us; and held up some furs." Cartier observed that the group "bartered all they had to such an extent that all went back naked without anything on them; and they made signs to us that they would return on the morrow with more furs."[8]

The ambitions of Cartier's expeditions from 1534 to 1542 went beyond trade, however, and most of these efforts focused on the St. Lawrence River Valley in the northern reaches of Dawnland in what is today Canada. Like many European explorers in the 16th and 17th centuries, Cartier was looking for an elusive passage through North America that would get him to the Pacific Ocean. Such a passage, many European explorers and policy makers hoped, would provide them faster access to the lucrative trade with Asia.

During his expedition on the St. Lawrence River in 1541, Cartier established a French colonial settlement just west of modern Quebec City. This French post was apparently built without the consent of the local Native American population. As a result, native fighters in the area besieged the settlement in the first winter. By 1543 due to harsh conditions and indigenous pressures, the French decided to abandon their colonial effort. The next French attempt at creating a colonial foothold in the region would not resume until the next century.[9]

There were several other failed efforts at establishing colonial posts in the region. One of those followed several English maritime expeditions on today's Maine coast, such as those led by George Waymouth in 1605 and by Thomas Hanham and Martin Pring in 1606. These missions spurred the establishment of a short-lived English colony in 1607 on the Sagadahoc River under the leadership of Geoge Popham and Raleigh Gilbert. This settlement was abandoned after a short period.[10]

European efforts at exploration and trade and failed attempts at establishing colonial beachheads were also accompanied by, as earlier discussed, the capture of Native Americans. Some of these individuals were taken for strategic reasons. The French mariner Cartier on at least two occasions captured several Native Americans. He abducted them with the intent that they would serve as guides and translators and to provide local knowledge. Cartier also presented several of these captives at the French court in the 1530s to garner support from the king for the explorer's colonial aspirations. This strategy proved successful, as the French king approved the establishment of the failed colony on the St. Lawrence River. Overall, however, likely the majority of Native Americans captured by Europeans during their maritime ventures on the New England coast ended up being sold as servants or as slaves on the markets of the Atlantic world.[11]

For many Native Americans, being captured and sold as servants or slaves meant eventual death in a faraway place. Available records suggest that many Native American captives died from disease. Others perished as a result of the often horrendous working conditions for slaves and servants. There are, however, some instances when Native Americans from Dawnland were able to return to their homelands. Arguably the two most famous examples here are Tisquantum, often still better known as Squanto, the diminutive version of his name, and Epenow. Their experience of captivity led each to pursue very different strategies in their approach to the European presence in their homelands.

Tisquantum, the subject of many children's books, myths, and legends, was captured in 1614 in Cape Cod Bay by an English mariner named Thomas Hunt. Hunt had been in the region as an officer in a flotilla led by John Smith during his explorations in the Atlantic Northeast. John Smith is usually better known to American audiences for his rescue by the Powhatan chief's daughter Pocahontas, a tale that Smith likely invented years after his stay in Chesapeake Bay in today's Commonwealth of Virginia. Incidentally, John Smith is also often credited for coining the term "New England," which he used as the title of a book, *Descriptions of New England* (1616). Hunt and his crew had been left behind by Smith, supposedly to explore the viability of a colonial English settlement in the region. Whatever their original intentions, Hunt and his men abducted Tisquantum and 20 some other Native Americans during this trip. They sailed toward Spain to sell as many of their captives into slavery as they could. Abductions conducted by English mariners such as Hunt led to a worsening of European indigenous relations in coastal Dawnland and, much to the chagrin of several mariners affiliated with the various joint stock companies that tried to operate in the region, also undermined the lucrative fur trade. While in the city of Malaga in Spain, a group of friars who opposed the sale of Native American slaves interrupted Hunt's plan to sell Tisquantum. Over the next five years, Tisquantum would eventually make his way back to his home region via England and Newfoundland. Once the Puritans established Plymouth Plantation, Tisquantum would emerge as a cultural broker between the English colonists, whose language he had learned in his days of exile, and the local Native American communities. But his actions gained him the ire of various indigenous peoples in the region. Tisquantum had used his close association with the colonists to gain payments of tribute and bribes from other Native Americans and was also likely aspiring to gain a leadership position among the indigenous people in the region. The tensions resulting from his ambitions are probably the reason why he ended up moving to Plymouth Colony for safety. There he assisted the colonists in figuring out how to farm, subsist, and survive in the new land. But he also helped the colonists explore southern New England's coastal waters. The Puritan settlers depended on Tisquantum to navigate the dangerous shoals of the region. He died of disease on such a mission late in November 1622.[12]

Like Tisquantum, Epenow was captured by English mariners. In 1611 during a journey on the southern New England coast, the English captain Edward Harlow abducted around 30 natives with the intention of selling them into slavery in Spain. Epenow was one of several individuals captured by Harlow and his crew on the island we today call Martha's Vineyard. Since Harlow had not been able to sell his human cargo to the Spanish, Epenow, alongside several others of the kidnapped Native Americans, was displayed to audiences in London. Such shows were popular in England at the time. Sir Ferdinando Gorges, a key player in and financial backer of the Plymouth Company and the early colonization efforts in the Atlantic Northeast, obtained Epenow as a servant. It was in Gorges's household that Epenow learned English from another Native American captive. Epenow apparently convinced Gorges that he knew of the location of a gold mine on Martha's Vineyard, which convinced this wealthy Englishman to send a mission to the island. Epenow and two other Native American captives accompanied the mission. During a military engagement between local Native Americans and the ship, likely instigated by Epenow, the captives escaped. After a fight that left several Native Americans dead and a few English sailors wounded, the crew decided to return to England. Another encounter in 1620 between Epenow and a group of Native Americans as well as Thomas Dermer, an English captain and employee of the Plymouth Company, and his crew led once again to a violent encounter. Dermer and Epenow had already had a relatively amicable encounter in 1619. During the 1620 mission Dermer had brought the native servant Tisquantum, whom the captain hoped could help to mediate and improve the tense relations between the region's Native American communities and the English. Dermer hoped that his diplomatic approach would further the trading interests of the Plymouth Company, with which he was affiliated. Based on the evidence, it is not clear why violence broke out during the encounter. Some sources suggest that Dermer outed Epenow as Gorges's servant during this meeting. Maybe Epenow felt threatened and might have initiated the attack to avoid being captured again. Maybe, given how angry the region's Native Americans were about the abductions of their kin, they decided to attack the crew to free Tisquantum. Or as some writers have speculated, Epenow had become convinced that violent confrontation was the best strategic approach for dealing with the English and other Europeans. Whatever the reason behind the outbreak in violence, the Native Americans took Tisquantum and killed several members of the English coastal party. Dermer barely escaped with his life; he suffered from severe wounds and died a few months after the incident in Chesapeake Bay likely due to complications of his battle wounds.[13]

The stories of Tisquantum and Epenow provide us a small glimpse into the disruptive impact that captive taking had on the Native American populations of Dawnland. Captured individuals were ripped from their families, loved ones, and communities. Both Tisquantum and Epenow are examples of how Native Americans of Dawnland participated in an Atlantic world that saw ever-increasing interactions between and movement of the peoples of Europe, Africa, and the Americas. Unlike Tisquantum and Epenow, however, the vast majority of captured individuals were never able to return to their homelands. For many of them captivity meant a deprived and abused life, a destiny often significantly shortened by death far away from one's homelands as a result of an Afro-Eurasian disease to which Native Americans had little immunity. Unfortunately and significantly limiting our understanding, the vast majority of these histories and experiences have been lost with the passage of time.

While this section only provides an incomplete discussion of some of the early contacts between indigenous peoples and Europeans in Dawnland, it underscores the central role that trade relations and raids for captives played in these early encounters. Yet, these early contacts had a devastating demographic impact on the Native American populations of the Western Hemisphere in general and of Dawnland in particular for another reason. The 1602 travels on the New England coast by Bartholomew Gosnold (the mariner who is credited with naming Cape Cod) and his crew and their contacts with various indigenous communities in the region seemed to have been accompanied by an outbreak of an epidemic in Dawnland. Disease seemed to have broken out among several indigenous peoples Gosnold traded with, and some researchers speculate that this maritime mission was the source of the epidemic. It is important to remember, though, that this particular disease outbreak was only one of many. The epidemics brought about dramatic change in the Native American societies of New England and had a destructive impact in the region. As we will explore below, disease that had likely had a negative demographic impact in the 16th century would continue to haunt Native Americans in the 17th and 18th centuries. Disease would significantly weaken and transform the indigenous societies of the region.

European Colonization and Disease

Afro-Eurasian diseases were a major force in reshaping the history of Native Americans in New England. European colonization accompanied by devastating epidemics killed vast numbers of the indigenous population. At the same time, despite devastating destruction, throughout the 16th and 17th centuries disease forced indigenous peoples to adapt in order to survive in their homelands.

The indigenous peoples of Dawnland suffered from what several researchers call "virgin soil epidemics." This term describes an outbreak of a new disease among a population that had not had prior exposure to it and thus had no immunity. The famous outbreak of the Black Death in the mid-1300s in Asia, Africa, and Europe, which killed tens of millions and maybe as many as 200 million people, is a historical example of a virgin soil epidemic. The pandemic is believed to have killed as many as 30–60 percent of the population in many regions throughout Afro-Eurasia. But while the Black Death is one example of a virgin soil epidemic in world history, starting in 1492 as a result of European colonization, Native Americans in the Western Hemisphere experienced one devastating disease outbreak after another.[14]

The indigenous people's susceptibility to Afro-Eurasian disease emerged out of divergent developments in the Western Hemisphere. The lack of domestic animals in the Americas, with the exception of the dog (and the llama in the Andes), led to the emergence of a very different disease environment in the Western Hemisphere compared to Afro-Eurasia. Pathogens from Afro-Eurasia had a harmful impact on indigenous societies and communities in Dawnland and all over the Western Hemisphere. The isolation of the Americas from the Afro-Eurasian landmass meant that the diseases that had developed there did not exist in the Western Hemisphere. Without prior exposure to these diseases, Native Americans had never been able to develop natural immunities to smallpox, leptospirosis, influenza, and many other diseases. Whereas societies in Afro-Eurasia had millennia to adjust to their disease environment and built up immunity, for Native Americans the exposure was much more expedited, concentrated, and immediate. Hence, the outbreaks of Afro-Eurasian diseases caused massive casualties among native communities over a relatively short amount of time and at an intense level.

Disease was the most effective weapon in the European arsenal to undermine Native American societies. Post-Columbian indigenous communities were hit hard by Afro-Eurasian pathogens to which they had no prior exposure and thus very little immunity. Some scholars estimate that native peoples in the Americas suffered from 50 percent up to—given continued interaction with Europeans and Africans over sustained periods—90 percent mortality rates. From the 16th through the 19th centuries, initially European fishermen, traders, explorers, shipwreck survivors, and slave raiders and, with later sustained contact, European armies and colonists, as well as enslaved Africans brought with them disease. As we have seen, epidemics spread along the long-established interregional exchange networks throughout the Americas. Disease had dramatic depopulating impacts, often long before active efforts at conquest and colonization took place. These developments were part of a process known as the Columbian exchange. This was a series of economic, biological, and cultural global exchanges that dramatically altered and shaped the modern world.[15]

However, several researchers who study the connections between Native Americans, European colonization, and germs caution us not to overestimate the impact of disease on indigenous societies. One of the critiques that these academics advance is that when many scholars write about the impact that Afro-Eurasian germs had on the indigenous peoples in the Western Hemisphere, they often do so as if they are talking about an isolated phenomenon rather than viewing disease as being tied up in larger historic trends and patterns. Thus, these scholars remind us that we should not underestimate the impact that warfare, massive dispossession, poverty, and enslavement had on the demographic decline among the indigenous peoples of the Americas.[16]

As we alluded to in the previous chapter, the limited primary source, oral historical, and archaeological records seem to suggest that in the Atlantic Northeast, disease spurred by colonization had a devastating demographic impact. We know little about disease outbreaks resulting from contact in the late 15th and 16th centuries, but epidemics likely had an impact on the region's indigenous peoples. Recall, for instance, Membertou, who in 1603 told Champlain that his people's number had dramatically declined throughout the 16th century.[17] Between Membertou's statement and the arrival of the English colonists on the *Mayflower* in 1620, at least two more epidemics seem to have struck the region. The first hit in the first decade of the 1600s, and another devastating epidemic haunted the region from 1616 to 1619. It is likely that this second epidemic led to the abandonment of indigenous settlements such as Patuxet, which would become the English settlement of Plymouth in 1620. In fact, the English colonists who arrived in Plymouth in 1620 saw "skulls and bones . . . in many places lying still above the ground where their houses and dwellings had been."[18] It seems that at Patuxet at least, the epidemic had hit so hard that the Native American survivors were unable to bury their dead.

Disease and colonization continued to have a dramatic impact after the establishment of English colonies in the region. New England's Native American population continued to be decimated by a series of disease outbreaks. In the early 1630s and then again later in that decade as well as in 1649–1650, epidemics broke out. Some researchers have identified the plagues that ravaged the native communities of the first half of the 17th century as epidemics such as smallpox and leptospirosis. Disease also struck in 1647 and again in 1659, the former blamed by some scholars on influenza, the latter on diphtheria. It is important to underscore, though, given the limited evidence and often confusing primary source record, that it is tricky to diagnose what specific disease hit indigenous communities during particular outbreaks. Determining the exact illness is an area of considerable scholarly debate. Yet, it is important to emphasize that contagion in the history of Native Americans of New England was closely linked to contact, trade, European permanent settlement, conflict, and captivity. The history of disease among indigenous peoples should thus not be understood as an isolated phenomenon but instead has to be understood in the context of colonization.[19]

Maybe even harder to determine are the exact population numbers and mortality rates among indigenous communities. Scholarly estimates about precolonial populations and the demographic decline that resulted from colonization vary widely. Gatherable information from primary sources is also limited. At best, these sources provide an incomplete glimpse and approximations into population numbers and trends in decline. The example of the Native Americans whom the English colonists called the "Pawtucket," a cultural, political, and economic conglomeration of indigenous communities in the Merrimack River Valley, helps to underscore this issue. Pawtucket was also the name of a large indigenous settlement in the first decades of the 17th century on the Pawtucket Falls of the Merrimack River, today in the city of Lowell. The primary documents and academic literature provide a confusing glimpse into the size of the population of the Pawtuckets. For instance, Daniel Gookin, a colonist and colonial official, citing indigenous informers as his source of information, estimated that the Pawtuckets experienced a significant population decline in the first half of the 17th century, from 3,000 Native American men "to not above 250 men."[20] Thomas Dudley, a colonial magistrate and governor, estimated the adult male population of the Pawtuckets at no more than 500 in 1631.[21] Meanwhile, historian Daniel Mandell maintains that by the early 1630s, "the natives in the region, known as the Massachusetts and Pawtucket tribes, had been devastated by the recent epidemic, and only about 200 remained."[22] While the above numbers underscore the dramatic impact that epidemics had on the indigenous peoples of Dawnland, it is impossible to verify which of the above-cited numbers provide the most accurate information.[23]

The issue of determining more precise numbers of indigenous populations is further complicated by the difficulty of figuring out what these names meant to 17th-century European writers. A speculation of what the nomenclature "Pawtucket" might have meant to the above-mentioned English observers might be elucidating here. When using the name "Pawtucket," might Dudley have been referring only to the inhabitants of the Pawtucket settlement or only to the groups living in the lower Merrimack River Valley, and therefore, might his numbers be much lower than those given by Daniel Gookin, whose indigenous informers might have counted the Native Americans of the whole drainage system, an alliance system that students of Native American studies today often call the Pennacook. We of course cannot know for sure based on the limited evidence.[24]

The issue of how to assess population numbers and decline is further complicated by the shifting alliances, migration, and adoption of outsiders into communities. Spurred by the impact of colonization, New England Native American communities and families were often open to the incorporation of outsiders into their ranks during the 17th and 18th centuries and beyond. These newcomers were often refugees who used to live closer to English settlements and fled from war and territorial dispossession. It was these realities that helped to create far-reaching, elaborate, and complex kinship networks throughout Dawnland. But this fluidity also meant that by the time of the colonial period several indigenous societies had become multiethnic and provided a home to refugees from other communities.

We will likely never be able to reconstruct reliable population numbers and demographic losses as a result of colonization and disease in Dawnland. Nevertheless, it is clear that English colonization and disease resulted in a demographic catastrophe for the Native Americans of New England. Epidemics destroyed indigenous communities and likely also some of the political and social structures of the precolonial past. Disease massively disrupted indigenous life and forced Native Americans to adapt to new realities in order to survive. Some English colonists adopted a sinister view on the public health crisis among the indigenous peoples. They maintained that God was "smiting the Indians with a sore Disease, even the small Pox, of which great numbers of them died."[25]

European Colonization and Changes in Native American Material Culture, Technology, and Warfare

European contact and colonization led to significant changes in the use of material culture, technology, and warfare among indigenous peoples in Dawnland, and these developments also had a demographic impact. While some historians tend to dramatize these processes, we have to also set these transformations into a larger historic context. As we have already explored in prior chapters, Native Americans had always changed their lifeways and had a long history of adapting their modes of subsistence, material culture, and technology. These changes were likely often spurred and influenced by adopting and being open to outside influences from within or beyond Dawnland. Thus, change was a constant in the life of indigenous peoples. However, it is important to underscore that colonization certainly accelerated the incorporation of European material culture and technology among Native American societies and brought about significant changes in indigenous ways of life and modes of warfare.

Native Americans were interested in European tools, metalware, decorative items, and other material objects. While Native Americans adopted European material culture for their intended uses, such items could also be incorporated in unique ways and put to new uses and given new meanings. Cloth, glass beads, and cooking pots were desired objects, and Native Americans also appreciated and were keen to trade for European knives, hatchets, and axes. Archaeological evidence suggests that they widely adopted these tools into their daily life.

Firearms might have been the most influential European technology to take hold in indigenous North American societies. Native Americans quickly realized that firearms were effective tools that made hunting easier. Moreover, Native Americans recognized the strategic importance that firearms could offer them on the battlefield. Native Americans adopted into their societies with a vengeance what the Narragansett called "thundersticks." In fact, Native Americans in the 17th-century Atlantic Northeast had a reputation for adopting new gun technology at a much more rapid rate than English colonists. Thus, while

English settlers in New England still widely used the more outmoded match-lock musket that needed to be ignited in order to be fired, Native Americans made wide use of the self-igniting and more expensive flintlocks rifles. Native Americans had another advantage. Likely due to their lifeways as hunters that necessitated good aim, Native Americans of Dawnland had the well-earned reputation of being much better shots than New English colonists.

The introduction of firearms and the need to obtain these weapons to be able to defend one's community against more powerful indigenous rivals with access to guns was one reason why intertribal warfare increased and likely became more violent as a result of contact with Europeans. Further-more, as we will explore in more detail below, the exposure to European modes of total warfare also led to an increase in Native American deaths compared to the more limited casualties suffered during precolonial aborigi-nal warfare. Thus, European colonization brought to Dawnland not only devastating disease but also more destructive warfare.[26]

The adoption of European technologies by Native Americans was accom-panied by an increase in trade. Beaver skins especially helped to pay for many of the material items desired by indigenous peoples. While such exchanges, especially that of fur, played an important role in the early con-tact period, Dutch, English, and French merchants and trading companies were interested not just in trade. Increasingly, they also desired another major North American resource—land. The establishment of colonies, which tended to expand quickly, came to play an ever important part in the impe-rial agenda of European states. Thus, the maintenance of their land basis, under increasing New English pressure to obtain more and more land, became an ever greater challenge to Native Americans of southern New En-gland in the 17th century.

First Permanent European Beachheads in the Atlantic Northeast

While there were brief and local interactions between Native Americans and Europeans, it was not until the early 17th century that the first perma-nent European colonies were established in Dawnland. While we call the region New England today, the Puritan colonists who created the first per-manent English colony in the region in 1620 were relative latecomers to the Atlantic Northeast. While as we have seen there were several English mari-ners who surveyed the region in the first two decades of the 17th century, so did the French, Dutch, and several other European countries. Already sev-eral years before the establishment of Plymouth Plantation, the French and the Dutch had created lasting colonial settlements in the Atlantic Northeast.

After the earlier-mentioned colonial endeavors by Cartier in the 1530s and early 1540s, the French renewed their efforts at empire building in the Atlan-tic Northeast in the early 1600s. The French mariner Samuel de Champlain was at the forefront of this initiative. Between 1603 and 1608, he was espe-cially interested in accessing the lucrative fur trade with local indigenous populations and wanted to organize this commerce into a more regular and systemic exchange network. While far from perfect, Champlain grasped the complexity of Native American trade better than many other Europeans. Such exchanges served to establish a relationship of reciprocity and political balance. Gift giving and supporting allies from an indigenous perspective were necessary to maintain a group's political status and power and were seen as essential parts of diplomatic decorum. Champlain grasped this polit-ical and economic reality, but the diplomatic procedures and gift giving would frustrate many a colonial official throughout the Eastern Woodlands. The North American past of the 17th, 18th, and 19th centuries is filled with examples of how failures in such understandings, often spurred by imperial arrogance, could lead to tensions in indigenous-European relations. While Champlain's efforts focused on the St. Lawrence River Valley in today's southeastern Canada, he also conducted several expeditions into parts of what is today the northeastern United States. He traveled inland and along the coast, and his writings provide researchers a valuable glimpse into the Native American societies of Dawnland in the early 17th century. Cham-plain's writings also give us a limited window into the change that happened over time. For instance, many of the large Native American settlements that Cartier had written about and interacted with during his expeditions seemed to have disappeared or shrunk in size by the time Champlain traveled in the region, likely due to the outbreak of epidemics.

Champlain's labors were accompanied by attempts to establish colonial settlements in the Atlantic Northeast to reinforce France's position in that part of the world. In 1608, Champlain helped to establish a French foothold in what is today Quebec City. Quebec became the first permanent French settle-ment in the region and would serve as a cultural and political center for the colony, which would become known as New France. But the French also looked farther to the south. Champlain, like several English mariners, had explored the place now known as New England, and France and England each claimed the region as their zone of interest. In 1611, for instance, French colo-nial officials and several traders set out on a diplomatic mission in what is today the state of Maine. They visited several river valleys, such as the St. John, St. Croix, Penobscot, and Kennebec, and sought to foster relations with the indigenous populations there to strengthen French strategic and economic interests. Notably, this expedition was also accompanied by Father Pierre Biard, who was interested in establishing a missionary foothold in the region, and the Jesuit order partially financed this mission. The English took an aggressive response to the French presence. In 1613, under the commission of the governor of Virginia, Samuel Argall led a mission to attack and destroy the French colonial holdings at Penobscot Bay as well as the Bay of Fundy.[27]

The French and English rivalry would dramatically shape the region's history in the 17th and 18th centuries. It had an especially long-term destructive impact on the indigenous societies of Dawnland, who were often caught up in the wars of empire. Moreover, as some of the discussion in later chapters will explore, the Anglo-French rivalry played itself out in the history and culture of several of the indigenous communities of northern Dawnland such as the Penobscot communities.[28]

The Dutch were also active players in the Atlantic Northeast. They established their first permanent colonial outpost, Fort Nassau, on Castle Island in the Hudson River in 1615. This site is not too far from the modern-day city of Albany. While this settlement served predominantly but not exclusively as a fur trading outpost, it was in the 1620s that the Dutch sent more settlers to the colony, which came to be known as New Netherlands. On paper at least, New Netherlands covered portions of the contemporary states of New York, Connecticut, New Jersey, Pennsylvania, and Delaware, though much of this territory was settled and controlled by indigenous groups. In the mid-1620s the Dutch also established an outpost called New Amsterdam that became a thriving city, today known as New York. While the European settler population never grew particularly large, especially compared to the neighboring New English colonies, the Dutch played an important role in the fur trade and were an important source for firearms and ammunition to several Native American communities throughout the northern Eastern Woodlands. While not a populous or necessarily strategically vital colony compared to several other of its holdings in the Americas and Asia, the Dutch Empire maintained control over this colony until 1664, when the English occupied this region during the Second Anglo-Dutch War.[29]

The Puritans who arrived late in 1620 in Cape Cod Bay and founded Plymouth Colony moved into a region where other European powers had imperial ambitions but also where Native American societies were in flux and had already experienced and would live through more devastating epidemics. The coastal communities were hit especially hard by disease, slave raids, and other colonial pressures, and many towns and villages faced pressures from groups in the interior that had been less devastated by epidemics or, through their trade with Europeans, had gained access to firearms. It was these calculations that likely led Ousamequin, often better known by his title "Massasoit" (which roughly translated means "leader" in Wampanoag) who was the sachem of the Pokanoket Wampanoag tribe, to not only tolerate the presence of the English settlement but also seek a defensive alliance with the colony. Ousamequin traded corn with the colony and permitted Tisquantum, who attempted to use this close association with Plymouth to increase his power and standing among the Wampanoags, to assist the colonists. While his exact motivations are hard to determine on the available evidence, Ousamequin likely pursued these strategies in the hope that Plymouth and the Wampanoags could create a relationship that would benefit both sides. Moreover, he likely grasped that access to European trade objects and a position as the intermediary in an exchange network between the English and other indigenous communities in the interior could heighten his status and position in the Wampanoag societies in the region. Over the decades Plymouth saw a growing number of English migrants arriving in the region. Much of this migration was based on entire families coming over, and many of these colonists were interested in obtaining land that they could farm. The changing demographic realities and the English desire for land put tremendous pressures on the Wampanoags.

The Global Fur Trade and the Great Land Rush

As we have seen, before Europeans were able to establish permanent settlements, Native Americans and Europeans often initiated contact and sustained relations through trade, and the exchange in fur played a central role here. For the indigenous peoples in Dawnland, this trade served not only an economic purpose to obtain desirable foreign goods; from a native perspective, such exchanges also served diplomatic and cultural goals of reciprocity. Native Americans saw them as a strategy to obtain closer ties with neighboring peoples.

Animal skins played a vital role in the early modern global commodities trade. The thick and soft furs appealed to consumers not only in Europe but also in parts of Asia and were distributed in complex global maritime and overland trade networks. Thus, an animal skin caught in North America could be shipped to London and then to a Russian harbor to be transported via overland trade routes of the Russian Empire into the commercial networks of Asia. European consumers especially desired beaver belts, which provided great raw materials for hat making because they were resistant to rain. Beaver hats were a central part of European fashion and featured prominently in markets from the 16th to the 19th centuries. Beaver hats also featured in the global Atlantic slave trade, where they were popular items among African merchants and consumers.

Native Americans did not just supply raw materials in the fur trade; they also processed it, work often done by indigenous women. Hunting parties often traveled long distances in pursuit of fur, especially as their own territories became overhunted due to their participation in the fur trade. These missions were often dangerous and could result in violent engagements with local indigenous groups on whose land these hunting parties encroached. Hence, the fur trade, which brought material benefits by introducing outside material objects to Native American societies, also reinforced and spurred indigenous warfare, as we explore below.[30] The demand for fur led to wider use of firearms by indigenous peoples, increased intertribal warfare, and growing numbers of Native American casualties.

Plymouth was the first permanent English colonial settlement in the Atlantic Northeast, but it was soon followed by settlements at Salem and Boston. Both communities developed into cities over time and became centers for trade. Boston especially emerged as the cultural and commercial hub not only for Massachusetts Bay Colony but also for New England more generally. As the New English colonial populations increased, so did the desire for Native American lands. The establishment of the colonies in New England in the 17th century occurred during Britain's ambitious drive toward global empire. As part of its imperial aspirations, Britain established settler and trading colonies the world over, a drive that would continue through the 19th century. The indigenous peoples of New England were among the first to face the nascent but expanding British Empire.

English pressures on Native American communities to surrender their land base in southern New England was a central part of the history of the region from the 1620s to 1670s, when land quickly became a more important commodity than fur. Furthermore, the dramatic demographic impact that disease and warfare had on weakening indigenous communities aided English colonial efforts tremendously. The appropriations of indigenous land were part of the larger worldwide process that the historian John Weaver describes as the "great land rush." From the 17th through the 19th centuries, British settlers appropriated indigenous land around the world in a variety of ways, and those same lands became gradually integrated into a global market economy. In southern New England this increased demand for land was spurred by a wave of English colonists, many of them farmers, who arrived in ever greater numbers in the 1630s–1650s. Historians of Puritan New England often describe this population movement as the "Great Migration."[31]

The land loss experienced by the indigenous societies exemplified the shifting power dynamics—a complex process of dispossession impossible to explore adequately in a book of this nature and frequently hard to reconstruct on the available evidence and often one-sided New English records. The depopulating impact that colonization and disease had on the region's Native American populations was a powerful ally in the English desire to obtain land. The first generation of English colonists often took Native American land, claiming that it was "vacant" or "wilderness." Moreover, indigenous populations had adopted various goods traded by Europeans into their daily life. Especially among some of the indigenous leaders, the exchange of less vital land became a way to keep up with consumption levels. These consumption patterns were encouraged by English traders who provided easy credit to Native Americans, a practice that encouraged further land sales because this became the only way for indigenous people to pay back their debts. When purchasing Native Americans lands, English colonists paid notoriously low prices. Other land transactions were just grabs or appeared questionable, coerced, fraudulent, or corrupt, or they were pushed through by colonial power players at the expense of Native Americans. At other times, the New English discontinued promised annuity payments to Native American groups whose land they occupied. English settlement expansion took its toll on the indigenous peoples in many parts of southern New England by the mid-17th century. Indigenous lands for agriculture and subsistence became more limited as pressure on Native Americans to surrender more of their territory increased.[32]

Indigenous Conflicts

The increasing European presence in the region reinforced interindigenous conflict. Recall that this type of violence was certainly not new. "Frequent conflict and fleeting alliances linked" Native American societies of Dawnland and beyond into what the historian Parick Malone calls a "dynamic system of organized violence."[33] Yet, the European colonial presence reinforced competition and changed warfare dynamics among Native Americans in the Atlantic Northeast. Old cultural traditions and norms as well as strategic goals, which had put restraints on the violent impact of indigenous warfare in precolonial times, came to unravel with the European presence.

Some communities in the early 17th century, for instance, were tied up in a conflict that English writers referred to as the "Tarenteen War." The Tarenteens were likely indigenous groups from northern Dawnland in what is today eastern maritime Canada and northeastern Maine. They were probably related to the contemporary Micmac nations. The Tarenteens had gained access to guns through trade with the French and undertook southerly raids to attack indigenous communities in what is today Maine, New Hampshire, and Massachusetts. The Tarenteens were involved in several violent conflicts with local communities there.

Oral histories and colonial records also suggest that there were a series of conflicts between the indigenous peoples of Dawnland and the Haudenosaunees that took place from precolonial times through the 17th century. The Haudenosaunees, or "Peoples of the Longhouse," were a Native American alliance system of several nations, probably originating in the 15th century, with homelands in the modern state of New York. They are commonly known as the Iroquois. Especially by the 1600s the Haudenosaunees were aggressively expanding in an effort to access new hunting grounds, establish dominance over neighboring peoples, and take captives to replenish their declining numbers as a result of disease but also to avenge their deaths through ritualized torture. Students of Haudenosaunee history often refer to these wars as "mourning wars."[34]

The easternmost nation of the Haudenosaunee coalition, the Kanienkehaka nation (their original name for themselves that loosely translates as "People of the Flint"), often better known by the name Mohawk (derived from their Algonquian-speaking neighbors and meaning "eaters of men") were at the forefront of these attacks into Dawnland. In the 1620s, the Mohawks and the Mahicans from eastern New York and western Massachusetts would begin an ongoing 50-year conflict over access to Dutch and later English trade, a competition that ultimately forced the Mahicans, despite the assistance of several Native American allies from Dawnland, to withdraw from the Hudson Valley and consolidate their holdings in western Massachusetts, especially around today's Stockbridge, Massachusetts. The Mahicans and the Mohawks also traded with the English in the Connecticut River Valley by the third and fourth decade of the 17th century, and the Mohawks obtained guns and ammunition through this trade as well as their interactions with the Dutch, which strengthened their military position in the region. Moreover, from the 1640s to the 1670s the Mohawks frequently raided east into New England, attacking indigenous settlements belonging to the Pennacooks, Sokokis, Pocumtucs, and other groups. A counterattack in the 1660s by an alliance of Native Americans from New England against the Mohawks apparently ended in a complete rout, killing several hundred fighters from Dawnland.[35]

As we have seen with the Mahicans, intertribal conflicts could be destructive to indigenous communities. In 1644, for instance, Bashaba Passaconaway of the Pennacook tribe decided to "subordinate" his people under the authority of the General Court of the Massachusetts Bay Colony in Boston due to repeated assaults by the Narragansetts, the Haudenosaunees, and other groups in the region. This is at least how English records described the act. It is likely that the Pennacooks saw their actions in a different light. Passaconaway and his kin probably hoped that the colony could help his people in this struggle, but the English provided no assistance to the Pennacooks against indigenous attackers. Moreover, the attacks by the Mohawks led the Pocumtucs to sell territory in the Connecticut River Valley to the English in the mid-1660s. Several of them abandoned their homelands and sought refuge with indigenous allies such as the Sokokis and the Pennacooks.[36]

Native American Conflicts with English Colonists

The establishment of English colonial settlements also led to conflicts and wars between Europeans and indigenous peoples. The establishment of Plymouth Colony in mid-December 1620, for instance, was accompanied by incidents of violence and tensions, and war and conflict between Native Americans and English also occurred in other parts of New England.

The colonists on the *Mayflower* were involved in several violent interactions with Native Americans. About a week before they arrived at the settlement site at Patuxet/Plymouth in mid-December 1620, the Puritans on the *Mayflower* had a military engagement with Native Americans. There was a short scuffle, likely with fighters from the local Nauset community, when, while searching for a suitable harbor and settlement site, some of the colonists had made camp at a place they christened "First Encounter" on Cape Cod. Arrows flew and gunshots were fired, but sources suggest that no one was killed or seriously injured. Leading the English in this skirmish was Miles Standish, a man hired by the *Mayflower* expedition as a military adviser. While roaming in the area prior to the engagement, the colonists had violated several Native grave sites and had taken four bushels of corn from a food storage, acts that likely enticed local indigenous fighters to challenge the English camp to encourage the colonists to leave their area.[37]

In 1623, Miles Standish again led a party of colonists and indigenous allies to launch an attack against the Massachusetts who lived to the north of the Wampanoags. Standish returned with the head of a Massachusetts sachem, placing it on a pike at the entrance to the Plymouth settlement. The display of the heads of Native American enemies was a tradition that New English colonists continued throughout the 17th century. After King Philip's War, for instance, New English colonists displayed various heads of Native American war leaders on pikes. Native Americans despised the beheadings and the display of the heads of leaders not only as acts of intimidation and victor's justice but also because they violated Native American beliefs and burial rites.

The 1623 display of the Massachusetts sachem also provides a glimpse into the tenuous relations between the Wampanoags and Plymouth Colony, as the symbolism of this act was not lost on the Wampanoags. It was a show of the English colonists' power and a visual display aimed to intimidate the Wampanoags. In fact, one Wampanoag openly challenged the display of the Massachusetts sachem and questioned the seriousness of the alliance. He asked the colonists of Plymouth "if we are allies, how cometh it to pass that when we come to Patuxet [Plymouth] you stand upon your guard, with the mouths of your pieces [guns] presented to us."[38] The defensive alliance between Plymouth and the Wampanoags was often strained and would decline further over the following decades when New English colonists obtained ever more aboriginal land. Despite tensions, the Wampanoags and the New English avoided an outright war until the 1670s.

At around the same time, a major source of tensions emerged in what is today the state of Connecticut. By the early 1630s, the Pequots were the principal regional trading partner with the Dutch. The Pequots were in control of significant portions of the fertile lower Connecticut River Valley, which provided this nation with rich farmlands as well as with access to the fur trade with interior groups farther to the north through this waterway. This location put the Pequots in an ideal intermediary position. Moreover, the Pequots came to play an important role in the production of wampum shell beads, which, as discussed in a prior chapter, were an important commodity in the indigenous regional trade networks as well as a key exchange good in the fur trade. In fact, wampum became increasingly treated as a form of currency in the Atlantic Northeast until the 1650s, when English colonists introduced minted coins. The Dutch quickly understood the value of wampum and encouraged groups such as the Pequots and the Narragansetts to increase the production of the beads. Local sachems were happy to comply, as wampum enabled them to obtain trade goods, which increased their status and power in their communities, and it was the Pequots who emerged as the major indigenous wampum producer and trading power. As a result of this development, the Pequots asserted their power over neighboring groups such as the Narragansetts, the Mohegans, and the Niantics. Some of these groups seemed to have been in a tributary relationship with the Pequots.

But with the ascendance to power, the Pequots also came to antagonize the interest of English colonists and several Native American tribes in southeastern New England. Several factors accompanied these changing dynamics. Massachusetts Bay Colony had begun to produce wampum by the mid-1630s, which challenged the Pequots' and Narragansetts' position. Indigenous groups such as the Narragansetts and the Mohegans also resented the Pequots' rise to power. In addition, the gradually expanding English population had established several settlements on the Connecticut in the 1630s, which included Windsor, Hartford, and Springfield, and colonists desired more of the fertile lands in the area. This desire for land, English demands for tribute in the form of wampum from the Pequots, and the murder of Englishmen, for which the English blamed the Pequots, created serious strains in the region.

It was these tensions that led to the Pequot War of 1636–1638. The English colonists found willing allies among the Mohegans and the Narragansetts, who believed that a close alliance with the English could increase their standing in the region. Given that in the late 1630s there were only a few thousand English settlers spread out over New England, the Mohegans and Narragansetts likely did not yet grasp the demographic impact that English migration and colonization would have long term on their societies. To the Mohegans and Narragansetts in the 1630s at least, the Pequots seemed like the worse threat, and weakening a strong and long-term regional rival with the help of the English must have seemed a sound strategic choice.

The most atrocious event in what was a drawn-out, small-scale, vicious conflict was a massacre that occurred at a major Pequot town, a site in modern Mystic, Connecticut. In 1637, English troops and their Narragansett and Mohegan allies surrounded the Pequot town, which was protected by a palisade structure. At dawn the English led a brutal attack that killed most of the community's residents. English militia set the town ablaze, burning many of the residents alive. English colonists and their Native American allies killed most of those Pequots who were able to make their way out of the firestorm.

The Puritan leader and colonist William Bradford, who also served frequently as the governor of Plymouth Plantation in the first decades of the colony's history, described the scene at Mystic:

> It was a fearful sight to see them thus frying in the fire and the streams of blood quenching the same, and horrible was the stink and the scent thereof; but the victory seemed a sweet sacrifice, and they gave the praise thereof to God, who had wrought so wonderfully for them, thus to enclose their enemies in their hands and given them so speedy a victory over so proud an insulting an enemy.[39]

Puritans such as Bradford described what happened at Mystic as a righteous, moral military victory for the English colonizers. It was a harrowing bloodbath of more than 500 mostly helpless children, women, elderly, and some warriors left behind to defend the palisaded Native American settlement. It was a massacre clearly intended to terrorize the Pequots. A Narragansett fighter expressed his shock and disbelief at the brutal conduct of English fighters in warfare. "It is too furious, it slays too many men."[40] The massacre at Mystic was not the end of the war. For another year English militias and their Native American allies pursued the Pequots throughout their homeland. During the duration of the war, many Pequots were killed. Others went into hiding, were able to survive in marginalized communities, or were taken in by Mohegan and Narragansett communities. Many other Pequots were forced into servitude in the English colonies.[41]

English warfare and combat displayed in the Pequot War and in the wars fought with Native Americans in the following decades were extremely violent and sought to destroy indigenous communities. The purpose of atrocious warfare was to create destruction, render Native Americans incapable of resisting, and undermine the future survival of indigenous societies. The killing of women and children as well as the destruction of harvests and food stocks to starve the enemy played an essential part in English military strategy. In future conflicts, the English and New English would again and again target and destroy indigenous settlements, women and children, farm fields, and food supplies. This strategy of attrition sought to drain Native American populations.

In the 1630s such modes of warfare seemed alien to indigenous peoples of Dawnland. This is not to say that Native Americans did not attack enemy settlements or kill their enemies, but it was not done on such a dramatic scale. English observers in the early 17th century were often dismissive of indigenous warfare, describing Native Americans as reluctant to kill and indecisive in their attacks. Rather than kill, Native Americans in Dawnland captured enemy women and children to bring them back to their home communities (and during the wars in the later decades of the 17th century and in the 18th century to sell as captives for ransom). But as we have seen, in the 17th century the old ways, which moderated and curtailed violence, were quickly on the decline. Due to experiences such as the Pequot War and the wide use of firearms, Native Americans in New England quickly changed their modes of fighting and adopted more violent strategies in war. Thus, like their English counterparts had done since their arrival in Dawnland, after the Pequot War, Native American fighters would also seek to destroy white settlements and targeted children, women, and the elderly on occasion. Both New English and the native peoples of the Atlantic Northeast, though at different rates of success and to varying degrees, embraced attrition as part of their warfare.

Native American Captives, Servitude, Labor, Land Loss, and Social Changes

It is important to reiterate, though, that it was not only conflict that helped to create the dramatic and often destructive changes. As discussed above, English colonization coincided with dramatic disease outbreaks, often enabled by wars, trade, and captive taking. With the establishment of English and other European colonies, epidemics continued. But colonization also led to the adoption of indigenous unfree labor in the English colonies. Moreover, English colonization also spurred the loss of land and other social changes.

The end of the Pequot War had a gradual influence on changing New English attitudes about labor, which had a direct impact on the lives of the Native Americans of southern New England in the 17th century. In the aftermath of the conflict, hundreds of Pequot prisoners were brought to the English colonies. Colonial authorities and leaders had proclaimed the conflict with the Pequots to be a "just war," which in the minds of several colonial stakeholders such as the governor of Massachusetts Bay Colony, John Winthrop, gave the colonists the right to use the war captives as laborers. While not necessarily historically accurate, they held the belief that since the Pequots had caused the conflict, the work done by Native American prisoners of war—or even the prisoners of war themselves—was to serve as a form of compensation to the English colonists for their losses, troubles, and expenses incurred during the conflict. Thus, hundreds of Pequots were employed on various colonial farms and estates. Moreover, it also appears that several Pequot war captives were exchanged for slaves of African origin in the West Indies. The habit of colonies to sell Native Americans from New England into Caribbean slavery would continue during other conflicts in the 17th century. The use of Pequot captives also spurred a debate, especially in the Massachusetts Bay Colony, about the use of war captives as servants and the nature of slavery in the colony. Slavery became increasingly embraced as an institution in the New English colonies in the mid-17th century, and some historians have linked the use of Pequot prisoners of war to the origins of American slavery.

Whether one accepts this overall argument, what does seem to be clear is that with the increasing acceptance of slavery in the New English colonies in the 17th century, a growing number of colonial households came to rely on gradually growing numbers of Native American and African slaves, servants, and workers as a source of labor.[42]

English sources suggest that colonial society had a constant need for workers. Occasionally, Native Americans who lived within or in close distance to colonial settlements would hire out their services to English employers. Moreover, colonists and colonial authorities often put pressure on indigenous communities to place their children as servants in English households. English colonists and authorities often argued that there were altruistic reasons for indentured servitude such as helping children to become Christians and productive members of colonial society. Regardless of the justifications used, it was foremost a strategy to provide labor to colonial households. Child servants were a cheap source of labor, as they generally earned little beyond room and board. Living with New English families also rendered indigenous children vulnerable. Life in colonial society exposed them even more to old-world diseases, and many Native American children died of epidemics during their servitude with New English families. Also, servitude could mean exposure to physical, emotional, and sexual abuse and violence. Such treatment must have come as a culture shock to many indigenous children, since traditionally native cultures of the Northeast relied far less on corporal punishment of youngsters than New English society.

The loss of indigenous land was the prime reason why a growing number of Native Americans sought employment in the colony. The earlier-discussed New English great land rush meant dramatic land losses for Native Americans. As we have seen, in southern New England from the 1620s to the 1670s, English colonists and colonial authorities exerted pressures on indigenous communities to surrender their landholdings. The devastating demographic impact of disease and warfare led some Native American leaders to sell excess lands. Debt was another factor that forced Native Americans to sell their land, and New English colonists and authorities purchased Native American lands for far below market value. Moreover, some surviving deeds and land transfer documents raise questions about such transfers. How much coercion, fraud, or official abuse of power might have been at play? At the same time, Native Americans adapted deeds as a means to protect their land basis. The history of land transactions is complicated and hard to assess on the limited evidence. Moreover, as discussed below in more detail, the creation of praying towns was also used by colonial authorities as a strategy to claim Native American lands for English settlement.

Many Native Americans understood the devastating impact that land loss had on their survival and on their modes of existence. English modes of agricultural production and settlement expansion dramatically altered the lifeways of Native Americans. They lost increasing amounts of territory, which inhibited their traditional modes of survival, and they also saw an increasing loss of their hunting grounds in close vicinity to their settlement. Miantonomi, a Narragansett leader who in the Pequot War had sided with the English, noted in 1642 the dramatic changes that threatened the world of the Native Americans of New England. "You know our fathers had plenty of deer and skins, our plains were full of deer, as also our woods, and of turkies, and our coves full of fish and fowl." All these changes brought on by English colonization made Native American ways of subsistence harder to sustain. Miantonomi reminded Native Americans in the region that "these English having gotten our land, they with scythes cut down the grass, and with axes fell the trees; their cows and horses eat the grass, and their hogs spoil our clam banks, and we shall all be starved." He would be dead only a year later after making this statement. Urged by the English to interfere, the Mohegans attacked the Narragansetts, captured Miantonomi, and executed the sachem to set an example for other Native Americans in the region. Realizing their vulnerable position after this incident, in 1644 the Narragansetts sought a closer relationship with the English. As with the Pennacooks, colonial records described the Narragansetts' efforts as a "submission" under English authority. Different from the Pennacooks, however, who had sought a closer relationship with Massachusetts Bay Colony, the Narragansetts did not want to deal with Rhode Island, Plymouth, or Connecticut Colony. Instead they reached out to the Crown in England. This suggests that the Narragansetts distrusted their Puritan neighbors and hoped that they might obtain a fairer treatment from the metropolitan English government, lobbying that the New English colonies vehemently opposed.[43]

In Native American communities in southern New England, poverty and alcoholism became increasing challenges. Daniel Gookin observed the changes:

> Their drink was formerly no other than water, and yet it doth continue, for their general and common drink. Many of the Indians are lovers of strong drink. . . . Hereby they are made drunk very often; and being drunk, are many times outrageous & mad, fighting with and killing one another; yea sometimes their own relatives. This beastly sin of drunkenness could not be charged upon the Indians before the English and other Christians nations . . . came to dwell in America.[44]

Alcoholism and poverty were challenges that often went hand in hand in Native American communities all over New England. At the same time, one needs to be careful with the frequently discussed issue of alcoholism in the historic sources. New English writers had many stereotypes about "drunken Indians" and propagated those in their writings.

From the 1620s through the early 1670s, for many Native Americans in Dawnland social change and partial adoption of European material culture happened gradually. Communities that lived on the margins of the New English colonies altered their trading practices with Europeans and incorporated European material culture over several decades. They adopted European firearms, iron tools, axes, kettles, cloth shirts, dresses, and blankets. Like their European neighbors, some Native Americans also began to adopt domestic animals such as horses and pigs, and some indigenous communities raised pigs and sold them for cash in Boston. Oftentimes these changes were self-driven, as Native Americans believed that such adaptations would improve their daily life or that they had become necessary. Throughout their long history in Dawnland Native Americans had adopted many changes, and indigenous groups likely saw the adaptations of the 17th century as little less than strategies to strengthen and improve their communities.[45]

Changes and transformations shaped the histories of indigenous peoples in New England in the 17th century. Disease, wars, trade, and land loss as well as indigenous slavery, servitude, and labor, alongside many other social changes, dramatically altered the lives of Native American communities, especially in southern New England. Natives adapted but also resisted these changes, and many worked to maintain their communities and adhere to their customs and traditions as much as they could. Such social changes and adaptations to new ways as well as indigenous efforts to maintain and continue their old ways are also observable in the Native American encounter with Christianity.

Indigenous Peoples, English "Civilization," and Christianity

"Come over and help us," proclaims a scantily dressed Native American on the 17th-century seal of the Massachusetts Bay Colony. While today the Native American is dressed and the word bubble is gone, this image still serves as the basis of the Commonwealth of Massachusetts's state flag. Historically the seal serves as a window into Massachusetts's and New England's ambiguous relationship with the region's indigenous peoples, providing a glimpse into the stereotypical views that the English held of Native Americans. How much the English colonists were interested in helping native populations is a point of debate. Seventeenth-century English colonists certainly wanted to build a stable, prosperous, and secure colony, and cosmopolitans in England had imperial global ambitions. The Massachusetts Bay seal was designed to help fund-raise toward that goal but also to justify the imperial endeavor of the colony. In the minds of Europeans in the 17th century, missionizing and converting Native Americans to Christianity was seen as a strategy to extend the benefits of their "civilization" to indigenous peoples. Compared to the efforts of the Spanish and French colonies, however, the energies of the New English to missionize Native Americans were much more limited. For much of the 17th century, the mission operations in Massachusetts Bay Colony were spearheaded by the aforementioned Daniel Gookin and a man named John Eliot.

Eliot played an instrumental role in the creation of Native American missionary settlements in Massachusetts Bay Colony, which the English settlers called "praying towns." Eliot was born in 1604 in England. He had been educated at Cambridge and migrated to Massachusetts Bay Colony, settling in Roxbury as a minister. In preparation for his missionary enterprise, he proceeded to try to learn Algonquin dialects and undertook, with much help from Native Americans, the arduous task of translating the Bible into Massachusetts, the language spoken by the surrounding Native American communities. The idea of praying towns played a key strategic role in Eliot's mind. He argued that the missionary settlements would lead indigenous peoples to convert to Christianity and get them to adopt English culture.

Historians vary widely in their assessment of Eliot's and the praying towns' impact on New England's Native American history. Several local historians and antiquarians have celebrated and eulogized the Puritan missionary as "one of the noblest spirits," a "friend," and a "helper" of the native peoples of the area. In contrast, the revisionist historian of the 1970s and 1980s Francis Jennings argued that the missionary was an "agent of empire" who assisted in the eventual subjugation of Native Americans in southern New England. Challenging Jennings assertion, the religious studies scholar Richard Cogley contends that Eliot saw praying towns as a way to protect Native American residents from white settlement pressures.[46] While it is beyond the scope of this book to insert itself into this debate, the discussion below underscores that the histories of the Native American praying towns and their relations with Puritan New England were complex and defy easy characterization.

Joining a praying town required some active changes in the life of Native American residents. Eliot envisaged Native Americans to learn the gospel. They were expected to build English-style clapboard housing and meeting-houses, live in a nuclear family, wear their hair in English fashion, and give up their traditional cultural practices. A regime of fines and physical punishment was meant to enforce this system.

The effectiveness of Eliot's plan to change Native American ways is difficult to assess. For instance, in many of the 14 praying towns residents continued to build their traditional houses and maintained some of their political structures. Furthermore, it is hard to assess how many traditional cultural practices continued under the radar of missionary supervision. It also appears that established Native American leaders tended to retain their prominence and positions in the praying towns. Moreover, there is also some evidence that suggests that residents in praying towns, such as Natick, resisted the demands by colonists and colonial authorities to have their children placed as servants in New English homes. Indigenous peoples in praying towns tried to survive and resist colonialism and attempted to maintain their land basis, kinship networks, and communities.[47]

The praying towns were spread out all over southern New England, and Eliot and Gookin supervised a number of them. Thus, their attention was divided between directing various missions, their many other professional obligations, and the need to raise funds for their mission projects. The praying towns were notoriously underfunded and received virtually no support from Massachusetts Bay Colony. In the mid-17th century, the distance and travel conditions were arduous and time-consuming. Moreover, Gookin complained that at some communities "vicious and wicked men and women" of neighboring native settlements, "which Satan makes use of to obstruct the prosperity of religion there," negatively influenced praying town residents. Gookin also noted the reluctance of Native American praying town residents to raise livestock and adopt English methods of agriculture.[48]

Praying towns certainly served as places that provided their communities with a more secure land base, at least for a while, but at the same time they also became vehicles that assisted in the dispossession of Native American lands. In 1653, Eliot successfully lobbied the colonial authorities to create a very small praying town of 2,500 acres called Wamesit in what is today downtown Lowell. While Massachusetts Bay Colony permitted the creation of Wamesit, the colonial legislature also used this opportunity to claim the lands surrounding the praying town to the south of the Merrimack River and granted these lands to English colonists from neighboring Concord and Woburn, a step that led to the founding of the towns of Chelmsford and Billerica.[49]

Given the absence of white missionaries, it was Native Americans who took on much of the spiritual and political leadership in the praying towns, and Wamesit again serves as an insightful example. In the mid-17th century, the distance and travel conditions up to Wamesit from Roxbury, where Eliot resided, were arduous and time-consuming. Numphow, a relative of Passaconaway and one of Eliot's first converts, was the leader of Wamesit. His son, Samuel Numphow, a former student of the Harvard Indian College, served as the praying town's teacher.[50]

With the limited insight that we can gather from documents, it is hard to assess why the Native Americans who gathered at Natick, Wamesit, and other praying towns embraced Christianity and to what degree. Were they politically or spiritually motivated to convert, or was it perhaps a combination of both? Given the destruction of disease, colonization, and the proliferation and rapid expansion of English settlements, might the religion offered by Eliot come across as more appealing to some indigenous peoples? Could they have believed that in combination with their old ways this religion might strengthen their spiritual position and maybe provide protection from further destruction and disaster? Was this a decision motivated by a desire to secure indigenous lands, sovereignty, and their position in the region? Did Native American leaders believe that conversion meant a gain in prestige and authority? Did they hope that conversion would bring about the support of colonial authorities or provide their people with access to trade goods or skills such as literacy? Did Native Americans believe that conversion would provide them acceptance in colonial society? Or was this a strategy pursued largely to placate the English colonial elites while, at the same time, guaranteeing the survival of their community? We can only speculate.[51]

A Storm on the Horizon

The intensification of New English colonization brought increasing pressures on indigenous communities. Trade and disease brought about by contact with Europeans began to alter the Native American world of Dawnland starting in the 16th century. The establishment of permanent European settlements brought further strains. As devastating epidemics continued, Native Americans also experienced military conflicts, unfree forms of labor, massive loss of land, and dramatic social changes and pressures. Thus, colonization had dramatically changed indigenous societies in New England—especially in the southern portions of the region. By the 1670s, the changes and pressures on indigenous societies hit a crisis point that erupted in an extremely violent and region-wide conflict known as King Philip's War.

Notes

1. For a discussion on the complex and diverse impact that conquest and colonization had on indigenous peoples across the Americas, see Christoph Strobel, "Conquest and Colonization," in *The Routledge Handbook to the History and Society of the Americas*, ed. Olaf Kaltmeier et al., 75–83 (New York: Routledge, 2019).

2. See, e.g., Lucianne Lavin, *Connecticut's Indigenous Peoples: What Archaeology, History, and Oral Traditions Teach Us about their Communities and Cultures* (New Haven, CT: Yale University Press, 2013), chap. 9.

3. Andrew Lipman, *The Saltwater Frontier: Indians and the Contest of the American Coast* (New Haven, CT: Yale University Press, 2015).

4. Kenneth M. Morrison, *The Embattled Northeast: The Elusive Ideal of Alliance in Abenaki-Euroamerican Relations* (Berkeley: University of California Press, 1984), 15.

5. Ibid., 16.

6. Ibid.

7. Ibid.

8. Ibid.

9. Ibid., 16–17.

10. For a glimpse into the complex history of early contact in Maine, see Emerson W. Baker, Edwin A Churchill, Richard S. D'Abate, Kristine L. Jones, Victor A. Konrad, and Haral L. Prins, eds., *American Beginnings: Exploration, Culture, and Cartography in the Land of Norumbega* (Lincoln: University of Nebraska Press, 1994).

11. Morrison, *The Embattled Northeast,* 16–17.

12. See, e.g., Neal Salisbury, "Squanto: Last of the Patuxets" in *Struggle and Survival in Colonial America*, eds. David Sweet and Gary Nash, 228–245 (Berkeley: University of California Press, 1981).

13. On Epenow, Tisquantum, and other captured Native Americans of Dawnland see, e.g., Alden T. Vaughan, *Transatlantic Encounters: American Indians in Britain, 1500–1776* (New York: Cambridge University Press, 2006), chap. 4.

14. For a readable introduction to the Black Death, see James P. Byrne, *The Black Death* (Westport, CT: Greenwood, 2004). See also Monica Green, ed., *Pandemic Disease in the Medieval World: Rethinking the Black Death* (Amsterdam: ARC Medieval Press, 2015).

15. Dobyns's wide-ranging work on disease and Native Americans has been influential in shaping many scholars' understanding. For a good summary that pertains to the Eastern Woodlands, see Henry Dobyns, *Their Numbers Became Thinned: Native American Population Dynamics in Eastern North America* (Knoxville: University of Tennessee Press, 1983). See also Alfred Crosby, *The Columbian Exchange: Biological and Cultural Consequences of 1492* (Westport, CT: Greenwood, 1973); Alfred Crosby, *Ecological Imperialism: The Biological Expansion of Europe, 900–1900* (New York: Cambridge University Press, 1986), 209–215; Charles Mann, *1493: Uncovering the New World That Columbus Created* (New York: Knopf, 2011); Charles Mann, *1491: New Revelations of the Americas before Columbus* (New York: Vintage, 2006). For a study on the demographic legacy of disease see, e.g., Russel Thornton, *American Indian Holocaust and Survival: A Population History since 1492* (Norman: University Press of Oklahoma, 1987).

16. The essays in *Beyond Germs,* edited by Cameron, Kelton, and Swedlund, underscore that conquest, land loss, slave raiding, and removal also had a devastating impact on the indigenous peoples of the Americas. Challenging Dobyns's and Crosby's historiographic assumption on this issue, the researchers in *Beyond Germs* suggest that the impact of conquest and colonization might have been more devastating for indigenous Americans than disease. Catherine Cameron, Paul Kelton, and Alan Swedlund, eds., *Beyond Germs: Native Depopulation in North America* (Tucson: University of Arizona Press, 2015).

17. For Membertou's account, see Reuben Gold Thwaites, ed., *The Jesuit Relations and Allied Documents: Travels and Explorations of the Jesuit Missionaries in New France, 1610–1791*, 73 vols. (Cleveland, OH: Burrow Brothers, 1896–1901), 1:177.

18. Jenny Hale Pulsipher, *Swindler Sachem: The American Indian Who Sold His Birthright, Dropped Out of Harvard, and Conned the King of England* (New Haven, CT: Yale University Press, 2018), 12.

19. My discussion on disease and colonization has been influenced by Bert Salwen, "Indians of Southern New England and Long Island: Early Period," in *Handbook of North American Indians*, Vol. 15, *Northeast*, ed. Bruce Trigger (Washington, DC: Smithsonian Institution, 1978), 170; Dean Snow and Kim Lamphear, "European Contact and Indian Depopulation in the Northeast: The Timing of the First Epidemics," *Ethnohistory* 35 (1988): 15–33; Pulsipher, *Swindler Sachem*, 12–17; Shephard Kreech, *The Ecological Indian: Myth and History* (New York: Norton, 2000), 79–94. For an essay that encourages researchers to look "beyond germs" when studying the history of New England, see Alan C. Swedlund, "Contagion, Conflict, and Captivity in Interior New England: Native American and European Contacts in the Middle Connecticut River Valley of Massachusetts, 1616–2004," in *Beyond Germs*, 146–173.

20. Daniel Gookin, *Historical Collections of the Indians of New England of Their Several Nations, Numbers, Customs, Manners, Religions, and Government before the English Planted There* (Boston: Belknap and Hall, 1674), 13–14.

21. Neal Salisbury, *Manitou and Providence: Indians, Europeans, and the Making of New England, 1500–1643* (New York: Oxford University Press, 1982), 104.

22. Daniel Mandell, *Behind the Frontier: Indians in Eighteenth Century Eastern Massachusetts* (Lincoln: University of Nebraska Press, 1996), 12.

23. On this issue, see Christoph Strobel, "Pawtucket and Wamesit: The Challenges of [Reconstructing the History of] Two New England Native Communities," in *Ethnicity in Lowell: Ethnographic Overview and Assessment*, Robert Forrant and Christoph Strobel (Boston: Northeast Region Ethnography Program, National Park Service, U.S. Department of the Interior, 2011), 14–15.

24. See Christoph Strobel, "Indigenous Peoples of the Merrimack River Valley in the Early Seventeenth Century: An Atlantic Perspective on Northeastern America" *World History Connected* 16, no. 1 (2019), https://worldhistoryconnected .press.uillinois.edu/16.1/forum_strobel.html (accessed June 6, 2019).

25. Pulsipher, *Swindler Sachem*, 16.

26. Patrick Malone, *The Skulking Way of War: Technology and Tactics among the New England Indians* (Lanham, MD: Madison Books, 1991), chap. 2. On the use of firearms by Native Americans in New England and in North America more generally, see David J. Silverman, *Thundersticks: Firearms and the Violent Transformation of Native America* (Cambridge, MA: Belknap, 2016), especially chap. 3.

27. On French colonization, see David Hackett Fisher, *Champlain's Dream: The European Founding of North America* (New York: Simon and Schuster, 2008).

28. See, e.g., Pauleena MacDougall, *The Penobscot Dance of Resistance: Tradition in the History of a People* (Hanover, NH: University Press of New England, 2004).

29. On Dutch colonization in the Americas, see Wim Klooster, *The Dutch Moment: War, Trade, and Settlement in the Seventeenth Century Atlantic World* (Ithaca, NY: Cornell University Press, 2016).

30. On the fur trade in the Atlantic perspective, see Susan Sleeper Smith, ed., *Rethinking the Fur Trade: Cultures of Exchange in an Atlantic World* (Lincoln: University of Nebraska Press, 2009). On the global connections of the North American

fur trade, see Claudio Saunt, *West of the Revolution: An Uncommon History of 1776* (New York: Norton, 2015), chaps. 1 and 5. For the role that Native Americans played in the global economy more generally, see Christoph Strobel, *The Global Atlantic, 1400–1900* (New York: Routledge, 2015), 96–99, 134–135, 144–145.

31. On the great land rush, see John C. Weaver, *The Great Land Rush and the Making of the Modern World, 1650–1900* (Montreal: McGill, 2006). On the great migration, see Virginia DeJohn Anderson, *New England's Generation: The Great Migration and the Formation of Society and Culture in the Seventeenth Century* (New York: Cambridge University Press, 1991).

32. Ian Saxine, *Properties of Empire: Indians, Colonists, and Land Speculators on the New England Frontier* (New York: New York University Press, 2019); Peter Leavenworth, "'The Best Title That Indians Can Claime': Native American Agency and Consent in the Transferal of Penacook-Pawtucket Land in the Seventeenth Century," *New England Quarterly* 72 (June 1999): 288–289, 293; Salisbury, *Manitou and Providence*, 199–202; David Steward-Smith, "The Penacook Indians and the New England Frontier, circa 1604–1733" (PhD diss., Union Institute, Cincinnati, Ohio 1988), 220; John Pendergast, *The Bend in the River: A Prehistory and Contact History of Lowell, Chelsmford, Dracut, Tyngsborough, Dunstable, (Nashua, NH), Massachusetts* (Tyngsborough, MA: Merrimac River Press, 1991), 65, 67–69.

33. Malone, *The Skulking Way of War*, 7.

34. On the Tarenteens and the Mohawks and indigenous warfare see, e.g., William Wood, *New England's Prospect,* edited by Alden T. Vaughan (Amherst: University of Massachusetts Press, 1977), 75–80. See also Lavin, *Connecticut's Indigenous Peoples*, 297–299. On the Haudenosaunees in general, see Daniel K Richter, *The Ordeal of the Longhouse: The Peoples of the Iroquois League in the Era of European Colonization* (Chapel Hill: University of North Carolina Press, 1992).

35. On this issue, see Neal Salisbury, "Toward the Covenant Chain: Iroquois and Southern New England Algonquians, 1637–1684," in *Beyond the Covenant Chain: The Iroquois and Their Neighbors in Indian North America, 1600–1800*, eds. Daniel Richter and James M. Merrell, 61–73 (Syracuse, NY: Syracuse University Press, 1987); Malone, *The Skulking Way of War*, 50–51.

36. On Passaconaway and the Pennacooks, see Strobel, "Pawtucket and Wamesit," 16. On Pocumtuc, see Lavin, *Connecticut's Indigenous Peoples*, 297–299.

37. Guy Chet, *Conquering the American Wilderness: The Triumph of European Warfare in the Colonial Northeast* (Amherst: University of Massachusetts Press, 2003), 15–18.

38. Robert V. Hine and John Mack Faragher, *The American West: A New Interpretive History* (New Haven, CT: Yale University Press, 2000), 59–60.

39. William Bradford, *Of Plymouth Plantation, 1620–1647*, edited by Samuel Eliot Morrison (New York: Knopf, 2002), 296.

40. Francis Jennings, *The Invasion of America: Indians, Colonialism, and the Cant of Conquest* (Chapel Hill: University of North Carolina Press, 1979), 223.

41. For more information on this conflict, see Alfred A. Cave, *The Pequot War* (Amherst: University of Massachusetts Press, 1996). See also Salisbury, *Manitou*

and Providence, 203–224; Laurence M. Hauptman, "The Pequot War and Its Leg-acies," in *The Pequots of Southern New England: The Fall and Rise of an Indian Nation*, ed. Laurence Hauptman and James D. Wherry, 69–80 (Norman: University of Oklahoma Press, 1990). See also Malone, *The Skulking Way of War*, 76, 78–80; Chet, *Conquering the American Wilderness*, 21–27.

42. For a scholarly work that draws a direct connection between the Pequot captives and slavery in New England, see Margret Ellen Newell, *Brethren by Nature: New England Indians, Colonists, and the Origins of American Slavery* (Ithaca, NY: Cornell University Press, 2015). Pulsipher, *Swindler Sachem*, chap. 2, sug-gests that the links are not quite as straightforward.

43. See "Submission to Old England," in *The World Turned Upside: Indian Voices from Early America*, ed. Colin Calloway, 79–83 (Boston: Bedford/St. Martin's, 1994). On this issue more generally, see Jenny Hale Pulsipher, *Subjects unto the Same King: Indians, English, and the Contest for Authority in Colonial New England* (Philadelphia: University of Pennsylvania Press, 2006).

44. Daniel Gookin, "Historical Collections of the Indians in New England," in *Collections of the Massachusetts Historical Society* (Boston: Massachusetts Histori-cal Society, 1792), 11.

45. Neal Salisbury, "'Red Puritans': The Praying Indians of Massachusetts Bay and John Eliot," *William and Mary Quarterly* 31, no. 1 (1974): 27–54.

46. For some typical examples, see Charles Cowley, *Memories of the Indians and Pioneers of the Region of Lowell* (Lowell, MA: Stone and Huse, 1862), 8–9; Pendergast, *The Bend in the River*, 45–49; Jennings, *The Invasion of America*, chap. 14; Richard Cogley, *John Eliot's Mission to the Indians before King Philip's War* (Cam-bridge, MA: Harvard University Press, 1984), 4.

47. For an insightful study of these issues in the praying town of Natick, see Jean O'Brien, *Dispossession by Degree: Indian Land and Identity in Natick, Massa-chusetts, 1650–1790* (Lincoln: University of Nebraska Press, 2003).

48. Gookin, *Historical Collections of the Indians of New England*, 186–188.

49. See "Patooket Graunted Indian Graunt," May 18, 1653, in *Records of the Governor and Company of the Massachusetts Bay in New England*, Vol. 3, *1644–1657*, ed. Nathaniel B. Shurtleff (Boston: Printer of the Commonwealth, 1854), 301. See also "Answr to Mr. Eliot's Peticion in Behalf of Indians and Condicion of Concord & Woobern Plantation," May 18, 1653, in *Records of the Governor and Company of the Massachusetts Bay in New England*, Vol. 4, Part 1, *1650–1660*, 136–137.

50. On Samuel Numphow, see Lisa Brooks, *Our Beloved Kin: A New History of King Philip's War* (New Haven, CT: Yale University Press, 2018), 82–83, 209–213, 215–219. On the central role that Native American and African missionaries more generally played in spreading Christianity in the Atlantic world, see Edward E. Andrews, *Native Apostles: Black and Indian Missionaries in the British Atlantic World* (Cambridge, MA: Harvard University Press, 2013).

51. My thinking here is shaped by Christoph Strobel and Robert Forrant, "'Into a New Canoe': Thinking and Teaching Locally and Globally about Native Americans on the Confluence of the Merrimack and the Concord Rivers," *New England Journal of History* (Spring 2016): 72–75.

CHAPTER FOUR

Native American Communities, War, European Empires, and the New English Struggle for Dominance

This chapter examines the history of Native Americans of New England from the eve of King Philip's War through the American Revolution. The text scrutinizes the destructive impact that King Philip's War had on the native people of southern New England. The chapter also examines the role that indigenous peoples such as the various Wabanaki communities of northern Dawnland played in the wars for imperial domination between New England and New France. Moreover, the text surveys the history of Native Americans in southern New England during this period. This chapter concludes with an examination of the role that New England's indigenous peoples played in the American Revolution.

King Philip's War and Anticolonial Resistance

King Philip's War was a cataclysmic event for the indigenous societies in New England. The conflict began in 1675 and involved several Native American tribes and the New England colonies. The war led to the death or enslavement of many of southern New England's indigenous peoples and dramatically undermined the position of the Native American tribes in the region. Given the complexity of the conflict and the limited space available in a narrative of this nature, this section can merely offer a glimpse into many of the complicated dynamics of King Philip's War.

By the 1670s, New English colonial expansion encroached upon the lands of Native Americans in New England. Especially in the southern portions of the region, the English had spread into the interior. Massachusetts Bay Colony easily reached to the midsection of the modern state of Massachusetts, and via and around the Connecticut River this part of western Massachusetts had also become a location for several New English settlements. Of course, farther to the south this river valley was a major population center in Connecticut, and the colony's coastline and the Thames River Valley were also locations where many growing English settlements could be found. English colonial settlements also covered parts of Rhode Island's coast especially around Narragansett Bay. Though more tenuous and spread out, some struggling English settlements could also be found on the coastline of today's states of Maine and New Hampshire. The English settler population in the New England colonies dramatically increased after 1620 and by 1670 had likely grown to over 50,000 people. The Native Americans of New England, on the other hand, faced a drastic demographic decline as the result of colonization. Historian David Silverman estimates that the indigenous population numbers in southern New England plummeted from an estimated 140,000 to 120,000 early in the 17th century, down by around 30,000 people by 1670—representing a demographic trend that underscores the challenges faced by the Native Americans of Dawnland at that time.[1]

As we saw in the previous chapter, in southern New England especially Native Americans faced increasingly limited options and challenges to their established ways of life. They faced problems connected to their ever-shrinking land base. Indigenous settlements were increasingly surrounded by the English, and to make matters worse, colonists pushed for more and more aboriginal land. Recall that Native Americans came to increasingly desire foreign material objects such as firearms, axes, cooking ware, and Asian and European cloth. Paying for this trade with Europeans became ever harder, reinforcing a vicious cycle of debt and land loss. Between the 1620s and the 1670s English colonists also cut down significant portions of the region's woodlands, which had a negative impact on the game population that Native Americans had traditionally relied on as a source for meat. Moreover, access to waterways became more limited due to English colonization, since most colonists refused to let indigenous people access "their" land. To make matters worse, there are frequent mentions in colonial records of the domestic animals of English colonists that grazed on and destroyed Native American farm fields. Colonists usually blamed New England's Native American populations for these trespasses, as in their opinion the indigenous people had failed to build fences or walls around their farm fields. Of course, Native American communities looked at these incidents through a different prism, feeling that it was the colonists' responsibility to control and enclose their beasts of burden and farm animals. To make matters worse, the available record also suggests that colonists at times deliberately let their animals lose to do harm to their Native American neighbors. In such instances but also in many other confrontations of this kind, New English authorities and colonists utilized the power of their laws, the threat of fines, and their military might to impose a colonial and social order on the indigenous populations in the region. Due to the loss of land, a growing number of Native Americans worked as servants or laborers in the colonial economy.

Despite some violent conflicts, Native Americans in southern New England had largely sought out peaceful relations with the New England colonies. They had submitted themselves and their territory under English authority and participated increasingly in the colonial economy, while many communities still tried to maintain as much of their autonomy and political sovereignty as possible given the circumstances. Some Native American groups resisted these trends and decided to sell or leave their lands. They moved west and north to join other tribal communities or sought out the protection of larger confederacies such as those of the Haudenosaunees and Wabanakis. By the 17th century many indigenous communities and confederacies had adopted refugees, either individuals or entire groups, and most Native American nations in the region must have been quite intertribal in their makeup as kinship relations were offered to outsiders in need.

In the 1670s the growing challenges, land loss, and English pressures led to a rising sense of frustration and discontent in many indigenous communities. Native Americans in southern New England increasingly felt their survival threatened and saw decreasing options in the region. Recall Miantonomi, the Narragansett leader who encouraged Native Americans in southern New England to adhere to intertribal unity in the early 1640s so as to create a stronger alliance to face English colonization but had been quickly assassinated for this activism. While this incident certainly created an understanding about the danger that an intertribal stance could mean in their relations with the English colonies—even if only intended for diplomatic let alone military purposes—by the mid-1670s it is likely that a growing number of Native Americans in New England considered such a strategy beneficial. Could a joining of forces, as Miantonomi suggested, strengthen the position of indigenous peoples in the region? Would an intertribal approach help to face and resist English colonization more effectively? These were likely questions that were on the minds of at least some Native Americans in southern New England in the 1670s.

The tense situation reached a boiling point by the 1670s in Wampanoag country. Metacomet, the Wampanoag leader whom the English called King Philip, had continued the alliance with Plymouth Colony initiated by Ousamequin up until this point. Beyond the overall above-discussed declining position of his people, in 1671 colonial authorities had also compelled the Wampanoags to hand over a substantial number of guns and sign a treaty that relinquished substantial control over their land. It is likely that policies and interferences such as this antagonized the Wampanoags and other Native Americans in southern New England. Such developments likely brought home to them that the indigenous-colonial relations worked increasingly less in their favor and likely led to negotiations and alliance building among some indigenous communities.

The situation escalated quickly in the spring of 1675, when New English–indigenous relations in southern New England were shaped by rumors, fears, and conspiracy theories. The murder of an English-educated Native American who worked for Metacomet and who some accused of spying for the English quickly escalated the situation. New English authorities swiftly proceeded with the execution of three Wampanoag men, an act that many in the indigenous communities perceived as unjust and a case of colonial overreach. Fearing conflict, Metacomet appealed to several of his neighbors for help to create a defensive alliance. Moreover, English settler society was rife with fear and rumors of a Native American rebellion.

Given the declining options and increasing frustrations with New English aggressive demands, several indigenous communities heeded the Wampanoag sachem's appeal. It was younger indigenous men, who made up the backbone of Native American military forces, who felt especially threatened by the loss and decreasing access to hunting and fishing grounds, developments that undercut and threatened their contributions to their communities. But such frustrations were also felt more broadly throughout many indigenous towns and villages. Such exasperations undoubtedly centered on the continuous efforts to try to work out compromises with the colonizers, negotiations that seemed to time and again lead to renewed New English demands for land and other encroachments on indigenous resources and established ways. The New English presence had increasingly undercut traditional gendered roles and sources of power that had long been established in indigenous societies. To a number of Native American communities in southern New England, war seemed increasingly the only way to resist English demands and attempt to strengthen their communities, cultures, and lifeways.

King Philip's War was, however, not a war between New English colonists on the one side and Native Americans on the other but instead was a complicated intercultural conflict. In southern New England, anticolonial resistance gained wide support among the Wampanoags, Narragansetts, and Nipmucs. Many Pequots, Mohegans, and Niantics, on the other hand, did not join the anti-English resistance and often supported the New English colonies in military campaigns. In addition, while the majority of New England praying towns either sided with the colonists or attempted to stay outside the conflict, some praying town residents joined the militant resistance.

Native American allies played a crucial role in the defense of the New English colonies during King Philip's War. Eliot's and Gookin's influence probably played a role in the decision of some praying town natives to side with the English. But the location of these praying towns might have played an ever more important role. Many of these communities were either completely surrounded by or in close vicinity to colonial settlements, which steered them toward seeking a close association with Massachusetts Bay Colony. That said, not all praying towns pursued this strategy. Some of the communities that were far enough away from a direct English threat joined the anticolonial resistance. Groups such as the Mohegans, Pequots, and Niantics had different motivations for joining with the New English shaped by their earlier experiences. They felt that an alliance with the English would serve their strategic purposes better and would help to strengthen their regional position, which motivated these nations to affirm their established alliances with the English.

Native American allies aided the colonies in their struggle against the indigenous anticolonial resistance struggle. Colonial records suggest that Native American soldiers were especially apt in the many military engagements that occurred in swamps, wetlands, and heavily wooded areas. Indigenous guides and scouts helped colonial troops advance much faster through parts of the landscape in which the New English had little fighting experience. Indigenous soldiers also frequently warned New English forces about surprise attacks. Thus, during much of King Philip's War, colonial forces benefited from the support of indigenous allies, guides, and scouts. Native allies also assisted the New English forces in staging effective defensive and offensive strategies against the indigenous resistance. When Massachusetts Bay Colony stopped relying on Native American guides, a decision motivated by English colonists' fears and Indian hating, the colony's defensive and offensive effectiveness suffered tremendously. When officials began again to rely on Native American guides and allies, a strategy that was also accompanied by the adoption of Native American warfare techniques, the colony's military fortunes improved. Compared to Massachusetts Bay Colony, Connecticut, which relied continuously on Native American allies as part of its military strategy, did not experience nearly as many military attacks during King Philip's War.

Some colonial records suggest that certain New English colonists were skeptical and resentful of their Native American allies. They complained, for example, that indigenous allies on the battlefield shot over their enemies' heads instead of killing them. Some critical voices also described them as displaying cowardly behavior in battle. How much this reflects actual Native American unwillingness to commit unnecessary acts of violence against fellow indigenous people, their desire to avoid foolish suicidal behavior on the battlefield, or the hatred that many New English felt toward Native

Americans is hard to gauge on the available evidence. Fragmentary evidence suggests that on occasion, Native American colonial allies protected indigenous captives from violence, abuse, or being sold into slavery. Such actions earned them the further ire of some New English colonists. Moreover, the resentment and hatred toward Native Americans in the New English colonies also led to violent acts and abuse of indigenous fighters, scouts, and guides who served the New English colonies as members of the militias.[2]

The name "King Philip's War" connects the conflict to Metacomet as the leader of the Native American anticolonial resistance struggle, but many influential leaders and complicated indigenous community dynamics shaped the conflict. Women also played a central role in the war, which was representative of the key position that female leaders had played in indigenous societies throughout the long history of Dawnland. The *sunksquaw* Weetamoo of the Wampanoags, for instance, was a major leader who commanded a large contingent of fighters in the conflict. She was a key ally of Metacomet, who was her brother-in-law. She died during the final stages of the war when she drowned in the Taunton River. The New English mutilated her body and displayed her head on a pike outside of Taunton.[3] Women also played an important role among the indigenous peoples who remained neutral or were allies of the New English. The *sunksquaw* called Weeounkkaas or Weunquesh is an oft-cited example here. Weeounkkass was the daughter of Ninigret, an influential sachem among the Niantics, and played a central role as a leader among her people during King Philip's War and beyond.[4] Women such as Weetamoo and Weeounkkas are often not featured in the conventional histories of King Philip's War. Because of the history of colonization and the gender biases of English colonists, who produced many of the written sources, indigenous women—leaders and commoners—have been largely written out of the mainstream histories of New England, despite the fact that they played an important role.

The war also targeted Native Americans who tried to stay outside of the conflict or attempted to remain neutral, such as the Pennacooks of the Merrimack River Valley. Many Pennacooks fled northward to find refuge in the interior of New Hampshire at the outbreak of the war. There they hid from attacks and attempted to put themselves beyond the easy reach of English colonists. Of course, this meant that they had to abandon their fertile farm fields in the Merrimack River Valley system, which made subsistence for these communities much harder.

Developments at the praying town of Wamesit, a community located in today's city of Lowell and a village closely affiliated with its Pennacook neighbors, underscores, however, the dangers that Pennacook communities were avoiding by seeking refuge in the interior northern Dawnland. Most of the Native Americans at Wamesit who had not decided to flee north with their Pennacook kin were arrested by colonial forces. In all, some 140 indigenous residents of Wamesit were forced to march to Charlestown to await a decision on what their destiny would be. After a likely harrowing experience in the city where English anger and fears about King Philip's War were accompanied by a tremendous hatred directed toward indigenous peoples, the colonial authorities decided to release most of the captives and encouraged them to return to Wamesit. But their troubles were not over. English colonists from the neighboring town of Chelmsford attacked Wamesit, killing a boy and injuring several women. Because of the failure of the Massachusetts Bay authorities to provide protection and fearing for their safety in the heated war climate, the vast majority of the Wamesits decided to abandon their settlement and join the Pennacook factions led by Wannalancet, the son of Passaconaway, and the other Wamesits who had fled earlier. There were, however, about a dozen individuals who stayed behind in Wamesit, people mostly too old or too sick to travel, as well as some dedicated family members who decided to take care of them. In an act of barbaric cruelty emblematic of the ferocious violence that defined King Philip's War, Chelmsford settlers returned to burn down the praying town and massacred several remaining residents.[5]

The praying town natives of Natick also fell victim to New English fears. As staunch allies of the colony, the praying town residents from Natick had aided the New English in several military campaigns early in the conflict. After these early military engagements when the Massachusetts Bay Colony authorities stopped using praying town soldiers, they ordered the residents of Natick to be relocated to an internment camp on Deer Island in Boston Harbor. Trapped on the windswept and exposed island, the Praying Indians suffered from inadequate shelter, lack of firewood, and exposure to the elements. Given the raw housing conditions, constant food shortages, and the lack of colonial society to adequately supply the camp, the praying town Indians must have suffered tremendously. While the sources are largely silent on the sufferings of internment camp residents, we know that they experienced "great distress and want for food."[6] Because of the insufficient available information, we also do not know how many Native Americans perished due to the horrendous conditions on the island.

The anti–New English resistance won several military engagements, committed atrocities, and attacked the majority of New English settlements during King Philip's War but failed to land a decisive blow against the colonies. While wreaking havoc in numerous settlements, indigenous resistance forces were generally unable to capture the defensive New English structures found in almost every colonial settlement. The New English fortified defensive housing structures called garrison houses, which were built to withstand Native American attacks and were a gathering place for colonists during assaults, saved the lives of many colonists and impeded Native Americans from making decisive inroads.

The Mohawks, after being encouraged to do so by the English governor of New York, Sir Edmund Andros, also violently interfered in the conflict early in 1676, which further undermined native resistance. They were eager to strike against Metacomet and his allies, as they did not favor the emergence of another powerful indigenous alliance system that could potentially compete with the Haudenosaunees in the Northeast. Thus, the Mohawks launched attacks on indigenous anticolonial resistance fighters. This intervention aided the New England colonies substantially in the conflict.

The New English committed many massacres during the war, such as the one discussed above at Wamesit. In the spring of 1676 at the waterfall in what is today Turners Falls, Massachusetts, on the Connecticut River, another horrific massacre happened. The area's indigenous peoples called the site Peskemskut, but the New English town later built on the massacre site still bears the name of the leader of this campaign: William Turner. At dawn colonial forces attacked the intertribal encampment of several hundred people, who likely had gathered at the falls to take advantage of the rich fishing grounds during spawning season. The Puritan clergyman and 17th-century historian William Hubbard described the attack in 1677 in one of the earliest histories of King Philip's War. Colonial troops "fired . . . into their very wigwams, killing many upon the place, and frighting others with the sudden alarm of their Gunns, made them run into the River, where the swiftness of the stream carrying them down a steep Fall, they perished in the waters. . . . [O]thers of them creeping for shelter under the banks of the great river, were espyed . . . and killed." While this was a particularly violent episode, it was typical of New English conduct during the war.[7]

Arguably one of the most decisive military engagements in King Philip's War was the Great Swamp Massacre. The Great Swamp is an area that can be found in the southern parts of modern-day Rhode Island in the homelands of the Narragansett. In the 17th century this was a large wetland area. The Narragansetts used this area as the base for their resistance and were joined there by many Wampanoag refugees. Hundreds of Native Americans involved in the anti–New English struggle had set up their *wetus* in the area, which was also the location of a large native fort that consisted of wooden palisaded walls strengthened by a stone wall. The thick vegetation and swampy landscape provided many opportunities to hide, made it hard for outsiders to penetrate, and offered plenty of cover for surprise attacks should enemy forces try to enter the Great Swamp. But an extremely cold period in late December 1675 froze the wetlands. This weather pattern allowed colonial troops guided by an indigenous informer to penetrate the area. Colonial forces engaged with Native American fighters but also indiscriminately slaughtered women, children, and other noncombatants. Just as during the Mystic Massacre during the Pequot War in the 1630s, colonial forces put the fort on fire but also burned Native American *wetus* and food stores. The estimates of Native American casualties during this extremely brutal episode range from 300 to 1,000 deaths.[8]

Fighting continued throughout New England, but another decisive blow to anticolonial resistance was the killing of Metacomet in August 1676 near Mount Hope in Bristol, Rhode Island. Citizens of Plymouth, Massachusetts, displayed the sachem's head on a pole in their community. Metacomet's wife and nine-year-old son were sold into slavery in the Caribbean. Representative of the destiny of many indigenous peoples in the aftermath of the war, they were among many hundreds of natives to share this fate. Many other Native Americans ended up enslaved or as serfs working for the New English colonists.[9] Court records suggest that many indigenous participants in the anticolonial resistance were put on trial. Many were found guilty and given the death penalty, while others were sold into Atlantic slavery. Another question arises that is hard to prove on the evidence. Were there Native Americans who were perceived as enemies of the New English who fell victim to extralegal killings? If so, how many were there?

The key to the eventual success for the New England colonies was that the colonists and their indigenous allies outlasted and wore down their Native American opponents by pursuing an extremely violent and bloody war. The total and atrocious warfare directed against the heart of their homeland—the civilian populations, farm fields, food supplies, and settlements—wore down the indigenous anticolonial resistance. English colonists effectively used violence and brutality as tools to quell the native resistance movement and subjugate the resistors. New English forces were effective at perpetuating atrocious war, and they were rarely stopped by Native American defensive structures. The forces annihilated entire settlements by burning indigenous towns and farm fields. While Native Americans were certainly at least a match in battle and kept the New English feeling under attack, in the long run the colonists could import supplies, firearms, and ammunition from Great Britain. As the war continued, the Native American resistance fighters were increasingly running low on ammunition. Moreover, they not only lost in the supply and logistics war but also lost the population numbers game. As we will explore below, thousands of Native Americans died in the conflict, and many others were sold into Atlantic slavery or faced bondage in the New English colonies.[10]

While the conflict came to an end in southern New England by the late summer of 1676, in northern New England war continued into the spring of 1678. The New English colonies and various Wabanaki communities participated in several military engagements as well as destructive raids and counterraids on each other's settlements. Moreover, some of the Wabanaki and Micmac coastal communities had their own flotillas, which struck effectively against colonial harbors and the New English fishing fleet in the region, putting many ships there out of commission. The maritime efforts of these indigenous communities served as an effective strategy for undermining New English efforts to colonize their homelands in northern Dawnland until the mid-18th century.[11] Thus, unlike in southern New England, where the English gained a decisive victory, King Philip's War in northern New England ended up in a standstill. The war was just an opening salvo in a series of conflicts that would last almost 100 years and involved the New English colonies, New France, and various Native American tribes and communities in the Atlantic Northeast.

Many Thousands Gone: Legacies of King Philip's War

While reliable data is impossible to gather given the very limited evidence, it is nonetheless clear that King Philip's War was a dramatic event that drastically reshaped the lives of indigenous peoples in southern New England. Recently some historians estimate that as many as 7 out of 10 Native Americans in southern New England perished in this conflict.[12] Whatever the exact numbers, it is clear that the conflict left a bloody mark on New England.

King Philip's War had a destructive impact on Native Americans of southern New England. The conflict brought dramatic casualties not only to those indigenous groups such as the Wampanoag, Narragansett, or Nipmuc tribes who resisted the New English colonies. Death also impacted those Native American communities who fought alongside the colonies such as the Pequot, Mohegan, and praying town communities. Native Americans from praying towns who were sent into the internment camp on Deer Island, as we have seen, likely also suffered high casualties. The war also impacted Native American communities who tried to stay neutral in the conflict. While Native American men of fighting age were certainly engaged in this war, it is also important to reiterate that it was Native American women, children, and the elderly who suffered high casualty rates in the conflict. As the New English colonies pursued an atrocious war, it was the indigenous civilian populations who suffered as a result.

As we have seen, for many of the survivors the aftermath of King Philip's War meant death, slavery, or servitude. At the end of the conflict, many Native Americans were given the death penalty for either participating in or allegedly being part of the anticolonial resistance. Moreover, likely over 1,000 New England Native Americans were sold into slavery in the Caribbean. One can only imagine how harrowing their experience was, being ripped from their homelands, often separated from their families and kin, and sent to an alien world where many were worked to death on a plantation or died of disease. Other Native Americans became slaves and servants in colonial households in New England.

King Philip's War, along with the 17th- and 18th-century conflicts discussed below, forced many Native Americans to leave their homelands on which their communities and ancestors had lived for hundreds of years and even millennia. For Native Americans, leaving the place of their ancestors was about so much more than giving up a town or village, farm fields, and fishing and hunting grounds. To stay alive, they abandoned the places where their ancestors were buried, which were to indigenous peoples of Dawnland locations filled with sites that had intrinsic cultural and spiritual associations, connections, and power. To many, diaspora meant a break with one's established spiritual and kinship connections and indicates how desperate the situation had become for many Native Americans in the region. Native Americans decided to flee horrendous circumstances and oppression. As occurred so often throughout their history, the indigenous peoples of Dawnland adapted to changing and shifting realities as a survival strategy. In the aftermath of King Philip's War, an Algonquian diaspora was established as Native Americans from the region sought refuge in or among the communities in today's Canada, while others moved under the protection of communities in the modern state of New York. Several of the descendants who ended up settling in New York relocated again in the first decades of the 19th century as a result of the federal removal policy of the U.S. government. Many were relocated to Wisconsin. Moreover, as we will discuss in the chapters below, shrinking homelands, changing economic realities, and interregional migrations led Native Americans to move to the region's cities, rural areas, suburbs, and different indigenous communities. The forced migration of Native Americans from all over southern New England to Bermuda, the Caribbean, and other slave markets of the Atlantic world was an especially sad and destructive experience for indigenous peoples and was also an important part in the story of this diaspora.[13]

The historian Daniel Mandell has described King Philip's War as "a fundamental turning point in relations between Indians and Anglo-Americans." In southern New England that was in many ways the case. The conflict, Mandell believed, also served as "an archetype for many of the conflicts" between Euro-Americans and indigenous peoples "in North America through the late nineteenth century."[14] King Philip's War is, however, not only of relevance in terms of national history as Mandell points out but is also of importance in the history of indigenous–Euro-American relations of New England. While in the southern portion of the region King Philip's War crushed Native Americans' ability to resist militarily, in the northern reaches of Dawnland this conflict was merely one war among many.

100 Years of Wars

Between King Philip's War and the American Revolution, the Native Americans of New England were tied into four major wars that the colonists referred to as King William's War (1688–1697), Queen Anne's War (1702–1713), King George's War (1744–1748), and the French and Indian War

(1754–1763). These conflicts were actually North American tangents of broader European, Atlantic world, and sometimes global wars. European and world historians thus refer to King William's War as the War of the League of Augsburg (or the War of the Grand Alliance), Queen Anne's War as the War of Spanish Succession, King George's War as the War of Austrian Succession, and the French and Indian War as the Seven Years' War (as it lasted in the European theaters from 1756 to 1763). These series of wars were part of a struggle between Britain and France over who would be the dominant power in Europe. They took place in Europe, but the rivalry also played itself out in a global theater as the two powers competed over and tried to strengthen their colonial holdings around the world. The Atlantic Northeast was at the center of the Anglo-French competition over power, and the Native Americans of New England often found themselves in the middle of this global war. This rivalry also played itself out in smaller regional conflicts such as Dummer's War (1722–1727), during which the Wabanakis in northern New England attempted to push back English colonization efforts. This proliferation of conflicts meant that many of the indigenous people of Dawnland lived through an almost continuous era of war.

While these wars featured battles at land and sea, targeted raids against the opponents' settlements also were a strategic feature of colonial warfare in the Atlantic Northeast. We have already mentioned the New English strategy of attacking Native American settlements and often burning down these towns and villages as well as farm fields and food stocks. This total warfare served one purpose—to leave Native Americans without places to shelter and to starve them into submission. New English writers have, however, generally paid more attention to the so-called Indian raids on New English settlements. During the wars of Anglo-French imperial competition, Native American allies of New France raided New English settlements. English settler colonial accounts tended to describe these attacks as violent assaults on innocent Puritan settlers who were victimized by their indigenous attackers. Moreover, these writers, generally Puritan contemporaries as well as later historians who were sympathetic to the English colonists, maintained that the French had manipulated their indigenous "allies" to participate in the raids. Thus, these writers argued that the indigenous "allies" served as "pawns" in the power game of the French. At the same time, the English colonists engaged in a "just" or "righteous" defensive war. This argument still holds a certain popular appeal to this day.[15]

This line of reasoning, which emphasizes New English victimization, tends to neglect that New English rangers and scouts struck against Native American settlements and ever more effectively interrupted Franco-indigenous raiding parties in what is today northern New England and Canada throughout the 18th century. Recall that the English attacks against indigenous settlements were especially harsh on the civilian population, and one of the most notable examples of this type of English raid happened during an attack on the native settlement of St. Francis (today Odanak in Quebec) in the fall of 1759. Throughout the late 17th century and the 18th century, this community had provided refuge to Native Americans from New England. Fighters from St. Francis had assisted French forces throughout their wars with the British. Thus, the community had become the focus of New English ire. At the time of the raid, St. Francis was mostly occupied by children, women, and the elderly, and what ensued was one of the most horrific episodes of the Seven Years' War. The New English ranger force supported by Mohegan scouts entered the settlement very early in the morning under the cover of darkness and slaughtered many of the sleeping residents. Individuals who tried to flee were shot on sight, and many were killed. While we will probably never get an exact casualty count, the number of deaths was likely in the hundreds.[16]

It is also important to emphasize that throughout the wars of the 17th and 18th centuries, and while historians often call these conflicts Queen Anne's War or King William's War, suggesting a united strategic front, New France and indigenous peoples often fought for and were motivated by different reasons. Thus, this was a tenuous alliance system at best. In many ways, the French and indigenous peoples fought disparate wars that sometimes loosely connected as strategic interests overlapped. The raids were a representation of the disparate nature of these conflicts. Wabanaki fighters were often reluctant to risk their lives on assaults on English fortified positions and were selective about the campaigns they participated in.

The Wabanakis had their unique reasons for participating in the conflict. Most important to these communities was that they wanted to maintain their political, economic, and cultural sovereignty in regard to the British as well as French colonies. The members of this alliance system drew from contemporary groups such as the Penobscot, Passamaquoddy, Maliseet, and Abenaki tribes and were often supported by the Micmacs and other first nations in Canada. Several of their communities, whose numbers had been strengthened by Native American refugees from southern and central New England, clearly understood the threat that New English colonization posed to their homelands. The Wabanakis realized that the New English claimed that they held sovereignty over their territory. Several of the Wabanaki communities also had Catholic churches or hosted French missionaries as well as traders, and some in these settlements engaged with Catholicism. Such cultural and economic networks helped to create ties between the Wabanakis and the French. Moreover, New France provided the Wabanakis with supplies such as iron tools, weapons, and ammunition, all of which had become of strategic importance to the Native American communities of today's northern New England and southeastern Canada. As this 100-year conflict continued, however, by the early 18th century as the French position in North America became weaker, so did New France's support to the indigenous peoples in northern New England. Because of these changing realities, Native Americans in the region received fewer supplies, ammunition, and weapons and less effective support. Given these changing realities, Wabanaki communities often pursued an independent policy toward the English, and the ties between New France and the Wabanaki nations were tenuous, but in conflicts many Wabanakis still often sided with the French until the end of the Severn Years' War. Yet after the French surrendered to the British in the Treaty of Paris in 1763, British colonists, who in prior decades had increasingly eyed the fertile lands of northern New England but had been contained by the Wabanakis, now swamped this region. This development confined the local Native American communities of northern Dawnland into ever-shrinking areas. For the Wabanakis, the Treaty of Paris meant that they had been transformed from being sovereign allies of the French into British colonial subjects by the stroke of a pen and with none of their input. As a result, some Wabanakis fled their homelands in the aftermath of the Seven Years' War. Some went north to Newfoundland to escape British pressures, and others fled to join communities in the upper Ohio Valley and the Great Lakes region.[17]

While raids played a significant role in the 100 years of war, historians have debated how much of a strategic impact they actually had in these conflicts. Some suggest that these campaigns were of strategic importance, while others argue that they were not an efficient use of military resources and capabilities. Regardless of the strategic advantages or disadvantages of raids, one thing seems to be clear: whether committed by European or indigenous assailants, as written sources and oral histories suggest, these surprise attacks created a culture of fear and panic throughout the Atlantic Northeast.[18]

Captive taking played a central part in the French-Indian raids. Hundreds of New English settlers were captured during these assaults. After the traumatic experience of the attack that often saw the murder of loved ones, the prisoners of war were usually taken on a trek several hundred miles north to New France. Because of the arduousness and the conditions of the journey, some of the captives perished during the ordeal. Once in New France, the lives of captives varied widely. Some captives went to colonial prisons, experiencing and suffering from the horrendous conditions that existed in early modern prisons. Other captives would stay with either French colonists or Native American communities. The vast majority of the surviving captives returned to New England, often either sold back for ransom or exchanged for French prisoners of war. Some captives chose to stay behind for some time and, after staying in French colonial or Native American society, would return to New England to serve as translators, cultural brokers, and diplomats. For others the integration into French colonial or indigenous society was permanent. Some of these individuals or their children obtained positions of rank in French and Native American societies. Individuals such as

Esther Wheelwright, for instance, embraced life in New France. Abducted during a raid as a child from Wells (in today's Maine), she lived first for several years in a Wabanaki community and then was placed in a convent in Quebec, where she was further educated. Wheelwright was eventually selected to be the mother superior of the Ursulines. Other captives such as Eunice Williams, the daughter of an influential Puritan minister in Massachusetts who was abducted as a young child from Deerfield in Massachusetts, spent the rest of her life among the Kahnawake Mohawks, a large indigenous community in the vicinity of Montreal. While Williams had multiple opportunities to return to New England, she chose to stay at Kahnawake and was accepted as a Mohawk into that community. Wheelwright's and Williams's stories are representative of a minority of captives who did not want to permanently return to New English society. While they might travel to visit their New English families in times of peace, these former captives embraced a life in either French or Native American societies. They learned indigenous languages and French, and some adopted Catholicism.[19]

While captive taking and captivity might seem particularly brutal from a modern perspective, it is important to underscore that the New English treated their prisoners of war as harshly or more so. While many New English captives were traumatized by the experience, many captivity narratives also underscore incidents of humane treatment of captives at the hands of their captors. Also notable in these narratives are the low incidents of forced sexual violence, so common in many war zones throughout world history.[20]

The taking of captives also had a dramatic impact on New English society and especially negatively influenced attitudes toward the region's indigenous peoples. The disdain and hatred felt toward Native Americans had already been prevalent in the English colonies during King Philip's War. These sentiments increased as a result of the taking of New English captives. Raids were highly publicized events, and the experiences and accounts of New English captives were widely read, discussed, and written about by New English colonists in the 17th and 18th centuries. Thus, the taking of captives by Native American raiders further spurred the hatred that many New English felt toward Native Americans.

There were many French-Indian raids that occurred throughout the wars and haunted the Atlantic Northeast. The raid on Deerfield in late February 1704 was arguably one of the more effective strikes of this kind and was a significant event during Queen Anne's War (1702–1713). The attack on Deerfield ranked among the deadliest raids and led to the capture of an unusually large number of prisoners. The raiding force of about 250 included French, Mohawk, Wabanaki, Pennacook, and Huron fighters. At the time, Deerfield was a newly established and insecure settlement on the northwestern reaches of the colony of Massachusetts. Fifty or so New English residents and soldiers were killed, and 112 individuals were captured. We do not know how many people were injured on the New English side. The attackers lost 11 people during the assault, and 22 members of their party were injured. While the Deerfield raid is representative of many other raids in terms of the way the attack was conducted, the process of captive taking, and the evacuation of the captives to the north, it was in other ways an anomaly. There were other raids that hurt the New English and yielded captives, but especially as the 18th century progressed, these strikes were increasingly ineffective and costly for the attacking party. In many ways the Deerfield Raid was an atypical event, as the attack was deadlier than many other raids and yielded more captives for the attackers.[21]

The Atlantic Northeast was close to being in a state of constant warfare throughout much of the late 17th century and the 18th century, and the unspeakable violent suffering had a significant impact on indigenous as well as New English and French colonial societies. War interrupted people's patterns of daily life, led to destruction of settlements and farm fields, and disrupted families who mourned and endured the loss of loved ones who were either killed as a result of the conflict or were captured as prisoners of war. Many Native American, New French, and New English communities also lived with the constant knowledge and fear that their village or town could be attacked at all points and that the horrors of war could be unleashed on them at a moment's notice.

Moreover, while we often tend to think of war as a male domain, across the Atlantic Northeast of the 17th and 18th centuries, Native American, French, and English women played an often central role during the conflicts. Conventional histories often depict women as playing a central role on the home fronts in their communities—attempting to support their families and neighbors to survive the extreme hardship of war. While many women certainly attempted to fulfill such roles, they also, as the historian Gina Martino demonstrates, served on the front lines of wars. They fought for and defended their families and communities using firearms, hatchets, and sometimes improvised weaponry.[22]

The impact of war on indigenous societies was often devastating, and at times New English wartime policies reflected the hatred and animosities of colonists. In 1755, for instance, lieutenant governor and commander in chief of "His Majesty's Province of the Massachusetts Bay in New England," at the behest of the Massachusetts General Court, offered a "proclamation" that provides a glimpse into the aggressiveness of the New English colonies directed against their Native American enemies. The proclamation required "his Majesty's Subjects of this province to embrace all Opportunities of pursuing, captivating, killing and destroying all and every of the aforesaid Indians."[23] Examining this proclamation from a contemporary perspective, one cannot help but to see the genocidal policies that are being advocated here.

This bounty proclamation promised huge sums of money to colonial invaders to capture or murder Penobscot men, women, and children:

For every Male Penobscot Indian above the Age of Twelve Years, that shall be taken . . . and brought to Boston, Fifty Pounds.

For every Scalp of a Male Penobscot Indian above the Age of aforesaid, brought in as Evidence of their being killed as aforesaid, Forty Pounds.

For every Female Penobscot Indian taken and brought in as aforesaid, and for every Male Indian Prisoner under the Age of Twelve Years, taken and brought in as aforesaid, Twenty-five Pounds.

For every Scalp of such Female Indian or Male Indian under the Age of Twelve Years, that shall be killed and brought in as Evidence of their being killed as aforesaid, Twenty Pounds.[24]

Thus, colonial policy encouraged the murder and scalping and the capture of not only men of fighting age but also civilian populations of women and children. After bringing the scalps of murdered people or the actual captives to Boston, colonists would be granted a lucrative payment from the public treasury. Given the danger and risk involved with having to transport captives over long distance, the problem of being slowed down by captives and the danger of facing Native American counterattacks and considering that the scalp would be compensated at 80 percent, there was little incentive to capture enemies alive. While this proclamation is one of the more open documents that points to this historical phenomenon, it is important to remember that there had been numerous bounty and scalp hunters who had very lucrative careers throughout the wars of the 17th and 18th centuries.[25]

A World Transformed

In the aftermath of King Philip's War and throughout the 18th century, the world of Native Americans in New England dramatically changed. These changes happened in southern New England first, but New English colonization's accelerated hold in the northern portions of the region by the 1760s also dramatically altered the lifeways of indigenous peoples there. Thus, throughout this period Native Americans and indigenous communities struggled with many political, economic, social, and cultural transformations. They lost part of their political sovereignty and land, needed to figure out strategies to integrate into the colonial economy, faced alcoholism, and interacted with colonial education and Christianity. Native Americans throughout this period changed their lifeways in an effort to maintain as much of their communities, autonomy, and culture as possible.

Native Americans in southern New England continued to experience challenges during this period. Disease persisted as an issue. Poverty was a problem in socially marginalized native communities. Debt was also a stress on Native Americans and reinforced further hardship. Many indigenous men and women joined the colonial labor force. They worked on New English farms; in towns and cities as day laborers, artisans, and workers; in households; and as migratory labor. Native American adults did so at times as free labor, but also often, either because of debt or because of their status as war captives, they served in New English households as servants or slaves. Children who were not excluded from their families' debt trap or from being prisoners of war often served as apprentices to New English employers. Thus, Native Americans remained on the margins of New English society. As native people were not citizens, they could not be taxed, but they also could not vote. Moreover, many indigenous communities in southern New England were controlled by government-appointed guardians who ran the communities' finances and often attempted to leave a social and cultural footprint on the native inhabitants they were put in charge of.

Indigenous men from southern New England also often served as sailors or in the military. As sailors they often spent extended periods, sometimes years, at sea with long separations from their families. Work on a ship was dangerous, often leading to fatalities or crippling injuries, and could expose indigenous sailors to alcoholism and disease. Likewise, serving as mercenaries in the conflicts of the late 17th century and the 18th century exposed Native American soldiers to many dangers. Dying or suffering an incapacitating injury as a result of fighting the wars in northern New England or in other parts of the Atlantic Northeast was only one danger for Native American soldiers from southern New England. They also disproportionately suffered from disease, and the rough-and-tumble martial culture also provided extended exposure to alcohol. Thus, both military service and working in the maritime trades were dangerous professions with high mortality for those employed in those sectors.

The disproportionately high representation of Native American men working as sailors or serving on active military duty, especially compared to white males, also explained their much higher mortality rate compared to Euro-Americans and further explains the continuous demographic decline among the indigenous populations in New England. In addition, as we will discuss at more length in the next chapter, the decline in the male population also led Native American women to seek partners outside of their tribal communities. Thus, throughout the 18th and 19th centuries a growing number of indigenous women married or sought out relations with African American and white men.[26]

English pressures on Native American lands continued after King Philip's War. New English colonists illegally trespassed on Native American lands to poach, grazed their animals on Native American pastures, stole timber, and even occupied indigenous lands. Moreover, New English colonists and colonies devised a variety of ways to dispossess indigenous peoples, a process that would continue after the American Revolution. Meanwhile, Native Americans fought hard to maintain as much of their land basis as possible. Throughout the 18th century many Native Americans fought for common landownership, believing that these strategies would most effectively stabilize their land base. Despite such efforts, the number of Native American communities throughout New England declined in this period. Smaller villages and hamlets within white towns dissolved, and even the communities that survived into the 19th century faced increasing loss of territory. This trend, as we will explore in more detail in Chapter 5, continued in the 19th century.

Colonial appropriations of Native American lands were an issue throughout the 18th century. The Native Americans at Mashpee on Cape Cod, for instance, petitioned the Massachusetts General Court in 1752 in protest that they were "much troubled" that their "English neigbors" took "away from us what was our land." Mashpee's indigenous peoples protested this dispossession and asserted their sovereignty and their strong connection to the land. "We shall not give it away, nor shall it be sold, nor shall it be lent, but we shall always use it as long as we live."[27] Like the indigenous peoples of Mashpee, Native Americans throughout New England understood that the maintenance of their land basis also meant that they could keep at least some of the political and economic sovereignty and independence in regard to mainstream New English society. As we will see in the next two chapters, the Mashpee Wampanoags' struggle over their homelands would continue in the following centuries.

Alcohol and alcoholism played a harmful role in the daily life of some Native Americans in New England throughout this period and beyond. The use of alcohol and the addiction to it among Native Americans had an often complex and diverse history throughout Dawnland. Alcohol-related problems impacted indigenous individuals of all backgrounds and communities throughout the region. Moreover, while alcoholism was a serious issue throughout the region's indigenous communities, New English colonists also often had stereotypical assumptions about alcoholism and Native Americans. Rather than providing an accurate historic depiction, these accounts more often than not offer us a glimpse into New English racist or stereotypical assumptions about Native Americans.[28]

While English colonial administrators, clergyman, and moral reformers often blamed alcoholism on the moral weakness of indigenous peoples, many Native Americans had a more complex historical and sociological understanding of this phenomenon. In 1722, for instance, the Mahicans, who lived in western Massachusetts and across the border in eastern New York, responded angrily to the accusations by New York governor William Burnet when he blamed them for wasting their corn harvest and belongings on the purchase of rum. They reminded the official that their addiction to alcohol was directly tied to the long history of the fur trade in the region and thus had roots as far back at least as the 17th century. The Mahicans reminded Burnet that when the Mahicans came "from hunting" to trade with Europeans for "Powder and Shot & clothing" during their first encounters, "they first give us a large cup of Rum, and after we get the Taste of it crave for more so that in fine all the Beaver & Peltry we have hunted goes for drink and we are left destitute either of Clothing or Ammunition." They also reminded Burnet that "for as long as the Christians will sell Rum, our people will drink it."[29]

Throughout the 18th century, several indigenous communities in southern New England became more engaged with Christianity, and this played a role in the education of their children. It is important to underscore, though, that the relationship between Christianity, education, Native Americans, New English, and other Europeans was a complex one that defies easy characterization.

Before King Philip's War Puritan clergymen such as John Elliot as well as Thomas Mayhew Sr. and Thomas Mayhew Jr. attempted to make inroads in bringing Christianity to Native American communities in southern New England, and the trend continued after this conflict. Some missionaries and New English clergyman tried to reach out to indigenous communities in an effort to missionize there. For instance, starting in the 1730s, English missionaries were active among the Stockbridge Indians of western Massachusetts. From the 1740s to the 1770s, German-speaking Moravian missionaries had a presence among several reserves in the region, such as at Schagticoke in northwestern Connecticut. Moreover, some Native Americans attended New English churches and the large outside religious meetings that were popular during the religious revitalization movements of the 18th century that historians often call the Great Awakening.[30]

As with the earlier missionary efforts of the 17th century, we have to be careful in our assessment of the successes of the attempts in the 18th century. Missionaries certainly tended to exaggerate the transformative impact of their efforts. This approach also often served as a strategy to increase their fund-raising potential with donors based both in the colonies and Great Britain who were interested in funding such enterprises. While the missionary outreach attempted to convert Native Americans to Christianity, it also often sought to have an educational impact. John Sergeant, a Puritan missionary among the Mahican people in Stockbridge, Massachusetts, for instance, ran a local school that catered to the children of that community in the 1740s. At the time of his death in 1749, he had begun to pursue an ambitious agenda to transform the local school into a boarding school that aimed to attract Native American children from communities situated some distance away from

Stockbridge. Sergeant had used his plans to create this school as a fund-raiser among groups in favor of missionizing indigenous peoples. Sergeant's boarding school survived for a few years after his death.[31]

In 1754, the minister Eleazar Wheelock founded the Moor's Charity School in Lebanon, Connecticut. The goal of this school was to educate Native American children. Wheelock used the school and several of his Native American students to fund-raise in order to support his agenda of Christian education for indigenous children. In the 1770s, the school eventually moved to Hanover in New Hampshire and became known as Dartmouth College. Much of the money that Wheelock had raised under the pretense to fund Native American education thus ended up helping to establish a school that became a college that for much of its history came to exclusively cater to a white student population, which drew especially from the ranks of the elite. In recent decades, though, Dartmouth College has again given greater emphasis to educating Native American students.[32]

Boarding schools were only one ineffective strategy for bringing education to Native American children in the 18th century. The early boarding schools were not popular with many Native American parents and communities, which explains the ultimate and relatively quick failure of these experiments. New England's indigenous populations were, however, interested in educating their children, and local schools that educated young Native Americans spread throughout southern New England.

In the second half of the 18th century, Native American schools proliferated in southern New England. But indigenous schools emerged not only on the reserves but also in smaller Native American communities that were not officially recognized by the colonial governments as sovereign indigenous territory. Indigenous communities actively promoted and supported their local schools to the best of their ability; they put themselves in charge of these schools and tried to maintain control over their educational systems. The teachers who taught in these schools were also often Native Americans.[33]

Native Americans equally played an active role in their complex and diverse interactions with Christianity. Historians such as Linford Fisher and Neal Salisbury caution us, however, not to describe the encounter of indigenous peoples with Christianity as a process of "conversion" or call Native American individuals religious "converts." Instead, Fisher describes Native American interaction with religion as "religious engagement" and "affiliation." He argues that this nomenclature better captures the "dynamism and inherent instability" of the process. "Native American engagement with Christianity," Fisher writes, "was a contested, multigenerational process that had at its cores an interest in education and was framed by concerns for the ongoing loss of land and a slowly eroding sense of cultural autonomy." It was such social and cultural developments that by the 19th century had led Native Americans in southern New England to create an indigenous version of Protestantism.[34]

In northern New England, indigenous engagement with Christianity was equally complex and also often driven by Native Americans. Until the late 18th century, it was predominantly Catholic priests and Jesuit missionaries who had established a foothold and worked with various Wabanaki communities. It is important to emphasize, though, that these priests had little effectiveness unless they had the approval and the respect of the communities they served. By the late 18th century, the Anglican Church also tried to establish a foothold in some of the Wabanaki communities of northern New England such as the Penobscot, Passamaquoddy, Maliseet, and Micmac communities. Again, it is important to emphasize Native American agency in such decision making. In the 19th century, whether Native Americans in northern New England identified with Catholicism, Protestantism, or neither said much about their political views and their cultural identity and norms.[35]

Several Native Americans came to play an active role in the religious leadership of their communities in the 18th century. Samuel Niles among the Narragansetts and Samuel Ashpo and Samson Occom among the Mohegans are well known for the impact they had in indigenous communities in southern New England and Long Island. As we discussed before, it is important to keep in mind that there were also many other individuals who served as unofficial ministers and educators in communities throughout the region and were not ordained.[36]

Occom, who had been an effective fund-raiser for Wheelock's Indian education program and became an ordained Presbyterian minister, wrote about the limited presence of Christianity during his childhood. He wrote that the Mohegans

> strictly maintain'd and follow'd their Heathenish Ways, Customs & Religion—tho' there was Some Preaching among them, once a Forthnight, in ye Summer Season, a Minster from N London used to Come up, and the Indians to attend, not that they regarded the Christian Religion, But they had Blankets given to them every Fall of the Year and for these things they would attend . . . and all this Time there was not one amongst us, that made a Profession of Christianity.[37]

On the one hand, Occom's observations underscore the feebleness of New English ministers and missionaries in getting Native Americans in southern New England to engage with Christianity. On the other hand, this passage underscores the effectiveness that indigenous ministers and missionaries eventually had in the 18th century and into the 19th century in their communities. Their work played a leading role in the creation of an indigenous version of Protestantism and in separating these churches and religious communities from mainstream New English religious institutions. As we will explore in the next chapter, Native American ministers often performed important roles as cultural, political, and moral leaders in their communities and fought for indigenous rights and cultural survival.[38]

Despite their effectiveness, impact, and hard work, the ordained indigenous ministers and missionaries faced unequal treatment and discrimination. Occom describes this issue. "Now You See What difference they made between me and other Missionaries; they gave me 180 Pounds for 12 years Service, which they gave for one years Service" to a New English missionary or minister. Not only was there tremendous inequity in pay, but Occom also had to perform more jobs than New English ministers and missionaries would have been expected to do. "I was my own Interpreter. I was both a School master, and Minister to the Indians, yea I was their Ear & Hand, as Well as Mouth."[39] The historian Linford Fisher points out that "in almost every instance, Natives in various towns preferred these Indian itinerants and ministers over settled paid Euro Americans."[40]

On the eve of the American Revolution, British colonization had dramatically transformed the political, economic, social, and cultural world of Native Americans of New England and aided in the continuous decline of their population. These developments had led to the fragmentation and disempowerment of many indigenous communities. Despite these processes, Native Americans all across the region adapted to new realities and struggled to persevere and survive. They fought for political sovereignty, autonomy, and land; continued to integrate into the colonial economy as a means to make a living; fought hard to alleviate their social ills; and sought strength in their experimentation with and increasing adoption of education and Christianity. These struggles of the colonial era, as we will see in the next chapter, would continue into the 19th century after New English colonists asserted their independence from Great Britain. In this revolutionary conflict, many of the Native Americans of New England emerged as key allies of the New English colonists in their struggle against the British Empire.

New England's Native Americans and the Revolution

Conventional and popular histories and mainstream perceptions of the American Revolution, when they consider Native Americans at all, still too often assume that indigenous peoples in North America exclusively sided with the British. Native Americans, these accounts suggest, chose the losing side in the conflict. In reality, however, Native Americans sided with both the British and the Americans and often would have preferred to stay neutral—unfortunately an option for only a few Native Americans in the Eastern Woodlands. The prevalent myth that Native Americans sided with the British certainly does not apply to New England. Here many of the indigenous communities joined the American colonists.[41]

Native American soldiers of Gay Head, Mashpee, Mohegan, Narragansett, Penobscot, or Pequot background, just to mention a few tribal communities, fought alongside the American revolutionaries, but it was the Stockbridge Indians who had an especially fierce reputation as the allies of the Americans. The Stockbridge Indian Company served in the battles at Bunker Hill, Bennington, and White Plains. They were also part of the Philadelphia campaign. They had a stellar reputation as scouts and skirmish fighters and as a unit that could spearhead larger armies during assaults. The "Indian Company," as it was often called, perished at the Battle of Kingsbridge (today in the Bronx) when they became victims of an ambush. But it is important to underscore that while the Indian Company has received attention by some scholars, Native Americans from across New England served in all branches of the American war effort from infantry to navy to cavalry and fought in many battles and campaigns of the American Revolution.

Moreover, indigenous allies supported the American war effort even beyond the battlefield. Native American oral traditions maintain, for instance, that the Stockbridge and Oneida communities supplied George Washington's desperate troops at Valley Forge with 300 bushels of corn. During the bitter winter of 1777–1778, the Native Americans snowshoed in these supplies, aiding the revolutionary troops who were in dire straits.[42]

For mainstream New English society, the long-term appreciation for the support that Native Americans in New England provided not only in the American independence struggle but also again during the War of 1812 was minimal. The Native Americans of New England reaped few benefits for their support in the successful American independence struggle and the War of 1812. Backing the Americans in these conflicts bequeathed no long-term benefits to the region's indigenous people. Their alliance with and support of the Americans, which aided the American colonies in gaining their independence and assisted the United States in their conflict with the British in the War of 1812, would be quickly forgotten and garnered few thanks and no long-term privileges or improvements to their tenuous position. As we explore in Chapter 5, in the newly independent American nation the native peoples of New England continued to face marginalization, economic hardships, dispossession, and social challenges. Some faced removal, while many others experienced the official elimination of their tribal status.

Notes

1. David J. Silverman, *Thundersticks: Firearms and the Violent Transformation of Native America* (Cambridge, MA: Harvard University Press, 2016), 105.

2. My argument on Native Americans and King Philip's War is influenced by Patrick M. Malone, *The Skulking Way of War: Technology and Tactics among the New England Indians* (Lanham, MD: Madison Books, 1991), 80–98; Silverman,

Thundersticks, chap. 3; Daniel R. Mandell, *King Philip's War: Colonial Expansion, Native Resistance, and the End of Indian Sovereignty* (Baltimore: Johns Hopkins University Press, 2010). For an example of a colonist complaining about the Mohegans' and Pequots' reluctance to fire at the Narragansetts, see Jenny Hale Pulsipher, *Subject unto the Same King: Indians, English, and the Contest for Authority in Colonial New England* (Philadelphia: University of Pennsylvania Press, 2006), 132.

3. On the Pocasset Wampanoag leader Weetamoo see, e.g., Gina Martino, "'As Potent a Prince as Any Round about Her': Rethinking Weetamoo of the Pocasset and Native Female Leadership in Early America," *Journal of Women's History* (Fall 2015): 37–60. On Weetamoo as well as other important players who have been too long neglected in the historiography, see Lisa Brooks, *Our Beloved Kin: A New History of King Philip's War* (New Haven, CT: Yale University Press, 2018).

4. See, e.g., Julie A. Fisher and David J. Silverman, *Ninigret, Sachem of the Niantics and Narragansetts: Diplomacy, War, and the Balance of Power in Seventeenth-Century New England and Indian Country* (Ithaca, NY: Cornell University Press, 2014), 105, 134, 139; Christine M. DeLucia, *Memory Lands: King Philip's War and the Place of Violence in the Northeast* (New Haven, CT: Yale University Press, 2018), 136.

5. Christoph Strobel, "Pawtucket and Wamesit: The Challenges of [Reconstructing the History of] Two New England Native Communities" in *Ethnicity in Lowell: Ethnographic Overview and Assessment*, ed. Robert Forrant and Christoph Strobel (Boston: Northeast Region Ethnography Program, National Park Service, U.S. Department of the Interior, 2011), 22–23.

6. On the internment camp on Deer Island but also for the struggle over commemorating this historic episode and site, see DeLucia, *Memory Lands*, 49–53 and chap. 2.

7. For the quote by Hubbard and a description of the massacre, see DeLucia, *Memory Lands*, 203–204.

8. My discussion draws from DeLucia, *Memory Lands*, 124–133.

9. See, e.g., Ruth Wallis Herndon and Ella Wilcox Sekatau, "Colonizing the Children: Indian Youngsters in Early Rhode Island," in *Reinterpreting New England Indians and the Colonial Experience*, ed. Colin G. Calloway and Neal Salisbury (Boston: Colonial Society of Massachusetts, 2003), 137–173.

10. My argument here draws from Silverman, *Thundersticks*, chap. 3; Malone, *The Skulking Way of War,* 80–98; Mandell, *King Philip's War.*

11. See Matthew R. Bahar, *Storm of the Sea: Indians & Empires in the Atlantic's Age of Sail* (New York: Oxford University Press, 2019).

12. See Christine DeLucia, "The Memory Frontier: Uncommon Pursuits of Past and Place in the Northeast after King Philip's War," *Journal of American History* 98, no. 4 (2012): 980; David Silverman, *Red Brethren: The Brothertown and Stockbridge Indians and the Problems of Race in Early America* (Ithaca, NY: Cornell University Press, 2010), 23.

13. My discussion here is influenced by DeLucia, *Memory Lands*, chap. 7.

14. Mandell, *King Philip's War*, 4.

15. No one represents this school of thought more eloquently than Francis Parkman. See especially Francis Parkman, *France and England in North America,*

Vol. 2, ed. David Levin (New York: Library of America, 1983). For a modern rendition of this particular school of thought, see Jay Atkinson, *Massacre on the Merrimack: Hannah Duston's Captivity and Revenge in Colonial America* (Lanham, MD: Lyons, 2015).

16. Stephen Brumwell, *White Devil: A True Story of War, Savagery, and Vengeance in Colonial America* (Cambridge, MA: Da Capo, 2005).

17. Ian Saxine, *Properties of Empire: Indians, Colonists, and Land Speculators on the New England Frontier* (New York: New York University Press, 2019); Pauleena MacDougall, *The Penobscot Dance of Resistance: Tradition in the History of a People* (Hanover, NH: University Press of New England, 2004), chap. 4; Neil Rolde, *Unsettled Past, Unsettled Future: The Story of Maine Indians* (Gardiner, ME: Tilbury House Publishers, 2004), chap. 6; Bruce J. Bourque, *Twelve Thousand Years: American Indians in Maine* (Lincoln: University of Nebraska Press, 2001), chap. 7.

18. On this, debate see Malone, *The Skulking Way of War*; Armstrong Starkey, *European and Native American Warfare, 1675–1815* (Norman: University of Oklahoma Press, 1998); Guy Chet, *Conquering the American Wilderness: The Triumph of European Warfare in the Colonial Northeast* (Amherst: University of Massachusetts Press, 2003).

19. On New English captives see, e.g., Emma Lewis Coleman, *New England Captives Carried to Canada: Between 1677 to 1760 during the French Indian Wars*, 2 vols. (Westminster, MD: Heritage Books, 2008). On Eunice Williams see, e.g., John Demos, *The Unredeemed Captive: A Family Story from Early America* (New York: Knopf, 1994). On Esther Wheelwright, see especially Ann M. Little, *The Many Captivities of Esther Wheelwright* (New Haven, CT: Yale University Press, 2016).

20. Alice Nash, "'None of the Women Were Abused': Indigenous Contexts for the Treatment of Women Captives in the Northeast," in *Sex without Consent: Rape and Sexual Coercion in America*, ed. Merrill Smith (New York: New York University Press, 2001), 10–26.

21. For an excellent study of the raid on Deerfield that ties this event into the larger developments of the Atlantic Northeast, see Evan Haefli and Kevin Sweeney, *Captors and Captives: The 1704 French and Indian Raid on Deerfield* (Amherst: University of Massachusetts Press, 2003).

22. Gina M. Martino, *Women at War in the Borderlands of the Early American Northeast* (Chapel Hill: University of North Carolina Press, 2018).

23. "Spencer Phips Proclamation" [November 3, 1755], in *Dawnland Encounters: Indians and Europeans in Northern New England*, ed. Colin Calloway (Hanover, NH: University Press of New England, 1991), 167–168.

24. Ibid., 168.

25. "Spencer Phips Proclamation," 167–169.

26. For a good discussion of the 18th century in southern New England, see Daniel R. Mandell, *Behind the Frontier: Indians in Eighteenth Century Massachusetts* (Lincoln: University of Nebraska Press, 1996). For a comparison with northern New England, see MacDougall, *The Penobscot Dance of Resistance,* chap. 4; Frederick Matthew Wiseman, *The Voices of the Dawn: An Autohistory of the Abenaki Nation* (Hanover, NH: University Press of New England, 2001), chap. 6.

27. Indians at Mashpee, "Petition to the Massachusetts General Court" [June 11, 1752], in *The World Turned Upside Down: Indian Voices from Early America*, ed. Colin Calloway (Boston: Bedford Books, 1994), 105–106.

28. On Native Americans and alcoholism, see Peter C. Mancall, *Deadly Medicine: Indians and Alcohol in Early America* (Ithaca, NY: Cornell University Press, 1995).

29. Mahican Indians, "Reply to William Burnet, Governor of New York, 1722," in *The World Turned Upside Down*, 88–90.

30. See, e.g., Patrick Frazier, *The Mohicans of Stockbridge* (Lincoln: University of Nebraska Press, 1992); Rachel Wheeler, *To Live upon Hope: Mohicans and Missionaries in the Eighteenth-Century Northeast* (Ithaca, NY: Cornell University Press, 2008).

31. Frazier, *The Mohicans of Stockbridge,* 96–101.

32. See, e.g., Colin Calloway, *The Indian History of an American Institution: Native Americans and Dartmouth* (Hanover, NH: Dartmouth College Press, 2010).

33. See, e.g., Linford D. Fisher, *The Indian Great Awakening: Religion and the Shaping of Native Cultures in Early America* (New York: Oxford University Press, 2012), 50–55.

34. Ibid., 5–12; Neal Salisbury, "Embracing Ambiguity: Native Peoples and Christianity in Seventeenth Century Massachusetts," *Ethnohistory* 50, no. 2 (2003): 247–259.

35. See, e.g., MacDougall, *The Penobscot Dance of Resistance,* chaps. 4 and 6; Bourque, *Twelve Thousand Years,* chap. 8.

36. Fisher, *The Indian Great Awakening*, chap. 5.

37. Samson Occom, *The Collected Writings of Samson Occom, Mohegan: Leadership and Literature in Eighteenth-Century Native America*, edited by Joanna Brooks (New York: Oxford University Press, 2006), 52–53.

38. Fisher, *The Indian Great Awakening*, chap. 5.

39. Occom, *The Collected Writings of Samson Occom,* 58.

40. Fisher, *The Indian Great Awakening*, 129.

41. For good introductions to the topic of indigenous peoples and the American Revolution, see Colin Calloway, *The American Revolution in Indian Country: Crisis and Diversity in Native American Communities* (New York: Cambridge University Press, 1995); Ethan A. Schmidt, *Native Americans in the American Revolution: How the War Divided, Devastated, and Transformed the Early American Indian World* (Santa Barbara, CA: Praeger, 2014).

42. On the Stockbridge Indians in the American Revolution, see Calloway, *The American Revolution in Indian Country*, chap. 3. On the Stockbridge Indian Company and Native American soldiers from the Northeast more generally, see Lucianne Lavin, *Connecticut's Indigenous Peoples: What Archaeology, History, and Oral Traditions Teach Us about Their Communities and Cultures* (New Haven, CT: Yale University Press, 2013), 337–339. On the Penobscots, see MacDougall, *The Penobscot Dance of Resistance,* chap. 5.

CHAPTER FIVE

Resisting Policies of Disappearance and Staying Visible

This chapter examines New England's Native American past from after the American Revolution to the mid-20th century. The text explores how Native Americans increasingly participated in the New England economy, working as domestic servants, farmhands, and craftspeople and as laborers in the mills, the whaling industry, and many other sectors. This period also witnessed mainstream society's efforts to obtain much of the remaining Native American landholdings, attempts that were often supported by the policies of the six New England states. White New Englanders often used arguments based on 19th-century racist assumptions as justification for these policies. They maintained that "real" Native Americans had "vanished" or were "disappearing" from the region and claimed that the communities who identified as indigenous people in fact were not.

Despite many challenges, indigenous peoples throughout New England adapted to the changing circumstances, as they had done throughout their history. Native American communities fought efforts by outsiders to take charge of their societies and participated in New English society on their own terms. They adopted changes that were conducive to improving their lives and supported the survival of their communities and families. Through political and cultural activism and by asserting their cultural and political sovereignty, New England's indigenous peoples continued to have a presence as Native Americans of New England on a regional, national, and sometimes global stage. Even as white New Englanders tried to convince themselves

that Native Americans had "disappeared" or "vanished," the region's indigenous peoples continued to maintain a presence.[1]

After the American Revolution, thousands of Native Americans lived in
New England. They often resided in poor communities and experienced
their share of social problems. Alcoholism remained a frequently reported
issue, and because of poverty, migration, and disease, the indigenous population in New England continued to decline during this period. Native Americans also continued to face racism from many of their white neighbors. In
fact, racist and stereotypical perceptions about what it meant to be an Indian
helped to shape and foster many negative images and accounts about the
region's indigenous populations in the 19th century.

Despite these realities, the Native American story in New England from
the 1780s to the 1940s was complex as indigenous people struggled to survive and fought to support and sustain their families and communities to the
best of their abilities. Facing tremendous challenges, some indigenous groups
were able to maintain a measure of autonomy, usually because of their
reserves and their legal status as Indians, which put them to some degree
outside the political, cultural, and citizenship system. At the same time, in
order to survive and counteract the attempts by state governments to undermine their special status as indigenous peoples, Native Americans had to
increasingly engage with New English mainstream society on a political,
legal, and economic level. In order to fight the challenges brought about during this period and guarantee the survival of their communities, indigenous
people used political lobbying and the courts with varying success. Beyond
political advocacy, Native Americans remained visible in other ways. As we
will see throughout this chapter, indigenous people contributed to New England culture and the economy in a variety of ways. They contributed as
scholars, preachers, activists, writers, journalists, performers, athletes, and
teachers and, as mentioned above, worked in many other sectors of the economy. Given their depleting land base and the quick disappearance of traditional ways of subsistence, indigenous people had to figure out new ways to
make a living and survive.

Native Americans and the New England Economy

The economic situation for indigenous people in New England was often
challenging. Like mainstream Americans, indigenous New Englanders faced
dramatic changes and had to develop strategies to adapt, persist, and survive
in a period that was shaped by dynamic economic changes. But as Native
Americans often found themselves in the lower strata of New England society and due in part to the unique status as Indians that they occupied in the
legal systems of several states, these transformations often provided more
intensive challenges to the region's indigenous populations.

Native Americans found themselves drawn into a whirlwind of dramatic transformations that were the result of some of the large changes that the New England economy underwent in the 19th century. The region saw a dramatic decline in the agricultural economy. Small farmers especially faced increasing challenges, and a growing number of small farms went under. As a result, many uprooted white New England famers migrated to the newly created states in the corn belt of the American Midwest. The 19th century was also a period of rapid industrialization and urbanization in New England, with an increasing percentage of the region's workforce laboring in factories and moving to growing cities. Moreover, New England's port cities and shipping industry continued to play a central and expanding role in the Atlantic and global trade of the 19th century.[2]

A significant challenge to Native American communities in New England was their shrinking territorial holdings in the late 18th century and the 19th century. Many smaller indigenous communities even disappeared entirely, and larger reserves lost significant portions of their landholdings. In southern New England in the second half of the 19th century, several reserves faced termination.

Native American reserves in New England were the result of a complex history of treaties and laws that originated in the colonial period. Reserves had some unique systems of land tenure and land use that resulted from a complex history of indigenous colonial relations. Among the Narragansetts in Rhode Island, for instance, the tribal council assigned land to members of the community, and by the early 1790s the government of Rhode Island also permitted the council to lease land to whites and to license timber production on reserve lands. Similar to the situation on the Narragansett reserve, systems of communal or joint land tenancy prevailed in many indigenous communities in New England in the early republic and the antebellum period. This meant that significant portions of reserve lands were either held in common by the entire community or were shared by several members of the community.

Even though economic realities were rapidly changing, many Native Americans in New England continued their established systems of farming and subsistence. Thus, many indigenous farmers preferred to produce on a small scale, catering mostly to their subsistence needs. These individuals showed little interest to produce for a market. Most importantly and continuing in precolonial and colonial era modes of indigenous agriculture, women did much of the farming, and they generally preferred to use a hoe rather than a plow to work the land. Thus, despite New English pressures to bring about change, Native American women persisted in their historic role as the main agricultural producers of their communities and continued to farm in traditional ways.

Nonetheless, there existed a growing number of Native Americans who sought out change and adaptation. In southern New England, some Native

American farmers successfully created larger farms, and more men worked as farmers compared to colonial times. In addition, on several of the larger reserves such as Gay Head and Mashpee, indigenous farmers also raised sheep, cows, hogs, and horses. Raising livestock, given the lack of domestic animals in the pre-Columbian Americas, had not been part of the traditional forms of Native American agriculture. Nevertheless, it was embraced by a growing number of indigenous farmers in the 18th and 19th centuries.[3]

Among the Penobscots and other Wabanaki communities in northern New England, the adoption of Euro-American–style agriculture was slower and showed mixed results throughout the 19th century. The homeland of the Penobscots in Maine is not easy farming country and can experience frost year-round. Still, the Penobscots, like other Native Americans in Maine, had farmed their lands before the coming of Europeans. By the 19th century, the Penobscots faced limited options. They lost significant portions of their homelands in the late 18th century and the 19th century, which confined them to an ever-shrinking territory. Compounding their situation, the massive timber industry in Maine that proliferated in the 19th century aided in deforestation and led to a significant decline in the wild animal and plant populations, which made it harder for the Penobscots to gather and hunt. Initially, officials of the Massachusetts General Court (Massachusetts controlled Maine until 1820, when the northeastern portion of New England gained statehood) and then the government of Maine advocated for a policy of so-called civilization. This program aimed to get the Penobscots to adopt Euro-American methods of agriculture (a system in which men would work the fields), convert the Penobscots to Protestant Christianity (as many among the tribe were devout Catholics), and settle in permanent clapboard houses and advocated for patriarchal and individual landownership. In many ways, however, the policy also provided a fig leaf for the dispossession of indigenous lands, as officials believed that the advocated changes among Native Americans would open up more land to white settlers. This policy ignored the racism of surrounding white settlers toward Native Americans as well as the desire by indigenous people to maintain their cultures and communities. In addition, while officials and white reformers publicly might have advocated for a policy of "civilization," ultimately they provided far too little assistance and resources to implement constructive change. The adoption of Euro-American agriculture moved at a modest pace and faced resistance. Still, despite the many challenges, by the mid-19th century Penobscot farmers raised hay, potatoes, oats, carrots, and fruit trees. Moreover, besides farming their land themselves, the Penobscots also leased some of their lands to white famers and loggers and pursued numerous other ways to make a living. Many Penobscots continued to adhere to their older ways as much as they could. They attempted to retain and, when possible, regain control over their lands and resources. In their struggle to remain independent, the Penobscots continued to hunt and gather, trade in fur, speak their language, fight to retain a Catholic priest, make baskets, and work as guides and lumberjacks.[4]

Beyond farming, the Native Americans in southern New England continued to supplement their diet with foods that they hunted, fished, or gathered. To the best of their abilities as natural availability allowed and as ever-shrinking access made possible, Native Americans hunted for deer and other animals, and especially in coastal areas and river valleys they fished and harvested shellfish. Where possible, indigenous women gathered plants, berries, and roots, some to be used as foods and others as medicine. In 19th-century southern New England, however, the options for mixed subsistence were ever diminishing as reserve lands were shrinking, providing community members with less common land to hunt, fish, and gather on. Moreover, New English communities increasingly denied access to Native American hunters, fishers, and gatherers. Thus, the traditional ways, while they still continued, did so in more limited ways. In the northern parts of New England, especially in Vermont and New Hampshire where traditionally agriculture was somewhat less central to Native American subsistence due to geography and climate, hunting, fishing, and gathering continued more commonly into the 20th century. That said, and as we have already explored, with the adoption of Euro-American forms of farming but also because of logging, groups such as the Penobscots and other Wabanaki communities of northern New England underwent significant changes in their lifeways.

Whether on or off the reserve, in the 19th century New England Indians participated in and integrated into the mainstream economy to an ever larger degree. Life sometimes required cash, as Native Americans needed money to pay for clothes, food, household goods, and health care. As we will explore in more detail below, some Native Americans joined the workforce off the reserves, while others occasionally left their homelands to make some money as peddlers. As aforementioned, indigenous groups and individuals at times rented their land to whites as farm or timber leases, but some Native Americans ran their own timber businesses and sold their wood on the market. Moreover, in the early 19th century, the Gay Head Indians (Aquinnahs) on Martha's Vineyard communally mined and sold the clay from the cliffs of their island. The clay was sold to New England population centers, where it was turned into clay pipes, glass, hearths, and many other products.

Life in the late 18th century and the 19th century also meant increasing threats to communal resources. White intruders committed land and timber theft, put fraudulent claims against Native American individuals and communities, and poached wildlife on indigenous lands. Participating in the market economy and partial integration into New England society was a complex and difficult process. Indigenous people often had to walk a fine line between participating in the mainstream New English economy and society and trying to maintain their cultures and communities. Individuals and groups responded to these challenges and changes in many different ways.

For many Native Americans in New England, work off the reserve more often than not, no matter what economic sector or industry they ended up being employed in, usually meant work in predominantly white society. Depending on what kind of employment a worker had, the separation from the reserve or home community could be for a day, several days, weeks, months, and sometimes years.

This trend aided in the declining use of Native American languages in New England. Off the reserves, away from their communities, interacting in a dominant culture where few if any spoke Native American languages, indigenous people stopped using their tribal languages and instead spoke English. This trend alongside others, such as the lack of formal teaching of indigenous languages, increasing white encroachment, and a shrinking indigenous population, reinforced the declining use of Native American languages.

Native Americans worked in many areas of the New England economy, and some of these economic interactions, as we have seen in earlier chapters, had a long history. In the 16th and 17th centuries, for instance, Native Americans traded European goods often in exchange for fur, and in northern New England, Wabanakis continued to exchange fur and deerskins into the early 20th century. In addition, in the New England colonies, as we discussed earlier, whites had employed Native Americans as slaves and indentured servants since colonial times.

Unfree forms of Native American labor, such as slavery and indentured servitude, continued into the mid-19th century. As we discussed in earlier chapters, New English colonists began to use unfree Native American labor in the aftermath of the Pequot War in the 1630s. But Native Americans had been captured and traded as slaves in the Atlantic economy as far back as the 16th century. Slavery and its legacies persisted for some time after American independence. Slaves who had Native American ancestry worked in urban areas as domestic help and artisans and on New England farms. While slavery became the jure illegal, the use of de facto slaves continued in New England. But this system was on the decline in the last decades of the 18th and ceased altogether by the first decades of the 19th century.[5]

Indentured servitude of Native Americans, on the other hand, continued into the mid-19th century. As we explored in prior chapters, this was a system that had started in the 17th century. Before and after the American Revolution, committing a small crime, suffering poverty, and being orphaned pushed many Native Americans into this system. Yet, the racial makeup of indentured servants changed in the 19th century. Even more so than in colonial times, this was a system of labor that disproportionately trapped people of color. It was indigenous children especially who were caught up in bonded labor. For instance, the 19th-century writer, Methodist minister, and political activist William Apess, a Pequot, was put into indenture at a very young age. While indenture did not provide an ideal environment, for the young Apess it might have provided a somewhat safer world than his home. The boy was abandoned by his parents and raised by an abusive grandmother who horribly hit him and used various other means of physical punishment. When he was four, Apess wrote, his grandmother hit him so hard with a stick that he believed that she might have killed him if it had not been for the interference of an uncle who saved his life. One should be cautious, however, not to romanticize indenture. For one, many indigenous children did not come from abusive families. Moreover, the white family that had raised Apess, much to his disappointment, had no qualms about selling his indenture to a judge in their area. Through much of his indenture and like many other servants, Apess experienced physical and emotional abuse, mistreatment, harsh conditions, and racism.[6]

Apess's experience was common for many indigenous children. Their parents were often poor and were thus at times forced to surrender their children into servitude. In many instances, parents were already indentured at the time of their children's birth, and their legal status brought the children into a system of bondage. Moreover, children who were orphaned or were considered to be neglected often ended up as indentured servants. This labor system and the taking of native children by "tribal overseers" continued into the 1870s.

The treatment of indentured servants often depended in large part on the master or mistress. Working for a kind and generous employer would be a different experience than being employed by an abusive one. That said, given the tilted power dynamics in this system, the bonded worker was always in a disadvantaged and vulnerable position.

Indentured servitude was also at times a strategy to impress Native Americans into the whaling industry, although most Native American whalers were free laborers. Whaling played an important role in the New England and Atlantic economies. Whale oil fueled many of the lamps used in North America and Europe in the 19th century, but it was also used in the production of soap and various other products. Southern New England's seaports, such as New Bedford in Massachusetts, played an active role in the hunt for whales and the production of oil.

Thousands of people from New England and around the world worked in this industry. While many Anglo-Americans worked on the ships, the ranks of mariners drew disproportionately from African Americans, Native Americans, mixed-race individuals, South Europeans, and persons of color from various corners of the world. Whaling played an important role in the U.S. economy and the New England economy and provided an opportunity to racial minorities, such as Native Americans from indigenous communities in southern New England, to participate in the burgeoning American and global economy. Whalers sailed and hunted the oceans and visited ports all over the world. The whaling ship was a racially diverse and complex space. While there could be racial tensions and violence on the ship, it was more often than not, given a paradoxical blend of rigid social hierarchy but also solidarity in its maritime environment, a world of relative fluidity and undisturbed interaction between different groups.

Native American whalers participated in an international maritime working-class culture. Among the Gay Head Indians on Martha's Vineyard but also in other indigenous coastal southern New England communities, many males joined this profession. Work as whalers provided a source of income, status, respect, and pride. But there were also problems affiliated with the trade. Many whalers carried high debts. Alcoholism and other excessive drinking were also endemic issues among mariners. Furthermore, whaling meant long voyages that separated mariners from their families and home communities for extended periods of time. Shipwrecks, accidents, and disease could occur on the high seas and in foreign ports. Being a sailor was a dangerous profession with high mortality rates and great risks of obtaining a crippling injury.[7]

After the American Revolution, as in colonial times, Native Americans continued to work in urban and rural households, on farms, and in businesses all over New England. They worked as maids, household servants, farm laborers, artisans, and craftsmen. Sometimes Native Americans worked for families in close proximity to their reserves or homelands, and in other instances they traveled some distance to find work. Being close to the reserve often meant that they could come home at night or on Sundays. For indigenous men, day labor on white farms did not pay the most lucrative wage, but it provided them with some flexibility and control over their time. Other workers lived on white farms, often in special servant quarters or houses, and paid white farmers in the form of labor in return for room and board.

Many indigenous women participated in the making and selling of traditional crafts and medicine. They were especially known and valued as basket and broom makers. These women and their children usually made their products in their settlements during the winter months, and once they had produced a critical mass by spring, they would travel around to sell their wares to white neighbors. Basket weavers often used traditional patterns, colors, and designs, and several Native American women had well-known reputations in the areas where they conducted their business for the high quality of their wares. Several indigenous women were also respected for their medical skills and were consulted and sought out for help by white, Native American, and African American patients alike. In the 19th century, indigenous medicine, as was the case with folk medicine, was often as successful in its forms of treatment and as sought out by clients as medical doctors. Like basket makers, indigenous herbalists and healers used their traditional skills to make a living in the mainstream economy. Being traveling merchants in the 19th century and their overall involvement and participation in the New English economy helped Native Americans to survive the dramatic economic transformations that occurred at the time and also aided New England's indigenous populations in staying visible within the dominant society.[8]

A well-known Penobscot trader in 19th-century Maine was Molly Molasses, who had a reputation for being a tough but also gifted negotiator and traveling merchant. Yet, Molasses's life story is also emblematic of how hard life was for the Penobscots in 19th-century Maine and Native Americans in New England more generally. Only two of her four children survived into adulthood, and her only surviving daughter had been raped by a well-known white entrepreneur in Bangor, Maine. Molasses spent much of her old days in poverty and was notorious and feared among white folks in several Maine towns. She drove a hard bargain and was often considered pushy, asking for assistance, begging, and demanding free passage on trains, ships, and carts. Such behavior must have at least in part been a result of her life in poverty and her experience of the hardships and mistreatment of her people, her loved ones, and herself. One wonders if she had to learn to put on a harsh demeanor, pick her battles, and push back strong and hard against abuse as her way to survive.

Some Native American traveling traders combined their business of selling crafts and medicine with performances and dances. Several of Molly Molasses's family members, for instance, gave performances as what white mainstream society would call "Indian doctors." Indigenous performance traders found that putting on traditional dress and a show helped to attract white customers and often became an additional source of income. Of course, these entertainers fed into white fantasies and stereotypes about Native Americans. But in reality, just like white New Englanders no longer dressed, lived, and acted like the Puritans of the 17th century, indigenous people in the region had changed as well.[9]

The 19th century was also a period of rapid industrialization in New England and saw the construction of factories all over the region, a development that did not pass by Native Americans, some of whom ended up working in the textile, boot and shoe, paper, armory, and other emerging industries. Industrialization dramatically changed the region, which had been a predominantly rural place, and turned New England into the manufacturing hub of the antebellum United States. The building of factories coincided with urban growth and happened all over New England. The 19th century saw the emergence of industrial cities such as Lowell and Lawrence in Massachusetts, Pawtucket in Rhode Island, Waterbury in Connecticut, Lewiston in Maine, and Manchester in New Hampshire, just to mention a few of the region's major and rapidly growing factory cities.

Mill girls such as Betsey Guppy Chamberlain, a person of mixed Native American and white ancestry, were the first generation of industrial laborers who worked the factory floors and machineries in rapidly growing cities such as Lowell, Massachusetts. While we know relatively little about Chamberlain's life, we know that she published several pieces in the *Lowell Offering* and the *New England Offering*. Chamberlain was born in 1797 as Betsey Guppy and spent her early life in New Hampshire. In 1820 she married Josiah Chamberlain. They had children together and operated a small farm in Brookfield, New Hampshire. When her first husband died in 1823 Chamberlain, struggling to make ends meet and to support her family, was gradually forced to sell her farmland. Eventually she moved to Lowell with her kids to find work in the factories to support her family. She likely worked in the mills for much of the 1830s and through the early 1840s, although she might have also worked for some time during this period as a boarding house keeper. Scholars also speculate that she might have had a short-lived marriage while in Lowell. In 1843 she married again. Like many New England farmers who ended up relocating to the midwestern corn belt in search of better opportunities, Chamberlain and her husband moved to Illinois to take up farming again. She was back in Lowell from 1848 to 1850, likely trying to make money, working in the factories, to help her family in Illinois. She also published a few more pieces during this period. In her writings, Chamberlain focused on rural life and women's rights, but a number of her publications also addressed the plight, mistreatment, and experience of Native Americans. Thus, Chamberlain's writings serve as a reminder of the continued presence of Native Americans in 19th-century New England. They provide us a glimpse into how indigenous people proudly reminded mainstream American society that they were still around and were not going away.[10]

Guardians and Indigenous Peoples

Colonial period laws had legacies that lasted into the 19th and 20th centuries and reinforced the treatment and the status of Native Americans as inferior members of New England society. For instance, like women and African Americans, Native Americans lacked the right to vote. Moreover, the treatment of several Native American communities in New England was akin to that of a minor or a ward of the state, since government officials appointed guardians, generally white clergy, lawyers, or other noted members of white society, to run and manage the affairs of such indigenous communities. While often seemingly well intended, this was at the same time a paternalistic policy that not only curtailed the rights of indigenous people but in several instances also inflicted serious damage on communities.

The initial appointment of a guardian was not necessarily an issue that was handed down by the state government. During the aftermath of the American Revolution, a period of rampant white settler encroachments on indigenous lands as well as illegal logging and poaching, some Native American communities in New England lobbied authorities, with varying success, to interfere on their behalf to preserve their rights, lands, and position. Such lobbying led state authorities in several cases to appoint guardians to manage affairs on certain reserves. In other instances, however, authorities appointed guardians without the consent of indigenous communities. In addition, other communities did not experience official supervision.

Because of the guardians, administrative precedents, and laws that regulated reserves, indigenous New Englanders had limited rights over their reservation lands, a fact that could be a double-edged sword. Native Americans who lived on reserves often had no individual land rights and without property lacked wealth. Still, it is important to underscore that such rules and regulations were also violated. Corrupt and morally questionable guardians sold reserve lands to interested friends or to people who had offered them a bribe or some other form of enticement. There were land speculators and officials pressuring Native Americans out of their land, and the legal restrictions were often bent (or violated) to accommodate such purchases. Moreover, Native Americans were not always the victims of land transactions. Instead, at times an affluent member of a community actively sold land to benefit him or herself, and these transactions often happened at the expense of their community. A far more likely scenario, however, was that land sales happened as a result of an incurred debt or out of financial hardship, and given the impoverished position that most indigenous New Englanders held in society, this was a common occurrence. The legal system often accommodated and, especially at times when Native American lands became more desired by New English society, even facilitated such transactions. Despite such occurrences, having communally held land made it harder for Native American individuals to sell property to members of New England's dominant society and also put checks and balances on official land sales. Hence, despite the many faults and abuses of the system, the regulations helped to preserve Native American lands in many areas of southern New England well into the 19th century.

Many Native Americans on the reserves of southern New England who experienced the guardian system saw it as a challenge to their rights, and they used the revolutionary political rhetoric of their day in an attempt to change this system. In places such as Mashpee, Christiantown, Chappaquidick, and many other communities, this was a struggle over political power, sovereignty, economic and cultural resources, religious control, respect, and authority. Indigenous activists deployed rhetoric that accused the guardians of being corrupt elitists who abused their power and privileges at the expense of Native Americans, who demanded self-rule. This phenomenon can be observed in the early 1830s during an event that historians today call the Mashpee Revolt. This incident was a struggle between state officials and guardians on one side and the Mashpee Wampanoags on the other. With the help of the earlier-mentioned William Apess, the Mashpees were able to regain control over their reserve lands and church. This type of Native American activism was representative of some of the broader trends in New England society at the time. Several groups who felt underrepresented and discriminated against used such strategies and manifestations to make their voices heard and demand more rights. State officials and guardians, on the other hand, tried to limit those challenges and often confronted them head-on. At times they exploited divisions, differences, and diversity of opinions in indigenous communities to their advantage. Thus, the strategy of divide and conquer, which had shaped New English warfare and diplomacy in the colonial period, was now applied in the political and cultural struggles over indigenous sovereignty of the 19th century.[11]

Indigenous Population Decline in New England

As their land basis shrank, so did the Native Americans' population. This was a development that was caused by a variety of factors, including continuously higher mortality than birth rates among New England's indigenous peoples. While Native American populations in the region in the 19th century did not experience the catastrophic demographic decline of the colonial years, populations continued to gradually decrease nonetheless. Mortality rates as a result of various disease outbreaks continued to haunt indigenous communities, though certainly not at the excruciating rates of the 17th century. Poverty also spurred indigenous vulnerability. Furthermore, indigenous men continued to work in dangerous industries and signed up at high rates for military service.

The population decline was further spurred by the outward migration of Native Americans who went to join indigenous communities outside of New England. Native Americans in northern New England, for instance, migrated to join communities north of the border in Canada with which members of these groups had close kinship ties. In addition, in the late 18th and early 19th centuries, the community of Brothertown in the state of New York attracted indigenous peoples from southern New England.

The Brothertown Indian reservation had been created by a conglomerate of Native American Christian converts especially from Connecticut, Rhode Island, and Long Island. Brothertown recruited its membership from tribes such as the Mohegan, Pequot, Narragansett, and several smaller groups from the region. During the aftermath of the American Revolution, the founders of the community were invited by the Oneida Indians, one of the six Haudenosaunee (Iroquois) nations of New York, to settle in their region. While the majority of the Haudenosaunees had sided with the British during the Revolution, recall that the Oneidas had sided with the Americans. Among the

Haudenosaunees, the Oneidas lived closest to the American settlements, which helped to push the Oneidas into the American camp. After the war, however, the Oneida position had become more isolated. Attracting new Native American settlements to their area by sharing their land and by encouraging these groups to start their own independent reservations, the Oneidas believed, could strengthen their regional position by gaining new allies. Strength in numbers, so went the strategic thinking, could help keep the growing and ever-encroaching surrounding Euro-American settlements at bay. The Brothertown Indians were one of the groups that took the Oneidas up on their offer. The Stockbridge Indians, from western Massachusetts, were another group that followed the Oneida invitation and relocated west.

For several decades, the communities of Brothertown and Stockbridge would continue to attract indigenous migrants from southern New England. Evidence suggests that some were in part attracted by these communities' efforts at preserving and maintaining the traditional ways of their peoples. Kinship ties and a desire to reconnect with family and distant relatives attracted others. Like so many migrants throughout U.S. and world history, others came in search of a brighter future. This low-flow migratory trend would continue through the first decades of the 19th century until the1830s. By that point, like many other indigenous communities and nations east of the Mississippi River, the Brothertown and Strockbridge Indians faced removal from their homelands in the state of New York to Wisconsin.

Processes of migration and consolidation occurred also internally within the New England region. In Massachusetts, for instance, Native Americans abandoned many of the smaller communities and moved to larger communities such as Gay Head and Mashpee. Indigenous hamlets generally consisted of several individuals to a few families and existed throughout the region. Usually the residents held a little land in common. But in the 19th century these small communities increasingly faced discrimination, legal challenges, wear on their limited land base, loss of land, poverty, and marginalization. Residents of such hamlets had long relied on the woods for hunting and gathering foods and medicines and on the waterways for fishing. Recall that New England towns increasingly barred Native Americans' access to the lands and areas they had used for generations for their subsistence. As life in smaller communities was increasingly getting harder in the early decades of the 19th century, larger reserves came to attract a growing number of residents of small indigenous enclaves who searched for a brighter future in those places.

Native American reserves in New England experienced fluctuating population numbers, which were influenced by the seasons as well as by the boom-and-bust cycles of the 19th century. The American market economy provided many challenges to the working poor, and given that Native Americans often belonged to the lower and lower-middling classes, they were particularly vulnerable in dire economic times. In periods of crisis, reserves provided a safe haven to Native Americans who had left their communities in search of labor and had lost their jobs. The reserve became a place to ride out a recession or depression not only for Native Americans who sought economic refuge there but also for some poor blacks and whites.[12]

Intermarriage and Identity

In 19th-century southern New England, just as in colonial times, intermarriage and sexual relations between Native Americans, African Americans, and whites occurred frequently. As we explored above, for various economic reasons many Native Americans moved off the reserves in pursuit of economic opportunities for themselves or to support their families and communities. During their life in mainstream New English society, some Native Americans entered into relationships with African Americans and whites. Moreover, given the shortage of Native American men on the reserves, some indigenous women also took African American or Euro-American spouses who would then live in the communities. The incorporation of outsiders could provide challenges and in part led to a reshaping of Indian identities. The history of intermarriage was thus an integral part in the continued adaptation, persistence, acculturation, and sustained Native American presence. Moreover, an examination of intermarriage provides a glimpse into the fluid personal relations—sometimes tense and conflict-ridden and at other times collaborative and tender—in the complex cultural mosaic that was New England in the 19th century.

Intermarriage and sexual relations among people of different racial backgrounds was also a factor that aided in the population decline among New England's Native Americans. This was often a complex process. New England's urban areas, especially the impoverished ones, were multicultural communities in which African Americans, poor whites (often recent immigrants), and Native Americans interacted and lived side by side. In such communities, persons of indigenous background at times abandoned their Indian identities, a process that historians today describe as crossing the color line. The individuals who pursued this strategy were generally people of mixed indigenous and African American or white ancestry. Over time, some individuals of such backgrounds would blend into African American or white communities, leaving their Native American roots and kinship relations behind. Other individuals of mixed-race background were often assumed to be either African American or white and were not considered Native American by members of mainstream New English society when they moved to non-Indian communities.

But did the passing as white or African American mean a total abandonment of indigenous identity? There is much that we cannot understand on the available evidence. A number of people likely made the decision to leave behind their indigenous roots and assimilate into other communities. But did some of those people continue to maintain their Native American identities in their homes or as part of their family history? In other words, while they did not outwardly project that they were part Native American to members in white or African American communities, was their indigenous identity still known about by close family members? Furthermore, did the Native American identity of their ancestors become a part of their family's history and cultural practice? Thus, while many would not outwardly appear as Indian to members of the dominant society, it is likely that a number of those individuals and households continued to maintain dual or multiple identities and that their Native American heritage and culture remained a part of their family identity.

Intermarriage alone did not lead to the incorporation of indigenous people into dominant New England society. Integration of newcomers also occurred in Native American societies. As we have explored in prior chapters, indigenous communities in the Northeast had long been open to the adoption and incorporation of outsiders. This trend continued throughout the early republic and the 19th century. Recall also our earlier discussion that reserves attracted African Americans and poor whites, especially in tough economic times, and that Native American men worked at sea or in the military, which meant that they were often gone for long periods of time and suffered high mortality rates. Thus, by the mid-19th century, Native Americans from southern New England communities had lived with and married African Americans and whites. These marriages were common on reservations, had been a regular feature since colonial times, and led several contemporary New English and European observers to comment on the racial mixing in Native American communities in southern New England.

It is important to underscore, though, that interracial marriage also caused tensions in southern New England's indigenous communities. Some Native American men resented the fact that some indigenous women found husbands outside of their community, and at times such dislikes were expressed in racialized rhetoric and showed a fear that the presence and adoption of outsiders could harm the survival of a group. The Mohegan and Narragansett tribes in southern New England, for example, rejected the inclusion of people in their communities who were not Native American. Overall, however, despite some tensions and racial anxieties, New England's Native American societies were generally more open to adopting and integrating outsiders compared to the dominant white society.

Some Native Americans raised concerns about the inclusion of outsiders and worried that this trend could lead to the loss of their indigenous identity in the eyes of New English mainstream society. There were certainly legitimate concerns regarding this issue, and they came to the forefront in the court case *Andover v. Canton* (1816).

This was a complicated court case that involved Lewis Elisha from the state of Massachusetts. He was the son of a Punkapoag Indian mother and an African American father who was also a slave. *Andover v. Canton* was in essence a welfare case. Elisha and his family had fallen on hard times, and the towns of both Canton and Andover in Massachusetts tried to avoid having to take them into their care. Ultimately the case went to trial. The court decided that as the son of a free mother, Elisha was born free. This took the social burden from Canton, a town south of Boston, which had a small community of Punkapoags, was the place of Elisha's birth, and, more importantly for the court case, was also the legal residence of his late enslaved father's owner. Given the court's decision, the responsibility fell to Andover, a town located some 20 miles north of Boston. Elisha had moved there as an adult after he got married. His wife, who was also a woman of mixed-race background, resided in this town, and he joined her in that community. The story of the court case was, however, vastly more complicated due to the legal implications that the decision raised. In fact, the court ruled that Elisha not only had the right to leave his tribe but had also in fact lost his status by leaving the Punkapoag community. Thus, *Andover v. Canton* established a legal precedent that the children of interracial Native American, African American, and white marriages could lose their status as Indians.[13]

Matters of identity were further complicated by the census. Today people self-identify their ethnic identities when they fill out the census form. In the 19th century, however, it was the census taker who decided the racial categories of the individuals and families whose data they recorded. Thus, if a person of mixed Native American, African, and European ancestry looked African American, mixed-race, or white to a census taker, that official would then mark that individual and family down in that category. Such decisions were further influenced by the racist understandings about blood quantum and preconceived notions and stereotypes about what Native Americans should look like and how they should act, which prevailed in U.S. mainstream society at that time. Such understandings helped to alter the identity of many indigenous New Englanders in the census records. On the reserves of southern New England, for instance, census takers often put down the residents as "non-white" or "Negro" but rarely as "Indian."

Religion, Reform, and Race: Indigenous New England in the Mid-19th Century

By the 19th century, Christianity was a well-established part of Native American life in New England. Given the loss of land, resources, economic pressures, and hardships, religious, political, and cultural leaders in indigenous communities attempted to stem the tide of this decline and advocated reforms. The hope was that these changes would help strengthen their communities' survival and lead to a brighter future. Religion played a central role in the indigenous people's struggle to maintain their sovereignty and keep their communities viable. Yet, the 19th century was also a period of intensifying racism, and mainstream society's views of Native Americans were increasingly influenced by these changes, a development that threatened the survival of many indigenous communities in New England.

As we discussed earlier, Christianity had taken hold in several indigenous communities since colonial times. All over New England, Native Americans had built and maintained tribal churches and successful schools. The Christianity practiced by indigenous New Englanders drew from and was inspired by Native American spiritual elements as well as by Catholic, Anglo-American, and Pietistic traditions. Moreover, due to the presence of schools, Native Americans in New England also had substantial rates of literacy in their communities.[14]

Given this history, by the mid-19th century there emerged a diverse religious landscape. In southern New England, indigenous communities had come to increasingly reject the state-appointed Congregationalist clergymen. Instead they came to favor Methodist and Baptist preachers, many of Native American background, such as the earlier-mentioned Pequot Methodist minister, activist, and writer William Apess, and the Baptist preacher Joe Amos of Mashpee. Among the Penobscot and Passamaquoddy tribes in Maine, an individual's Christian sect could often provide insights into their identity and politics. Both communities were split between Catholics, who tended to worship and educate their children in French-speaking churches and schools, and Protestants, who favored English and close ties to the state of Maine. The two factions also disagreed on how their tribes should be run. The Protestant factions among the Penobscot and the Passamaquoddy tribes, for instance, favored the long-established system that chiefs in the community would serve for their lifetime, while the Catholics favored a system that gave members the right to vote out leaders.[15]

The economic decline on Native American reserves in the first half of the 19th century in southern New England was felt in churches and schools. In their efforts to stem this tide, indigenous religious and political leaders reached out to white New Englanders who described themselves as reformers. In southern New England states, special legislative commissions took an increasing interest in the conditions on reserves, supported programs to study social challenges, and financially backed reform programs. In earlier times, such agendas had been largely financed by religiously affiliated groups and churches. In the first decades of the 19th century, state authorities began to provide supplementary monetary sources to communities but also aided Native Americans to some degree in their effort to protect their land. In the later decades of the 19th century, however, New England states would work to undermine the presence and sovereignty of indigenous communities by not only going after the communal land base, which they had done to several native groups before, but also passing laws that terminated reserves. This shift had a devastating impact on indigenous communities in the region.

This dramatic transformation occurred in part because of changing attitudes about race. Throughout the 17th, 18th, and 19th centuries, Native Americans in New England had succeeded in integrating themselves at least partially into the regional culture and economy while also maintaining separate communities and lives as Native Americans. This strategy had enabled their survival, despite complex pressures and challenges. But changing attitudes about race and Native Americans eventually aided in the termination of many reserves in the region. White New Englanders had increasingly convinced themselves that real Native Americans had vanished from the region. In the minds of many whites, indigenous New Englanders had not changed and adapted their ways in order to survive but instead they had disappeared entirely. This imagined outcome found reflection in the writings of many 19th-century white New Englanders who wrote about Native Americans. These authors imagined the indigenous people of the region as noble or as evil savages, sometimes both. However, a unifying theme in many novels, poems, and history books was that Native Americans had disappeared. The historian Daniel Mandell puts it succinctly: By the 1850s, this "emphasis on a special past, celebrated or criticized, along with the new scientific notions of race and popular images of western Native Americans, made contemporary Indian descendants in the region seem part of the general population of color rather than the heirs of Massasoit, Uncas, or Metacomet."[16]

By official estimates, from 1780 to 1865 the Native American population in Massachusetts, Connecticut, and Rhode Island had declined from over 2,100 to about 1,800 people. Of course, many individuals who self-identified as Native American were not counted in these figures, because in the racial and cultural views that predominated at the time, these Native Americans had vanished. Mainstream New English society refused to see many people with indigenous ancestry and kinship ties as anything other than low-class whites or as persons of color. Another phenomenon of great gravity by the mid-19th century was the dissolution of many Native American communities. By the time of the American Civil War, at least half of the 1,800 persons lived on three reserves: Mashpee on Cape Cod, Gay Head on Martha's Vineyard, and Narragansett in Rhode Island. Many of the small enclaves and communities that could be found all over New England in the aftermath of the American Revolution had now been dissolved due to the many pressures faced by indigenous peoples. Yet, the challenges on the few remaining Native American communities in New England would certainly not cease. During and in the aftermath of the Civil War, the well-established reserves would face an onslaught of pressures that threatened their survival.[17]

Termination and Citizenship: An Assault on Indigenous Communities in Southern New England

Between the 1860s and the 1880s, the southern New England states targeted the sovereignty of Native American communities and continued to push for individual property ownership at the expense of communal landholding. The self-proclaimed white reformers and politicians who supported these transitions maintained that such policies would give Native Americans the right to vote and that individual landownership would help indigenous people become more productive, integrated, individualistic, and aspiring members of society. Moreover, this approach was also driven by and reflected mainstream New England's society's views of what it meant to be a pure Native American.

Like many other white New Englanders, the advocates of termination and citizenship believed that indigenous New Englanders, as a result of their racial mixing with other groups, had ceased to be Indian. This perception was influenced by 19th-century mainstream American beliefs that race was determined by blood quantum. This meant, for example, that if a person's father was African American and the mother was Native American, this individual had a blood quantum of 50 percent black and 50 percent indigenous blood. But prevailing racial thought, influenced by the complex history of slavery in the United States, also adhered to the concept of the one blood rule, which implied that a person with African ancestry was considered black. Hence, in mainstream American thought at the time, having African American blood was considered to be a more determining factor of race than having indigenous ancestry.

The debate over termination and citizenship reflects and provides a glimpse into the peculiar mix of racism and the desire for creating more egalitarian political structures and enfranchisement that shaped these policies. While some individuals and families welcomed these strategies because they advocated for this right to own their land as private property, the majority of Native Americans disliked the policies of termination and citizenship and resisted them. By the 1880s, the efforts at resistance among many indigenous communities had proved to be unsuccessful, as many lost their reserve or tribal status and were granted citizenship, a privilege that seemed hollow to many Native Americans who were devastated that they had lost their tribal status. As a result of the consorted efforts by the states of Massachusetts, Connecticut, and Rhode Island, it was only a few small Native American communities that did not lose their distinct protected legal status in southern New England.[18]

Between 1859 and 1870, the Commonwealth of Massachusetts terminated all the tribes in the state. During the first phase of termination, Massachusetts targeted the smaller enclaves in the state. By 1862 with the exception of larger communities such as Mashpee and Gay Head where the opposition to termination was strong, the state granted full citizenship to Native Americans. The larger reserves only got a short-term respite, as state leaders were set to terminate all tribes. By 1870, all remaining indigenous communities had been terminated. Mashpee and Gay Head, by far the two largest communities in the commonwealth, became separate towns, in part because the surrounding white communities rejected the incorporation of so many Native Americans. This development proved fortuitous to these communities in the long run.

The story of termination and citizenship was a complex and diverse process in the state of Connecticut. Like Native Americans all over New England, indigenous communities in the state had suffered the loss of territory and political and judicial encroachment before the era of termination and citizenship. Certainly these policies were driven by the same motivations as in other New England states, which we discussed above. But given Connecticut's unique local circumstances, the power that county courts had in managing Native American affairs (although state officials often superseded those courts if it was in their interests), and the fact that the state often used termination to enforce business interests locally (even more so than in other parts of New England), each Connecticut tribe had its diverse and complex history during this period.

The enforcement and responses to termination and citizenship were therefore especially diverse in Connecticut. For instance, the Niantics, who had a reserve in East Lyme, welcomed termination. They were, however, the only tribe to do so, and they did not endorse or desire the state's policy. Rather, most members of this shrinking community had found a home on the Mohegan reserve and saw this as an opportunity to sell their reserve lands, which only a few were still using. The State of Connecticut moved fast on this opportunity, taking over the land and terminating the Niantics, and granting the members of the newly dissolved tribe full citizenship. Other indigenous groups in Connecticut outwardly resisted termination and citizenship, most with little success. In 1860, for instance, Connecticut had already allotted the Mohegan reserve, meaning that individual members and families had been assigned small parcels of land, and officials put the reservation under state guardianship. In 1861, the state reclaimed its authority over the tribe from the local county court. By 1872, the state's legislature moved ahead and detribalized the Mohegan nation, granted its members full citizenship, and the reserve and tribal school were annexed by the Town of Montville. The Mohegan Indians who occupied an allotted parcel of land gained legal title to the property and had to pay taxes. In Connecticut, unlike in Massachusetts, not all native tribes faced termination. The Paugussetts, while losing much of their land, did not face termination during this period. Moreover, the Pequot and Schaghticoke nations survived termination into the 20th century not only as legally recognized tribes but also with intact reserves (though their landholdings were very small, given significant territorial losses earlier in the 19th century).

In Rhode Island, the Narragansett had also long fought the encroachment on and meddling with their land basis and resisted the political pressures to push for these policies, with some limited success. The Narragansetts opposed termination and citizenship by a wide margin. Still, in 1881 Rhode Island state officials moved ahead with terminating the tribe, paying $5,000—to be shared among the members of the nation—for the remaining reserve lands.

While the resistance against termination had not resulted in the outcome that many had hoped for, Native Americans continued their struggle to maintain their communities and cultures. Termination had a disruptive impact on the region's indigenous peoples who had lost their protected legal status. Many Native Americans continued to be part of the lower segments of society, a status shared with other minorities in New England, and the detribalization of their communities now posed an additional challenge to their survival. This policy hit smaller indigenous New England communities and groups the hardest. Indigenous communities such as those of the Mashpees and Gay Heads, who occupied their own towns, were able to preserve some political and cultural sovereignty into the 20th century, when new challenges emerged that we will explore later in the book. Other indigenous communities such as the Mohegans, Narragansetts, and Nipmucs maintained family, social, and cultural networks that aided in the survival of their peoples.[19]

Despite the dreaded developments and policies, Native Americans throughout New England aimed with some success to guard their tribal histories and presence by marking and protecting some of their cemeteries and sacred sites. For instance, Nipmuc descendants lobbied for an official marker to be put up in 1930 at the now three-acre Hassanamisco Reservation in Massachusetts. The sign reads "Indian Reservation: These four and one-half acres have never belonged to the white man. Having been set aside in 1728 as an Indian reservation by the forty proprietors who purchased the praying Indian town of Hassanamesit." Such markers of a continuing Native American presence can be found throughout New England.

Staying Visible, 1880s–1940s

Native Americans in New England continued to confront challenges and showed resilience in the late 19th century and the first half of the 20th century. Despite mainstream reformers' and politicians' naive beliefs that termination would integrate Native Americans into New England society, it is important to underscore that racist assumptions in mainstream society did not aid in their integration. Moreover, indigenous New Englanders did not want to cease to be Native Americans. In order to survive, they maintained their cultures, traditions, kinship networks, communities, tribes, intertribal connections, and their identities. Indigenous people from the Northeast continued to stay visible to mainstream New England and American society and sometimes even to audiences from around the world.

Economic survival continued to be a challenge for indigenous people in New England in the late 19th century and the 20th century. Surviving in one's home community and making a living was often difficult. Some Native Americans were able to get jobs in factories or other places of employment in surrounding towns or urban areas. Others worked in agriculture. Many Micmacs from communities in northern Maine and Canada worked as migratory farmworkers. The Penobscot, Passamaquoddy, and various other Wabanaki bands from northern New England worked in lumber and logging camps. They also worked as drivers and labored in the timber, lumber, paper, and textile industries. The Penobscot community of Old Town in Maine became a center for canoe construction, an industry that employed Penobscot and Passamaquoddy workers from surrounding communities. Catering to an expanding tourist economy, Native Americans in Maine would make crafts such as toy canoes, tomahawks, and baskets; stage Indian shows; and worked as guides for white hunters and fishermen. The disappearance of whaling jobs required new strategies of survival in several indigenous communities in southern New England as well. To support their families at home, some Native Americans spent long seasons away from their home communities working in construction and other jobs. Other families, as we will explore below, moved entirely to cities for jobs. Some Native Americans joined the armed forces.[20]

The Penobscots provide a nice case study on how Native Americans from New England tried to maintain a presence on a regional, national, and global stage. Members of the tribe exhibited their traditions and culture at the World's Columbian Exposition in Chicago in 1893, an event staged by its organizers to celebrate the 400th anniversary of Christopher Columbus's transatlantic voyage. This world fair lasted many months and attracted exhibitors from 46 countries and many diverse cultures. More than 27 million people from the United States and beyond came to see this spectacle.[21] Many Penobscot writers and artists also played an active role in the late 19th century and in the first half of the 20th century. In 1893, for example, the earlier-mentioned Joseph Nicolar published *The Life and Traditions of the Red Man,* a history of the persistent values and traditions of the Penobscot people. The book provided a refreshing new perspective at a time when academic writing focused on the disappearance of indigenous peoples and their cultures.[22] The Penobscot Nation also produced a number of artists such as the musician Lucy Nicolar and Molly Spotted Elk (Mary Alice Nelson). Molly

Spotted Elk was born on the Penobscot Indian Island Reservation in Maine. From an early age she performed as a dancer, but she also wrote stories, poetry, and fiction. During the 1930s her dancing career took her to Paris, where she married a Frenchmen with whom she had a daughter. She and her daughter fled France during the German invasion, which separated her from her husband. Molly Spotted Elk spent the rest of her life between her home reservation and New York City, and while her dance career often played to the prevalent racial stereotypes and sexual fantasies among Euro-Americans and Europeans about Native American women, her career as a performer introduced and raised an awareness among her audiences in the United States and Europe about Penobscot culture and traditions. Furthermore, Molly Spotted Elk also published a book of Penobscot stories and a dictionary.[23]

Penobscot Indians and other Native Americans from New England played an active role in the world of sports. Figures such as Louis Francis Sockalexis and Ellison Brown are just two such examples. Both athletes were known on the national as well as the international stage in the late 19th century and the first half of the 20th century and played a pathbreaking role in the history of sports.

Louis Francis Sockalexis, a Penobscot Indian from Maine, was a well-known baseball player. Unlike many of the famous Native American star athletes at the time, he had not attended Indian boarding school and instead had gone to a local Catholic high school. In high school and later at Holy Cross College in Worcester, Massachusetts, he excelled at various ball games and was also a fast runner. Sockalexis's greatest talent was baseball—especially pitching. From 1897 to 1899 after playing a few months of college ball at Notre Dame University in Indiana, he became a player with the major league baseball team in Cleveland. Then the team was called the Cleveland Spiders, but today it is known as the Cleveland Indians. This name change occurred in the first two decades of the 20th century in part as result of the nickname the team was given because Sockalexis caused such an excitement in the fan base.

But the story of Sockalexis is also emblematic and provides a window into the challenges that many Native Americans faced in the late 19th and early 20th centuries. For one, he struggled with alcoholism, which resulted in him needing to leave Notre Dame, and it was also the reason why his extremely promising career was cut short in Cleveland. Moreover, it is important to remember that Sockalexis played baseball as a person of color 50 years before Jackie Robinson became the first African American player in the major leagues. The late 19th century was a period in American history of open racism, discrimination, and racial violence. During games, Sockalexis faced many racist chants and slurs from opposing teams' supporters and players. His presence in Cleveland was also the object of many a racist cartoon.

Observers wrote that he seemed to not be phased by it when he played on the field, but one wonders if there was deeper nonvisible trauma and hurt that resulted from such abuse and if such cruelty also helped to spur his alcoholism. Based on the available evidence, we can merely speculate. Of course, sports commentators at the time and in later years, given the racist currents and stereotypical assumptions, blamed Sockalexis's alcoholism on the fact that he was Native American.

After leaving Cleveland, Sockalexis got his alcoholism under control and was able to eke out a career as a minor league player for a few more years in various New England cities such as Waterbury, Lowell, and Bangor. Later in his life he played on town teams close to his reservation, coached younger players, and worked on a riverboat on the Penobscot River and in the logging industry. He died in 1913, only in his early 40s, of a heart attack while working a logging job.

While Sockalexis's cousin Andrew was an accomplished marathon runner who placed second (1912) and fourth (1913) in the Boston Marathon, Ellison Brown, a Narraganset from Rhode Island, was the strongest New England Native American marathon runner of the 20th century. Given the nickname "Tarzan Brown," he was the only Native American to win the Boston Marathon twice. He won in 1936 and in 1939, a race during which he set a record. Brown also competed in the 1936 Olympics in Berlin, but after a promising beginning to the race he unfortunately was forced to drop out due to incapacitating cramps.[24]

The Abenaki communities in Vermont and New Hampshire in the late 19th century and the first half of the 20th century provide another case study of the indigenous struggle for survival. Some Abenaki families lived in communities on marginally desired lands such as forests and marshes. There they maintained as much of the traditional ways of subsistence as possible. Like other indigenous groups in northern New England, they farmed, hunted, fished, and gathered food. Other Abenakis sought exile in indigenous communities in Canada, especially in the former mission villages on the St. Lawrence River. Still others lived transnational lives, moving back and forth between their Canadian and northern New England home communities. New English observers described some Abenakis as "river rats" and "pirates." The term "river rats" described people of Abenaki descent who resided in small shantytown communities on riverbanks, while "pirates" lived on houseboats on the region's lakes. By staying outside of mainstream New English society, both groups attempted to maintain as much of their independence as possible. They subsisted by fishing, hunting, and working odd jobs especially on boats and in river log driving. Like Native Americans in other parts of New England, some Abenakis passed as white and blended into either the Anglo-American or French Canadian communities of northern New England. People of Abenaki descent also owned or worked on farms and in the timber, lumber, paper, and textile industries. Others made baskets and produced arts and crafts for tourists; manufactured snowshoes, moccasins, and canoes; or served as guides for hunters and fishers.

Like other indigenous communities in New England, the Abenaki communities in Vermont and New Hampshire had to confront the challenges of living in racially charged times. In the 1920s and 1930s, for instance, Ku Klux Klan rallies in cities such as Barre, Vermont, targeted Abenaki and French Canadians alike. These were also the heydays of eugenics and scientific racism, and such beliefs were used as a justification to take indigenous children from their families to give them to white New English families. As we explore in the next chapter, this was a horror faced not only by the Abenakis but also by other indigenous people in New England and all over the United States. In 1931, the eugenics movement in Vermont also helped to push for the passage of the Act for Human Betterment by Voluntary Sterilization. This policy, according to Abenaki historian Frederick Wiseman, led to the sterilization of over 200 people of Abenaki descent in Vermont who had been targeted and harassed to submit to this inhumane procedure.[25]

Southern New England tribes, despite the loss of their reservations during the termination period, continued to maintain their communities, traditions, and identities. Like earlier generations, many members from these communities had to engage with mainstream society's economy and educational system. As aforementioned, even though they no longer lived on a reserve, the Mashpees and Gay Heads of Massachusetts lived in a separate town where they were able, despite land losses, to maintain political control into the 20th century. Many Mohegans and Narragansetts also remained either on or in the vicinity of their old reserve lands. The Narragansetts kept their church, continued to have a council, and had unofficial chiefs, and members of the tribe continued to meet on a regular basis. For much of the late 19th century and the first half of the 20th century, the activism of the community focused on undoing termination and regaining recognition as a tribe on the state and federal levels. While these efforts remained unsuccessful at the time, they set the essential groundwork for the tribe's continued lobbying and activism, which helped the Narragansett Nation to gain federal recognition in the 1980s. The Mohegans also continued to exist as a distinct community in Montville. Mohegan life centered on a church (which was also open to whites). The Mohegans had their own cemetery, had chiefs, and continued to hold their Wigwam Festival in September. For the Mohegans these cultural elements all served as pillars of the community, which aided their survival into the 21st century. Smaller communities no longer were able to maintain separate enclaves and integrated into towns. But they still worked hard to maintain their kinship networks and their tribal identities. Moreover, in many places all over New England, Native Americans asserted their identity by wearing indigenous dress during public meetings and at events.

Elders played an important role in the survival of their peoples and cultures. Among the Mohegans, for instance, Fidelia Fielding (1827–1908) and Gladys Tantaquidgeon (1899–2005) helped to preserve their people's languages, cultures, and medicinal and other knowledges. Tantaquidgeon had been trained by her elders in Mohegan medicine and culture, but she also earned a degree in anthropology at the University of Pennsylvania. She studied traditional Native American medicine for her entire life and published several books on this subject. She was also active in cultural preservation among western tribes when she worked for the federal Indian Arts and Crafts Board during the Great Depression. Moreover, she preserved records, documents, and artifacts of relevance to Mohegan history and, with her father John and her brother Harold, helped to create the Tantaquidgeon Museum in the early 1930s, which is still run by the Mohegan Nation today. Eventually, Tantaquidgeon's efforts helped the Mohegan Nation gain federal recognition.[26]

Starting in the 20th century when Cape Cod became a growing vacation destination for Euro-Americans, the Mashpee Indians' relative isolation from mainstream New England society began to increasingly break down. For much of its history, the community had been in a place that was relatively undesirable to Euro-Americans. Thus, the Mashpees had remained in charge of their town, a reality that gradually unraveled in the 20th century. The growing influx of outsiders was, however, also accompanied by cultural and political revitalization. Reaching out to the indigenous groups at Gay Head and at Herring Pond in Plymouth, these three communities formed the modern Wampanoag Nation in 1928. The Wampanoags held their first powwow shortly thereafter in Mashpee, which coincided with the yearly summer homecoming, an event that the Mashpees had held for over 200 years. The powwow took place for two days and included a pipe ceremony, political speeches emphasizing Wampanoag culture and identity, a memorial to the 17th-century leader Metacomet, races, baseball games, songs, dances, games, and a beauty pageant. In the first half of the 20th century, such powwows and cultural events gained increasing popularity across New England and were a visible sign that Native Americans would not disappear in the region.[27]

In the early 20th century, Native Americans in New England also attempted to strengthen their position by pursuing intertribal political strategies. Indigenous peoples in the region not only revitalized their own tribal identities, as we saw above, but also in 1923 founded a short-lived organization called the Indian Council of New England. This group was supported by the anthropologist Frank Speck and several other Euro-Americans and brought together Native Americans from various tribal backgrounds all over New England. The council celebrated intertribal ideals and advocated that New England's indigenous communities and tribes work together to maintain their cultures, traditions, and languages. The Indian Council of New

England aimed to create a more united political front. At public functions members of the council also dressed like Great Plains Indians, a clothing style often worn by Native Americans in the eastern United States from the 1880s to the 1960s. Native Americans in New England likely adapted this style of dress because it made them more easily recognizable as real Indians in the distorted and stereotypical perceptions of mainstream Americans. Thus, by using this kind of attire, indigenous New Englanders made their presence known to the outside world in the only fashion in which mainstream New English and American society would see them as Native Americans. While the Indian Council of New England only survived for a short period of time, the organization reinforced certain legacies in the region's Native American history of the 20th century. The council helped intertribal collaboration, strengthened government, and reinforced the indigenous presence, identities, and awareness.[28]

As in earlier times when New England's Native Americans significantly contributed to the militias and various war efforts, indigenous New Englanders continued to serve in the armed forces in the second half of the 19th century and throughout the 20th century. Native Americans from New England participated in the American Civil War and both world wars. This participation was reflective of the generally high participation rate and the contributions of Native Americans to U.S. war efforts. During World War I, about 16,000 Native Americans joined the armed forces, serving at about double the rate of other ethnic American groups. During World War II, about 25,000 Native Americans would serve on active military duty. Alongside other Americans, whether white, Latino, Asian American, African American, or Native American, indigenous New Englanders who identified as Penobscot, Narragansett, or Mashpee as well as with other indigenous communities from all over the region served in this conflict, fighting either abroad or serving on the home front. Military service provided indigenous people from New England the opportunity to meet Native Americans and other minorities from all over the United States and created greater intertribal awareness but also fostered the realization that indigenous Americans had the status of a minority in the United States. While U.S. propaganda told Americans that they were fighting racism and imperialism abroad, indigenous soldiers knew that they were also experiencing discrimination at home.[29]

Just as in the 19th century when economic transformation and industrialization in New England aided in urbanization, cities attracted Native Americans in search of employment. The phenomenon of urban indigenous communities would continue into the 20th century. As we will explore in more detail in the next chapter, the presence of indigenous New Englanders in cities would therefore increase again during the economic boom that began and continued after World War II. In search of better economic opportunities, indigenous peoples from New England and beyond were drawn to northeastern metropolitan areas such as Boston and New York City. While most ended up staying permanently in their newly adopted cities, many maintained close and regular contacts and ties with their indigenous relatives and sending communities and visited their families and homelands as often as they could. However, life in the city had its unique challenges. Native American urban migrants had to find and build community. In an intertribal effort that united Native Americans from a variety of tribal and community backgrounds, they created meeting places to socialize, find assistance, and create organizations to lobby on their behalf. Two organizations founded in 1969, the Boston Indian Council and New York's American Indian Community House, are just two examples of this development. Such organizations exemplified the need that Native Americans had for community but also show how such institutions were built by pursuing intertribal strategies.[30]

Conclusion

Still, to many in mainstream society, Native American communities in New England remained hidden in plain sight. While signs of a continued Native American presence could be found all over the region, many white New Englanders believed that indigenous peoples had long disappeared.

Despite the political, economic, and cultural challenges that shaped Native American lives from after the American Revolution into the 20th century, indigenous people continued to maintain a presence in the region. As during the colonial period, indigenous New Englanders continued to demonstrate a keen skill at surviving in a complex and often hostile multiethnic world. Native Americans in New England survived and existed often on the margins of society. Some did so in their families and extended kinship groups. Others survived in indigenous communities. While the officials of several New England states had argued that the termination of reserves would assimilate Native Americans and lead them to join mainstream society, this reality never materialized. Native Americans continued to face racism and nonacceptance in New English society, further enticing them to retain their old communities and kinship networks. Indigenous people continued to carve out an existence on their old homelands, now, however, without the official recognition of local and state governments and the federal government. Even if the dominant society had convinced itself that Native Americans had disappeared, indigenous life continued in the region. Places such as Mashpee in Massachusetts and the Native American communities in places such as the Penobscot River Valley in Maine were just a few among the various places and communities where indigenous people lived.

Native American networks—the connection and bonds among and between different groups—in New England also helped in the survival of indigenous peoples. Such connections became a source of strength but also brought about a continued awareness that was built on long-existing family, tribal, and intergroup networks. These networks created an awareness that there existed other indigenous groups and individuals who shared experiences and had lived through similar challenges. This awareness helped the survival of Native Americans in New England.

Therefore, family, community, and regional indigenous networks played an essential role in the Native American history of New England from the end of the American Revolution far into the 20th century. They became pillars on which indigenous peoples built a continued Native American presence in the region. These institutions helped indigenous New Englanders and their communities to survive and thrive into the 21st century.

Notes

1. This chapter's title and conceptualization draw from part of a chapter by Neal Salisbury on Native Americans in the Atlantic Northeast and is meant as a compliment to my former teacher and mentor. Neal Salisbury, "The Atlantic Northeast," in *The Oxford Handbook of American Indian History*, ed. Frederick E. Hoxie, 352–355 (New York: Oxford University Press, 2016). This chapter also draws from the study by Daniel R. Mandell, *Tribe, Race, History: Native Americans in Southern New England, 1780–1880* (Baltimore: Johns Hopkins University Press, 2008).

2. For a useful overview of the history of the New England economy, see Peter Temin, ed., *Engines of Enterprise: An Economic History of New England* (Cambridge, MA: Harvard University Press, 2000).

3. This section on agriculture draws from Mandell, *Tribe, Race, History*, chap. 1, which provides a general overview on the economic participation and involvement of Native Americans in southern New England.

4. For a more detailed discussion, see Pauleena MacDougall, *The Penobscot Dance of Resistance: Tradition in the History of a People* (Hanover, NH: University of New Hampshire Press, 2004), chap. 6 and 140–149.

5. This section draws from Mandell, *Tribe, Race, History*, chap. 1.

6. See William Apess, *A Son of the Forest and Other Writings*, ed. Barry O'Connell (Amherst: University of Massachusetts Press, 1997); Philip Gura, *The Life of William Apess, Pequot* (Chapel Hill: University of North Carolina Press, 2015); Drew Lopenzina, *Through an Indian's Looking Glass: A Cultural Biography of William Apess, Pequot* (Amherst: University of Massachusetts Press, 2017).

7. On New England Native Americans and the global whale hunting economy, see Nancy Shoemaker, *Native American Whalemen and the World: Indigenous Encounters and the Contingency of Race* (Chapel Hill: University of North Carolina Press, 2015); Nancy Shoemaker, ed., *Living with Whales: Documents and Oral Histories of Native New England Whaling History* (Amherst: University of Massachusetts Press, 2014).

8. Mandell, *Tribe, Race, History,* chap. 1; MacDougall, *The Penobscot Dance of Resistance,* chaps. 9 and 10.

9. Bunny McBride, *Women of the Dawn* (Lincoln: University of Nebraska Press, 1999), chap. 3.

10. On Native Americans and factory labor and for an insightful discussion of Chamberlain's biography and writing as well as a collection of her published work, see Judith Ranta, *The Life and Times of Betsey Chamberlain: Native American Mill Worker* (Boston: Northeastern University Press, 2003).

11. This section draws from Mandell, *Tribe, Race, History,* chap. 3; William Apess, *Indian Nullification of the Unconstitutional Laws of Massachusetts: Relative to the Mashpee Tribe; Or, the Pretended Riot Explained* (Boston: Press of J. Howe, 1835); MacDougall, *The Penobscot Dance of Resistance,* chap. 8.

12. This discussion draws from Mandell, *Tribe, Race, History,* chap. 1. On the Brothertown and Strockbridge Indian communities, see David J. Silverman, *Red Brethren: The Brothertown and Stockbridge Indians and the Problem of Race in Early America* (Ithaca, NY: Cornell University Press, 2010).

13. My section on interracial relations draws from Mandell, *Tribe, Race, History,* chap. 2.

14. Ibid., chap. 4.

15. My discussion in this section draws from Salisbury, "The Atlantic Northeast," 353; MacDougall, *The Penobscot Dance of Resistance,* chaps. 6–7.

16. Mandell, *Tribe, Race, History,* 173. For a general discussion, see 172–184.

17. Salisbury, "The Atlantic Northeast," 353; Mandell, *Tribe, Race, History,* chap. 5.

18. Salisbury, "The Atlantic Northeast," 353.

19. For a more detailed discussion on termination and citizenship in southern New England, see Mandell, *Tribe, Race, History,* chap. 6.

20. Salisbury, "The Atlantic Northeast," 354; MacDougall, *The Penobscot Dance of Resistance,* chaps. 9–10. See also Bunny McBride and Harald Prins, *Indians in Eden: Wabanakis and Rusticators on Mount Desert Island, 1840–1920* (Camden, ME: Down East Books, 2010).

21. Norman Bolotin and Christine Laing, *The World's Columbian Exposition: The Chicago's World Fair of 1893* (Champagne: University of Illinois Press, 2002).

22. Jospeh Nicolar, *The Life and Traditions of the Red Man,* edited by Annette Kolodny (Durham, NC: Duke University Press, 2007).

23. McBride, *Women of the Dawn,* chap. 4.

24. On Sockalexis and Brown see, e.g., Donald Fixico, *Daily Life of Native Americans in the Twentieth Century* (Westport, CT: Greenwood, 2006), 97–98, 100.

25. Frederick Matthew Wiseman, *The Voice of the Dawn: An Authohistory of the Abenaki Nation* (Hanover, NH: University Press of New England, 2001), chap. 7.

26. For southern New England after termination, see Mandell, *Tribe, Race, History,* epilogue.

27. Peter Iverson, *"We Are Still Here": American Indians in the Twentieth Century* (Wheeling, IL: Harlan Davidson, 1998), 63.

28. Salisbury, "The Atlantic Northeast," 354–355.

29. Iverson, *"We Are Still Here,"* 50, 107; Salisbury, "The Atlantic Northeast," 355.

30. Salisbury, "The Atlantic Northeast," 355.

CHAPTER SIX

Native Americans in Modern New England

This final chapter provides a brief glimpse into the history of Native Americans of New England from World War II to the present. The text explores the survival of groups such as the Maliseet, Mohegan, Narragansett, Niantic, Nipmuc, Passamaquoddy, Penacook, Penobscot, Pequot, Schaghticoke, and Wampanoag tribes in modern New England. While tribal communities played an important part in the life of Native Americans, many individuals of indigenous descent, as this chapter explores, also lived in urban areas. This chapter continues by examining the impact that residential schools and family separation had on Native American children, families, and communities. The chapter also surveys the impact of indigenous nationalism and the efforts of Native American communities to gain federal and state recognition. Moreover, the text examines indigenous pursuits of economic and cultural revitalization. This chapter concludes by briefly examining some of the continuous challenges that Native Americans in New England face today.

Native Americans and New England Cities

While there is still too often a common misperception in much of mainstream American society that Native Americans live predominately on reservations, throughout the United States many individuals of indigenous descent reside in rural, suburban, and urban communities. This fact can also be observed in the Northeast. Thus, as in the 18th and 19th centuries, cities have continued to play a central role in contemporary indigenous life in New England.

The Native American community of Boston, especially compared to such communities in New York City, San Francisco, and Seattle, is widely understudied. There is still much we can and need to learn. During her fieldwork in the 1960s and early 1970s, still among only a few studies on this subject, the anthropologist Jeanne Guillemin estimated that about 2,500 to 3,500 Native Americans were residing in the greater Boston area at that time. Guillemin's research focused on the Micmacs from the Canadian Maritimes who had a noticeable presence in the Hub, as Boston is sometimes called, and frequently circulated between the city, their Canadian reserves, and other urban areas in Canada and the northeastern United States. Many of the Micmacs lived in the diverse low-income areas of the greater Boston area. They worked in low-skill jobs, in construction, or in factories. Often they lived with members of their extended family or members of their tribe. Tribal and intertribal networks were also used for such things as ride sharing to commute to work, traveling back and forth between one's urban residence and home community, and childcare. In addition, some native parents who worked in urban areas sent their children back to their sending communities to have them raised by family members there. Thus, in urban areas, just as on reservations, the peer network played an important role in the community's survival. As in other urban indigenous communities such as those in New York City and San Francisco, bars played a special role as meeting places for natives in the greater Boston area. Since the early 1970s the Native American population in Boston has only increased and become more diverse.[1]

Various centers and associations seek to serve the interests of indigenous peoples who live in urban communities. Some Native Americans in the greater Boston area created the North American Indian Center of Boston over four decades ago to support the urban indigenous community. Other urban communities in New England also have indigenous organizations. The Greater Lowell Indian Cultural Association, for instance, is another group active in the region.

Targeting Indigenous Children: Boarding Schools and Family Separation

New England, just as the rest of the United States, has a complicated history of neglect and abuse of indigenous children. Many Native American children were forced to attend boarding schools (sometimes referred to as residential schools) away from their home communities and families. Many of New England's indigenous children, like native kids throughout the United States, also were pulled away from their families to a disproportionate degree, especially when compared with kids in white society. Boarding schools and the family separation system destroyed many lives and caused intergenerational trauma among many Native American families and communities.

Native American boarding and residential schools, created by the federal government and various Christian churches in the late 19th century, have a complicated and often disturbing history. Native American children from New England ended up in boarding and residential schools. There, they were forced to give up their traditional dress and put on uniforms. School authorities and disciplinarians also forbade indigenous children to speak their languages, and if they did they often faced harsh physical punishment and solitary confinement. Boys were forced to cut their hair, which was a sign of mourning in several Native American cultures. Moreover, boarding schools were often rampant with physical, sexual, and emotional abuse. The goal of the boarding school was to separate Native American children from their cultures of origin. Their goal was to "kill the Indian and save the man."[2]

The mind-set that enabled the cruelty of the boarding schools also pushed for a policy of family separation across the United States throughout the 20th century. Advocates of family separation aimed to pull indigenous children out of their families and place them within white society. This was a policy implemented in the name of the "welfare of Indian children." Its advocates believed that it would be beneficial to native children if they were brought up away from indigenous society and cultural influences. Thus, often without much cause thousands of Native American children were ripped from their families throughout the United States. Horrible abuse happened as a result of the policy of family separation. For much of the 20th century, social services and police officers pulled native kids out of their families and placed them in the "child welfare system." The policy of family separation meant that Native American children were placed in group homes, with foster parents, and often back and forth, with stints in hospitals and crisis intervention centers. Reports of painful and atrocious sexual and physical abuse are rampant in depositions in front of Congress in the 1970s as well as in testimonies collected in later years. While the advocates of this system maintained a belief that indigenous children would be better off not growing up Native American and thus advocated to have them taken away from their families, the realities of these policies provide a glimpse into a world of neglect, abuse, and trauma. Congressional hearings in the 1970s on the abuses of the family separation system eventually aided in the passage of the Indian Child Welfare Act (ICWA) in 1978, a law that tried to tackle systemic mistreatment and pushed for native children to be placed with indigenous families.[3]

In Maine, a truth and reconciliation commission has examined the treatment of Wabanaki children within the state's welfare system post-ICWA. This commission had the mandate of Maine's governor and the leaders of the state's Wabanaki communities. It was the first effort of this kind in the United States. Testimonies collected by the commission found that Maine's child welfare system had a horrible history of family separation before 1978 and that the state violated ICWA and continued to fail Native American children into the 21st century. Truth and reconciliation is a fraught process. Dealing with survivors' trauma and abuse as well as uncovering generational trauma, depression, and severe mental health issues as communities are undergoing the process of discussing this horrific past is a challenging and gut-wrenching experience. The legacies of trauma and abuse of the cultural genocide of residential schools and family separation will be hard to overcome.[4]

Native Nationalism and Sovereignty

Native nationalism, a force that in the words of historian Kent Blansett serves "to protect and uphold the rights of Native peoples and indigenous sovereignty," was a phenomenon that underwent a resurgence in New England in the second half of the 20th century.[5] This nationalism has been a defining feature in native communities' struggles for federal and state recognition, played an essential role in indigenous economic and cultural revitalization, and shapes Native American activism in the region. Thus, native nationalism became a defining feature in the recent history of indigenous New Englanders's pursuit of sovereignty and self-government.

Blansett identifies native nationalism as a phenomenon "that covers a long history of efforts to promote and protect the explicit rights of an Indigenous nation's governance, lifeway, language, community, land, law, and peoples." It is a force "that has always inherently existed" in the Native North American communities, and, which has the maintenance of indigenous sovereignty as a central pursuit. To Native Americans, indigenous sovereignty is not something that is given by the powers or mercy of the colonizing or mainstream society. It is instead transcendent. It acknowledges "individuals, families, clans, bands, genders, sacred spaces, societies, communities, marine spaces, and lands." A dominant feature of native nationalism is to protect indigenous rights and independence, but it is not to seek integration into mainstream American society. These desires can astonish members of mainstream American society. But given that native people have and still experience the United States as a colonial state and also given the history of conquest, colonization, violence, dispossession, racism, termination, and assault on sovereignty, this desire should not come as a surprise. Moreover, intertribalism—connections, exchanges, interactions, and cooperation between different indigenous communities—is also an important part of native nationalism. In their pursuit to preserve and regain sovereignty, many Native Americans realize that alliances beyond one's own tribal community can improve their odds and position.[6]

Federal Recognition and Land Claims

At the center of indigenous nationalism and the struggle for Native American sovereignty in New England in the post–World War II period was the fight for nation and land. These efforts played themselves out in the areas of federal recognition as well as in land claims. Much of this political and legal action came as a result of the unique history of the region. At the center of indigenous legal and political activism was the 1790 Trade and Intercourse Act. A rather boring document that discusses issues of the operation of trading forts as well as how to conduct and finance trade with Native Americans, the act also established that there existed a federal prerogative when dealing with Native Americans. In other words, the document established the legal precedent that only the federal government of the United States was allowed to negotiate for the sale or cession of Native American lands. As we discussed in the previous chapter, it was, however, the state governments in New England that not only terminated the standing of several of the tribes in the region but also sold indigenous land. Many of the Native American communities in New England argued that this was a violation of law. In the late 19th century and through much of the 20th century, many native peoples in the region saw the termination of their tribal status as well as the dispossession of their lands by state governments as an injustice and as a violation of federal law. As a result, community leaders, activists, and the rank and file in indigenous communities argued for the rerecognition of their tribal status and a reinstatement of some of their lands. They filed several lawsuits and held protests, but it was into the 1960s and 1970s that their political activism was widely ignored and legal measures were struck down. Up to this point, courts maintained that due to a long colonial history, the original 13 states that had founded the United States had maintained a special legal position that excluded these former British colonies from the federal prerogative. However, a U.S. Supreme Court case between the Oneida Indians and the State of New York overturned these prior decisions and maintained that the Trade and Intercourse Act and the federal prerogative it established also applied to the original 13 states.[7]

Many indigenous communities in the Northeast also saw their struggle for land and nation in global terms. In many native communities, veterans who returned from wars abroad played a leading role in the reassertion of indigenous sovereignty. During their tours of duty they had been exposed to rhetoric that they were fighting for the "rights of nations to self-determine" or that they fought to "make the world safe for democracy." Moreover, Native Americans in New England were aware that in Africa and Asia many former colonies gained their independence in a successful struggle for national liberation. Some wanted to emulate these efforts, at least in part, and were inspired by these struggles for national liberation.[8]

In the 1970s, tribal and intertribal political activism showed some promising results for native peoples. In 1976, for instance, several Native American groups requested state recognition by Massachusetts and Maine. This request was based on a 1776 treaty with Massachusetts, which at that time was in control of both states. Moreover, in 1978 the Wabanaki Confederacy reconstituted and became active again, an especially dramatic occurrence since this indigenous alliance system had not met for over 100 years.[9]

Starting in the mid-1970s, several tribes in New England began their struggle for federal recognition and to seek compensation for the land losses they had incurred as a result of New English appropriation of their lands. In the 1970s, the Passamaquoddy and Penobscot tribes had won in federal court against the State of Maine, arguing that they had lost lands to Maine in violation of the Trade and Intercourse Act.[10] President Jimmy Carter's administration took a proactive position and restored some of the lands of the two tribes and provided a monetary compensation package to the groups for the dramatic land losses they had incurred, and both nations were granted federal recognition. But this was only the first of several cases in New England where the federal government recognized a Native American tribe. In 1980, the Houlton Band of Maliseet Indians gained federal recognition. In 1981, the Gay Head Indians (Aquinnahs) on Martha's Vineyard were federally recognized. The year 1983 saw the federal recognition of the Narragansetts, and that of the Mashantucket Pequot followed in 1984. Moreover, in 1991 the Aroostook Band of Micmac in Maine and in 1994 the Mohegan Nation gained federal recognition.

More recently there have been other groups that have gained federal recognition, but these recent cases have been more complex and tense. In 2002 in Connecticut, for instance, the secretary of the interior recognized the Eastern Pequot Nation and then in 2004 the Schaghticoke Tribal Nation. In an unprecedented decision in 2005, the Bureau of Indian Affairs revoked the federal recognition of the Eastern Pequot and Schaghticoke tribes after lobbying by Connecticut officials, the state's members of Congress, and private landowners. The issue of gaming, which we will discuss below, had been a factor in leading to this negative outcome. Roughly at the same time and also in Connecticut, the efforts to obtain federal recognition by the Golden Hill Paugussett Indian Nation were denied by the government. To the north of Connecticut, while the Commonwealth of Massachusetts had recognized the Nipmucs in 1976, the tribe was denied federal recognition in 2004 and again in 2018.

Also in Massachusetts on Cape Cope, the Mashpee Wampanoags, after a struggle that began in the mid-1970s, finally gained federal recognition in 2007. For the last decade, the Mashpees have been in discussions with the Commonwealth of Massachusetts about the creation of a gaming complex, since the state has been pursuing the creation of several such facilities as a source of additional revenue. The Mashpees have also sought to secure land. However, President Donald Trump's administration has actively sought to undermine the Mashpee Wampanoags' efforts to secure land and to open a casino, even questioning the legitimacy of the tribe. This has happened despite the support of the tribe by several Massachusetts members of Congress and several of the politicians from the town of Mashpee. In 2019, Congress voted to support the Mashpee Wampanoags. These recent developments suggest that the position of Native Americans in New England, even after federal recognition, remains politically fraught, a concern shared by indigenous communities throughout the United States.

There are several other smaller indigenous groups, such as the Chappaquiddick Wampanoag, the Abenaki Nation of Missisquoi, and the Cowasuck Band of the Pennacook, just to mention a few here, that have not obtained or have not pursued federal recognition. These communities have been halted by mainstream society's stereotypical perceptions and racism toward Native Americans, the expense of the endeavor, the lack of resources, or the fact that they have hit other roadblocks on the way to federal recognition. While some of these groups are recognized by the state in which they reside, such as the Nipmucs in Massachusetts and some of the smaller communities in Connecticut, others are not recognized by the states in which they live.

There are high stakes—political, economic, and cultural—for indigenous communities that undergo the process of federal recognition. The Branch of Recognition and Acknowledgement of the Bureau of Indian Affairs and recognition by an act of Congress requires an arduous and time-consuming process in which communities have to provide substantial evidence in order to be federally recognized. This process requires much time and financial resources, luxuries that many indigenous groups do not have. The process of who fits the rigid criteria of federal recognition is also a political one, and often a current presidential administration's perspective on Native American rights has an impact on how a decision on an issue will turn out.[11]

It is important to underscore that the issue of recognition is an inherently political process that at times can create distrust and frustration among indigenous peoples. Recognition gives federal or state bureaucracies the power to decide which indigenous groups qualify as tribes. Many feel that federal and state officials should not have such a right or that they do not have adequate knowledge to judge who qualifies as Native American and who does not. Given the prior termination of tribal status and the long history of racism, they also fear that 19th-century understandings of racial purity still shape modern perceptions. Native peoples in New England have previously had substantial negative experiences with such policy decisions. Furthermore, recall that to many Native Americans, indigenous sovereignty is not something that has to be obtained through federal or state recognition by a colonizing power; it is something that is inherent to their nations.

Economic and Cultural Revitalization

Economic and cultural issues play an important role in many indigenous communities in New England. Building and maintaining a strong economic infrastructure on reservations is a key challenge. Having tribally owned businesses provides jobs and also helps to raise revenue for communities. Cultural revitalization, such as language retention as well as continuing many of the cultural traditions, is seen as equally important. Native peoples see both forms of revitalization as critical strategies for maintaining their sovereignty and guaranteeing the cultural survival of their peoples into the future.

Economic development is a key issue in many indigenous communities. How can tribes provide an adequate standard of living to their members without being economically dependent on the federal government? How can communities establish viable entrepreneurship and businesses? How can these developments reflect tribal resources, customs, and traditions? What strategies can indigenous peoples pursue to emerge out of their long histories of dispossession, oppression, and marginalization? And finally, what are the costs affiliated with economic development, and how can these harm indigenous peoples and their environments? All these questions are being asked in indigenous communities across North America and beyond. Many indigenous activists and community leaders maintain that without economic strength, sustainability, and autonomy, indigenous communities will not have political sovereignty, as the two, they believe, go hand in hand.[12]

There are a wide variety of indigenous businesses all over New England. Emerging out of their long history with the tourist trade, Native Americans in northern New England still cater to this sector. The Aroostook Band of Micmac Indians, for instance, runs a gift shop that sells Native American crafts. The Passamaquoddy and the Penobscot tribes used a portion of the money they gained in their land claims to invest in the economic future of their peoples. The Passamaquoddy tribe, for instance, invested in securities and land. Moreover, the tribe bought a large blueberry farm and other businesses and invested into a large cement factory through a leveraged buyout. The Penobscot Nation also runs various businesses and ran a tribally owned company called Olamon Industries. This company produced cassette tapes in a plant, but as tapes fell out of use, the company fell on hard times throughout the 1990s. The plant reinvented itself as a custom molding and contract manufacturing company but eventually faced closure again. In 2010, the Penobscot Nation tried to relaunch the abandoned factory as a defense contractor. For the Penobscots, as for many other Native American tribes in the United States, to maintain, rebuild, and sustain their economic base is a continuous struggle.[13]

Gaming also has an economic impact on some native communities in the Northeast, a historic development that was enabled by the Indian Gaming

Regulatory Act, which was passed by the U.S. Congress in 1988. Since its enactment, some tribal communities pursue gaming in their search for economic sovereignty. The act compels tribes to seek compacts with state governments, a fact that is often ignored by nonnatives who are critical of indigenous gaming. Thus, Native American gaming benefits the state coffers, and governments often seek out such arrangements with tribes.[14]

Native American gaming is especially established in Connecticut. The Mashantucket Pequot tribe opened Foxwoods Resort Casino there in 1992. The Mohegan Nation followed suit with the opening of the Mohegan Sun Gaming Resort in 1996, just 10 miles from Foxwoods. Both casino operations have been highly profitable and have become popular destinations in the Northeast. The State of Connecticut has also financially benefited from the two casino resorts. The profits made from gaming have also allowed the Mashantucket Pequot tribe to open a museum and a library—great cultural resources that present Pequot history to a broad audience.

Native American gaming has also revitalized long-established resentments against Native Americans in New England, just as across the United States. Native Americans are often decried for having "unfair" access, as often epitomized in claims of an "Indian takeover" of the gaming industry. Of course, these arguments ignore the revenues and benefits gained by state governments. The financial success of Foxwoods and Mohegan Sun in Connecticut had an especially noticeable impact, as historian Neal Salisbury writes, as it has spurred "tropes of racial purity, authenticity, and [white] American innocence." Such narratives often depict indigenous communities "as 'special interests' rather than [as] sovereign nations." Moreover, as we discussed above, such resentments have "stymied the acknowledgements efforts of other tribes in the Atlantic Northeast."[15]

Just as many Native Americans see economic and political sovereignty as an essential part of their community's future viability, the cultural revitalization of their tribes is also considered a key component in creating sustainable societies. Some indigenous communities, such as the Mashpee Wampanoag tribe, are attempting to expand, revive, and revitalize their language. Native American musical groups, such as the Penobscot Burnurwurbskek Singers, try to maintain and strengthen their heritage, while at the same time they are influenced and enriched by intertribal musical influences. Many Native American tribes also have vibrant art and artisan communities, which are busy revitalizing, preserving, and reinventing indigenous New England forms of cultural expression. The Native Americans of New England have also come to play an active role in the preservation and representation of their past for many decades. Many tribes have museums, such as the one mentioned earlier of the Mashantucket Pequot tribe, through which they preserve their people's past. The Passamaquoddy tribe is also reclaiming its culture through a digital repatriation project. The tribe is seeking to repatriate cultural artifacts and is attempting to preserve its heritage through digital means. Thus, the Passamaquoddy tribe, just like other Native Americans of New England, tries to recover from a long past of having its culture and artifacts appropriated by museums, other institutions, and nonnative writers. Thereby, the tribe is able to represent and tell its history on its own terms.[16]

Native American Activism in New England

Since World War II, Native Americans in New England have continued to participate in many forms of activism. These forms of political expression serve as reminders to mainstream society that indigenous peoples are still very much present in the region. They are part of the long and proud struggle of Native Americans to adhere to as much of their ways of life and sovereignty as possible, but they also remind white Americans of the destructive impact that the history of colonization had on the indigenous peoples of the United States.

Since 1970, the 350th anniversary of the arrival of the *Mayflower,* Native Americans from New England and beyond gather annually for a national day of mourning on Thanksgiving day in Plymouth, Massachusetts. The site of the first permanent New English colonial beachhead is now a seaside town and a historical tourism attraction due to popular historic sites in the community such as the Mayflower, Plymouth Rock, and Plimouth Plantation, a living history museum. These sites attract visitors from all over the United States who may not realize that the town was built right on the former Native American settlement of Patuxet. Every year on the fourth Thursday in November, Native Americans march in town and gather on the hill next to Plymouth Rock, a memorial built over a specimen of a rock on which, so goes the story, the Puritan colonists once landed. The place where the main gathering occurs is called Cole's Hill. It is the location of a statue that claims to depict Ousamequin (Massasoit), the 17th-century sachem who, as we learned earlier, led an alliance of indigenous peoples in the region. Here speeches and musical performances are given to commemorate and protest the Native American loss of life and land as a result of the long, destructive, and painful history of colonization as well as the continuous oppression of Native Americans. Indigenous activists have also installed a plaque on a boulder on the hilltop that reminds the public of "the genocide of millions of their people, the theft of their lands, and the relentless assault on their culture." Yet the speeches, organized by groups such as the United American Indians of New England, also emphasize indigenous survival in New England and beyond. Speakers address the challenges faced by modern Native American societies such as alcoholism, suicide, poverty, drug addiction, crime, sexual violence, language retention, and other issues. To Native American activists the ceremony serves as a reminder that indigenous people in New England have not disappeared, have not been conquered, have not vanished, and are still here.

In 2005, activism also finally led the Massachusetts Legislature to repeal a law from the King Philip's War era in 1675 that banned Native Americans from entering Boston—330 years after its initial passage. Native American activists were helped in their mission by an organization of minority journalists who threatened to hold their conference in another city if the law was not changed. Beyond the negative publicity that this story generated, Boston city leaders were also afraid to lose an estimated $4.5 million of revenue if the conference was canceled.[17]

21st-Century Challenges

The diverse challenges for Native Americans in New England continue into the 21st century. Each community faces its unique challenges emerging out of complex histories of colonization and indigenous-white relations. This chapter merely scratches the surface of these trials. Issues of tribal recognition, economic sustainability, and cultural retention, which we have discussed above, will continue to challenge New England's indigenous communities into the future. Moreover, the protection of water rights and fishing rights and the fight to end addiction, which we will discuss below, are only some of the additional issues that contemporary indigenous New Englanders face.

The Penobscots in Maine are involved in a struggle over water-quality standards and river rights, a confrontation that is symptomatic of the kind of challenges that indigenous peoples across North America face today. The roots of this dispute stem from competing interpretations of Maine's 1980 Indian Claims Settlement Act. The tensions between the Penobscots and the State of Maine are based on two varying understandings of the legal meanings of islands. The act states that the Penobscot reservation consists "solely of Indian Island, also known as Old Town Island, and all the islands in that river northward." On the one hand, since the 1980s the Penobscots have argued that this settlement included the portions of the river adjacent to their islands, since the river has always played an important role in their daily life, subsistence, and survival. On the other hand, Maine maintains that the reservation ends at the islands' riverbank. The state government claims that the Penobscots have no legal and historical rights to the river drainage system that bears the name of their people. These issues are contentious in Maine, and the Penobscots' position is often vilified and oversimplified in media coverage and misunderstood in much of mainstream society. But the legal dispute has played itself out in various instances in the U.S. court system. In August 2017, however, the U.S. Supreme Court sided with the Penobscots' definition of "islands."[18]

The debate over who controls the river came again to the forefront in 2018 in a fight over Environmental Protection Agency (EPA) water safety standards. The Maine Department of Environmental Protection has sued the EPA over the standards. The Penobscot Nation has also become involved in this suit, as it is claiming sovereignty over the river as confirmed by the 2017 U.S. Supreme Court decision. The Penobscots have pointed out that their stewardship and protection of the river is essential if strict water-quality standards are to be maintained and that the upper river valley falls under the jurisdiction of their reservation. As many Penobscots still procure food from the river, they support the stricter EPA standards as being essential for the community's health. Meanwhile, many of the state's residents and the state government continue to maintain that the Penobscots are looking for conflict and are trying to claim the entire river without providing access to others, a position that the Penobscots and their allies condemn as divisive and far from the truth. The Penobscots, numerous state residents, and environmental advocates instead argue that they have a right to a sustainable and healthy life without being threatened by toxins. Instead, they argue, the state government is beholden to special business and energy interests at the expense of the environmental and health concerns of Maine's citizens. This debate and the resulting legal arguments and confrontations over the Penobscot River are likely going to continue into the foreseeable future.[19]

The fishing and hunting rights of indigenous peoples can also be contentious issues in New England, as they are across several communities in the United States where Native American–white relations can be tense. Some in mainstream society resent the fact that Native Americans have certain rights that result from treaties or other legally binding agreements. In early March 2018, for instance, the Mashpee Wampanoag Tribe and the Town of Mashpee held a joint meeting. The tribe's chairman, Cedric Cromwell, described this assembly as "historic." The meeting is an indicator that Mashpee is currently a place where there are relatively good relations between tribe and town, but fishing rights have still been a source of contention. During the meeting, tribal and town governments joined each other in their respective ritual, which included the Pledge of Allegiance and an opening prayer. The joint meeting had constructive discussions on issues such as wastewater management and the creation of affordable housing—areas in which tribe and town have been cooperating. The issue of tribal fishing practices, especially in relation to shellfishing, tends, however, to sour relations. Mashpee is trying to manage a problem of excess nitrogen in its water by announcing that it planned to seed about 20 million quahogs and oysters to clean the water. During the meeting, Mashpee selectman Andrew Gottlieb mentioned his "concern" that "if there is not an adherence by all fishermen to the regulations that we have in place to allow the shellfish to mature, there will be fewer animals in the water for the required time." This comment was directed straight at the Mashpee Wampanoags. Wampanoag Tribal Council vice chairwoman Jessie "Little Doe" Baird reminded Gottlieb of the tribe's "aboriginal rights to fishing, hunting, and gathering." Baird acknowledged that this was a complicated issue and expressed the Mashpee Wampanoags' willingness to investigate joint solutions, but she also emphasized that it was the tribe's "responsibility, while we are alive, to protect our rights for other tribal citizens."[20]

Addiction, which has a long and devastating history in the region, remains a challenge in contemporary Native American communities. Indigenous New England has been especially hard hit by the opioid crisis. While this epidemic is devastating communities throughout the United States, rural indigenous peoples are disproportionately impacted, with deaths from overdose rising by 519 percent from 1999 to 2015 alone. This increase is more than double the national upsurge.

The Penobscot Nation in Maine has developed an interesting strategy to deal with addiction. The tribe argues that the much higher substance abuse among its membership is linked to "intergenerational trauma" and has come up with a unique strategy to deal with criminal drug offenders. The Penobscot Nation pairs conventional counseling, social assistance (i.e., help with housing), harm-reduction services, drug testing, and check-ins with the courts with additional programs that introduce felons to tribal traditions. Journalist Zeke Spector describes this process: "Guided by cultural advisers, participants are required to take part in activities that include sweet grass picking, basket making, and sweat lodge ceremonies that offer both healing and spiritual benefits. Because addiction can lead to isolation from the larger community, these cultural activities allow offenders an opportunity to reconnect with the community and embrace their identity," a strategy that helps in their healing.[21]

Conclusion: "We Are Still Here"

Native Americans in New England have experienced many trials and tribulations since 1945. These challenges emerged out of the complex and diverse histories of colonization and indigenous white relations of the last 500 or so years. Despite this often challenging past, as we have explored throughout this book, Native Americans have also survived in New England. This happened often against seemingly insurmountable odds. This resilience emerged from the oppressive struggle experienced by native peoples with New English colonization and has been shaped by the strong and enduring indigenous cultural traditions that originated in the millennia before 1492 and have helped Native American survival in New England to this day.

Notes

1. See, e.g., Jeanne Guillemin, *Urban Renegades: The Cultural Strategy of American Indians* (New York: Columbia University Press, 1975).

2. For an introduction to boarding schools, see Alice Nash and Christoph Strobel, *Daily Life of Native Americans from Post-Columbian through Nineteenth Century America* (Westport, CT: Greenwood, 2006), 241–245.

3. For an international perspective on this issue, see Margaret D. Jacobs, *A Generation Removed: The Fostering and Adoption of Indigenous Children in the Postwar World* (Lincoln: University of Nebraska Press, 2014); Margaret D. Jacobs, *White Mother to a Dark Race: Settler Colonialism, Maternalism, and the Removal of Indigenous Children in the American West and Australia, 1880–1940* (Lincoln: University of Nebraska Press, 2009).

4. *Dawnland: Documentary,* directed by Adam Mazo and Ben Pender-Cudlip (PBS: Independent Lens, 2018).

5. Kent Blansett, *A Journey to Freedom: Richard Oakes, Alcatraz, and the Red Power Movement* (New Haven, CT: Yale University Press, 2018), 3–4.

6. Ibid., 7–8.

7. Kathleen J. Bragdon, *The Columbia Guide to American Indians of the Northeast* (New York: Columbia University Press, 2001), 83.

8. On this issue, see Daniel Cobb, *Native Activism in Cold War America: The Struggle for Sovereignty* (Lawrence: University Press of Kansas, 2008). For a global perspective of the national liberation struggle, see Vijay Prashad, *The Darker Nations: A People's History of the Third World* (New York: New Press, 2008).

9. Neal Salisbury, "The Atlantic Northeast," in *The Oxford Handbook of American Indian History*, ed. Frederick E. Hoxie (New York: Oxford University Press, 2016), 355.

10. For a detailed study, see Paul Brodeur, *Restitution: The Land Claims of the Mashpee, Passamaquoddy, and Penobscot Indians of New England* (Boston: Northeastern University Press, 1985).

11. Bragdon, *The Columbia Guide to American Indians of the Northeast,* 83.

12. For a study of these issues see, e.g., Robert J. Miller, *Reservation "Capitalism": Economic Development in Indian Country* (Santa Barbara, CA: Praeger, 2012).

13. See, e.g., "The Penobscot Indian Nation Now Molds High-Tech Parts for Aviation," Plastics Today, December 21, 1998, https://www.plasticstoday.com /content/penobscot-indian-nation-now-molds-high-tech-parts-aviation/989117 9041045 (accessed May 2, 2019); Robert M. Cook, "Tribal Works: Defense Contracts Position Penobscots for Long-Awaited Prosperity," Mainebiz, August 23, 2010, https://www.mainebiz.biz/article/tribal-works-defense-contracts-position -penobscots-for-long-awaited-prosperity (accessed May 2, 2019).

14. On gaming see, e.g., Ambrose I. Lane, *Return of the Buffalo: The Story behind America's Gaming Explosion* (Westport, CT: Bergin and Garvey, 1995).

15. Salisbury, "The Atlantic Northeast," 356.

16. See, e.g., the website Wôpanâak Language Reclamation Project, http://www.wlrp.org/ (accessed May 9, 2019); Jeanne Morningstar Kent, *The Visual Language of Wabanaki Art* (Charleston, SC: History Press, 2014); E. Tammy Kim, "The Passamaquoddy Reclaim Their Culture through Digital Repatriation," *New Yorker*, January 30 2019, https://www.newyorker.com/culture/culture-desk/the-passamaquoddy-reclaim-their-culture-through-digital-repatriation (accessed January 31, 2019).

17. Chris Reidy and Janette Neuwahl, "Legislature Votes to Repeal 1675 Hub Ban on Indians," *Boston Globe*, May 20, 2005.

18. Francis Flisiuk, "'Maine Has Its Own Standing Rock'—The Penobscot River Fight Explained," *Conway Daily Sun*, October 1, 2017, https://www.conwaydailysun.com/portland_phoenix/news/maine-has-its-own-standing-rock---the-penobscot/article_5a1679fa-a800-5f89-9e71-c5a7b63222c2.html (accessed April 18, 2019).

19. Marina Villeneuve, "Maine Tribe Pushes in Court to Retain Strict Water Quality Standards," centralmaine.com, December 7, 2018, https://www.centralmaine.com/2018/10/30/maine-tribes-are-skeptical-of-federal-move-to-revisit-river-water-standards/?rel=related (accessed December 13, 2018). See also Flisiuk, "'Maine Has Its Own Standing Rock.'"

20. Tanner Stening, "Mashpee and Tribe Officials Hold Rare Joint Meeting," *Cape Cod Times*, March 5, 2018, http://capecodtimes.com/news/20180305/mashpee-and-tribe-officials-hold-rare-joint-meeting (accessed April 24, 2019).

21. Zeke Spector, "A Native American Tribe Is Using Traditional Culture to Fight Addiction," VICE News, March 15, 2018, https://news.vice.com/en_ca/article/59knjz/a-native-american-tribe-is-using-traditional-culture-to-fight-addiction (accessed August 13, 2018).

Epilogue
The Story Continues

I am often reminded of a walk that my family and I took on Deer Island in Boston Harbor on September 9, 2016. The island today is connected by a causeway to the mainland and is the location of a massive sewage plant that serves the Boston metropolitan area. At that time, only one marker on the island commemorated the history of the internment of the praying town Indians during King Philip's War. (There is now a Deer Island Native American Memorial in the works.) My family and I went there on the tail end of a storm. There were spectacular waves and conditions of high wind. I could not help imaging myself being incarcerated here in similar stormy conditions during much colder months with little shelter, trying to help my family survive, and coping with the loss of loved ones, all as a result of an arbitrary politically motivated imprisonment as once Native Americans had had to do in the mid-1670s.

As my family and I were heading off the island, I noticed a woman walking who was wearing a sweatshirt: "Hannah Duston fighting terrorism since 1697." Hannah Duston was a New English woman captured during a raid in March 1697 in Haverhill, Massachusetts. Like many New English captives, she experienced trauma and violence during her ordeal. But it is also important to remember that the Native Americans who participated in these raids had also experienced trauma and brutality as a result of colonization. Many of the participants in such raids had been pushed out of their homelands as a result of the establishment of New English settlements, had found refuge in indigenous communities to the north, and felt that they had a score to settle. A few weeks after her capture from Haverhill, Duston found herself in a small camp on the Merrimack River, close to the confluence of the Contoocook River, today in central New Hampshire. Duston and two other captives who were left behind in the company of two Native American men (one middle age, the other an old man), two indigenous women, and seven children decided to strike. While the Native Americans were sleeping, Duston led the two captives in the murder of the two men, then the two women, and finally six of the seven children. The last Native American child was able to escape. The now-free captives scalped the dead bodies, took their flintlock gun and some hatchets, and fled in one of their captors' canoes. While her contemporaries gave the Duston story attention, the story became popular again—and many aspects of it fictionalized—during the 19th century. As during the colonial period, the Duston stories of the 19th century were often used as a tale to vilify Native Americans and depict indigenous people as brutal "savages" and to justify the commitment of violence against Native Americans during the U.S. period of westward expansion. The Hannah Duston sweatshirt that I saw on Deer Island provides in some ways a modern continuation of the white settler as victim narrative. Yet, it is an important task for historians to remind mainstream society that the victimization of New Englanders, just as that of Native Americans, might make for good myth, but it is bad history. My personal experiences and impressions on this day often remind me of the contentiousness of how we remember and memorialize this past.

This book merely scratches the surface of this past—the history of Native Americans of New England in the last several millennia. Many important stories, voices, and histories are not covered or are barely glanced at in this book, and researchers will likely uncover much more in the future. The issue of how we preserve and acknowledge the indigenous past of the region will continue to be part of this ongoing history.

In the 21st century, indigenous New Englanders are living complex lives. They straddle the worlds of indigenous and mainstream societies in diverse ways, a reality often shaped by individual experiences and by one's community of origin. This is an existence in multiple realities, competing value systems, and complex identities.

As we have seen, despite what some mainstream society myths about the "vanishing New England Indian" claim, indigenous peoples have persisted through often challenging and difficult times. Colonization and racism—with their legacies of disease, dispossession, poverty, discrimination, detribalization, and social challenges—have had an often destructive impact. Still, despite often horrific challenges, through adaptation, resilience, change, and perseverance and by continuing their established ways and struggling to maintain their sovereignty, Native Americans have survived in New England through often unimaginable odds. Today's descendants of communities such as the Abenaki, Maliseet, Mohegan, Narragansett, Niantic, Nipmuc, Passamaquoddy, Penacook, Penobscot, Pequot, Shagticokes, and Wampanoag tribes as well as other indigenous kin groups and people of indigenous descent who live in the region's cities, suburbs, and rural areas all have been influenced by this complex past and will continue to help shape New England's future.

This interpretive history provides merely a glimpse into the complex story of Native American survival in New England. While this epilogue provides an end point for this narrative, the story of Native Americans in New England very much continues into the future.

Chronology

ca. 2.6 million–ca. 11,700 BP	Pleistocene epoch, a geological period in which significant portions of the world were covered by glaciers and average global temperatures were an estimated 5–10 degrees Celsius colder.
ca. 115,000–ca. 11,700 BP	Last Ice Age.
ca. 17,500 BP	Almost all of New England is believed to be still covered by glaciers.
ca. 15,000–ca. 9,000 BP	Paleo Indian period.
ca. 9,000–ca. 2,500 BP	Archaic period.
	Early Archaic (ca. 9,000–ca. 8,000 BP)
	Middle Archaic (ca. 8,000–ca. 6,000 BP)
	Late Archaic (ca. 6,000–ca. 3,800 BP)
	Terminal Archaic (ca. 3,800–ca. 2,500 BP)
ca. 2,500 BP–ca. 1500 CE	Woodland period.
	Early Woodland (ca. 2,700–ca. 1,650 BP)
	Middle Woodland (ca. 1,650 BP–ca. 1000 CE)
	Late Woodland (ca. 1000–ca. 1500)
1200	Cahokia is at the height of its influence. Close to present-day St. Louis, Cahokia was one of many earthwork building societies in the Eastern Woodland region and is believed to have been the largest city in pre-Columbian North America.
1492	In search of a trade route to Asia, Christopher Columbus stumbles across the Western Hemisphere. This journey, while likely not the first contact between the peoples of the

	Americas, Africa, and Europe, establishes sustained and permanent contact.
1497–1498	The Venetian mariner Giovanni Caboto (John Cabot) and his crew, sailing under the English flag, explore the eastern coast of North America reaching from today's Nova Scotia down to the coastal Carolinas.
ca. 1500–1620	Early contact period/Final Woodland period.
ca. 1500	Beginning and increasing presence of European explorers, fishermen, and whalers on the northeastern North American shore. This presence initiates exchanges and ever more complex interactions between Native Americans and Europeans. Such relations also aid in the introduction of various diseases that have a devastating demographic impact on the indigenous populations of the Western Hemisphere.
1507	Geographer Martin Waldseemueller calls the Western Hemisphere "America" in honor of the Florentine mariner Amerigo Vespucci, a term that would eventually be commonly used.
1524	Mariner Giovanni Verrazzano interacts with various coastal indigenous New England peoples during his voyage in the region.
1534–1542	Jacques Cartier's voyages and attempts to establish a foothold in the St. Lawrence River Valley in modern-day Canada.
1602	Bartholomew Gosnold travels the North American Atlantic coast from southern Maine to Narragansett Bay. He names Cape Cod. Disease (likely smallpox) breaks out among the indigenous peoples with whom Gosnold traded and likely spreads throughout the region.
1603	Martin Pring commandeers an English mission that explores the New England coast from today's Casco Bay in Maine to the area of the Native American town of Patuxet. A few years later this site would be occupied by the British, and their colony became known as Plymouth Plantation. Plymouth became the first permanent English colony in the region.

1603–1608	Samuel de Champlain leads various expeditions throughout the northeastern Woodlands region of today's southeastern Canada and the northeastern United States. He travels inland and along the coast, providing ethnohistorians a valuable glimpse into the region and the indigenous societies of Dawnland.
1605	George Waymouth's expedition to what is today coastal Maine.
1606	An expedition led by Thomas Hanham and Martin Pring investigates coastal Maine.
1607	The year in which Ousamequin (Massasoit) is believed to have become the leader of the Wampanoag Confederacy.
	English colonists, led by Geoge Popham and Raleigh Gilbert, establish a short-lived colony on the Sagadahoc River (in today's Maine).
1608	Champlain establishes a French foothold at Quebec City, the first permanent French colony in the region.
1609	Henry Hudson explores New England and other parts of the eastern North American coast and travels up the Hudson River.
1610	Adrien Block travels along the New England coast and notes many Native American settlements in the region.
	Samuel Argall, on behest of the Jamestown colony, explores the New England waters from Penobscot Bay to Cape Cod. He is especially interested in the viability of the region as a fishing ground. Due to the success of this mission, Jamestown decides to send yearly fishing expeditions to New England.
1611	French colonial officials and several traders set out on a diplomatic mission to visit several of Maine's river valleys, such as St. John, St. Croix, Penobscot, and Kennebec, to foster relations with the indigenous populations there and to strengthen French strategic and economic interests in the area via the English. Notably, this expedition is also accompanied by the Jesuit Pierre Biard, who is interested

in establishing a missionary foothold in the region. (The Jesuit order partially financed this mission.)

The English captain Edward Harlow, during a journey on the southern New England coast, abducts five Native Americans, including Epenow.

1613 Under commission of the governor of Virginia, Samuel Argall leads a mission to destroy French colonial holdings at Penobscot Bay as well as the Bay of Fundy.

1614 John Smith explores and names "New England." In 1616 he publishes his book *A Description of New England*, which also includes a map that shows the region from Cape Cod up to the Bay of Fundy.

English mariner Thomas Hunt, an associate of John Smith, abducts a group of some 20 Native Americans during a maritime venture along the southern New England coast. One of the captured Native Americans is Tisquantum (Squanto).

1615 Dutch settlers establish the colonial outpost of Fort Nassau (not far from Albany, New York).

1615–1619 Taranteen War, a series of violent conflicts among the Native American peoples in Dawnland.

1616–1619 New England's Native American population is decimated by a series of disease outbreaks.

1620 Native Americans on Martha's Vineyard led by Epenow attack Thomas Dermer and his crew.

Puritans establish a colony at Patuxet/Plymouth on land that had been cleared and worked by its earlier Wampanoag inhabitants, who abandoned their settlement during the epidemics that ravaged the region from 1616 to 1619.

1621 The Pauquunaukit Wampanoag (Pokanoket) tribe in what is today southeastern Massachusetts signs a treaty of defensive alliance with Plymouth Colony.

1624–1626 The Dutch initiate a more sustained colonization effort in the Hudson River Valley and establish a settlement called New Amsterdam (New

York). The Dutch claim imperial control over the region until 1664, when their colonial holdings are lost to the English during the Second Anglo-Dutch War.

1625	Jesuits arrive in Quebec. From 1632 to 1674 their writings, called *The Jesuit Relations*, provide a valuable glimpse into the history of the indigenous peoples of the northeastern Woodlands.
1626–1628	English colonists establish a foothold at the mouth of the Naumkeag River (so named after the indigenous peoples of the land), which becomes Salem, Massachusetts.
1630	Founding of Boston. The community emerges as the administrative, cultural, and economic center of the Puritan colonies in New England.
1632–1642	The Great Migration. About 20,000 English settlers (mostly Puritans) arrive in New England.
1633	Founding of Windsor in what is today the state of Connecticut.
1635	English colonists commence the colonization of the Kwinitewk/Connecticut River Valley.
1636–1637	The Pequot War.
1642–1643	Kief's War.
1640s–1660s	The Haudenosaunees (Iroquois) launch devastating raids against various Native American groups in New England as well as other parts of the northern Eastern Woodlands.
1646–1675	John Eliot's mission among several southern New England communities. These efforts lead to the creation of several praying towns.
1661	Death of Ousamequin (Massasoit).
1663	With the help of indigenous scholars, John Elliot publishes a translation of the Bible in the Massachusetts language.
1665	Caleb Cheeshahteaumuck, a Wampanoag from Martha's Vineyard, is the first and only Native American to graduate from Harvard's Indian College.
1675–1676	King Philip's War. Several Native American tribes in New England engage in a conflict with the New England colonies. The war leads to the

death of a significant portion of New England's Native American population and kills many English colonists. Many indigenous survivors were sold into slavery in the Caribbean.

1689–1697	War of the League of Augsburg (War of the Grand Alliance)/King William's War. Indigenous peoples in New England and Acadia are participating in an imperial war between France and England that involves their respective colonists.
1702–1713	War of the Spanish Succession/Queen Anne's War, a continuation of the war for imperial supremacy between Britain and France involving again the colonies and various Native American nations.
1722–1727	Dummer's War. Wabanakis in northern New England attempt to push back English colonization efforts.
1728	The Hassanamesit community of the Nipmucs is sold to create the town of Grafton. Several Nipmuc families obtain shares in the community.
1736	Connecticut grants a reservation to Schagticoke Indians.
1740s–1770s	Moravian missionaries are present in several reserves such as Schagticoke in northwestern Connecticut and Duchess County, New York.
1744–1748	King George's War/War of Austrian Succession. New England's Native Americans continue to be involved in the British and French struggle over imperial dominance.
1749–1755	Father Le Loutre's War.
1754	Eleazar Wheelock founds the Moor's Charity School in Lebanon, Connecticut. The goal of the school is to educate Native American children. The school is eventually moved to Hanover in New Hampshire and since 1770 has been known as Dartmouth College.
1754–1763	French and Indian War/Seven Year's War.
1759	Samson Occum (Mohegan) becomes an ordained Presbyterian minister.

1763	Treaty of Paris. France cedes its Canadian holding to Great Britain.
1775–1783	American Revolution.
1783	Treaty of Versailles. Great Britain recognizes the independence of the United States.
1790	Non-Intercourse Act. This act suggests that states cannot sell the land of Native American tribes without federal approval.
1830	Indian Removal Act.
1833	The Mashpee Revolt.
1860s–1880s	Many southern New England Native American communities face policies of detribalization and termination.
1879	Establishment of the Carlisle Indian School in Pennsylvania, first among many Indian boarding schools throughout the United States.
1885	Major Crimes Act.
1886	The State of Connecticut recognizes the Golden Hill Reservation.
1887	General Land Allotment Act.
1924	Native Americans are given U.S. citizenship.
1965	American Indian Civil Rights Act.
1975	American Indian Self-Determination and Education Act.
	Mashpee land claims trial.
1976	Massachusetts recognizes the Nipmuc tribe.
1978	American Indian Religious Freedom Act and American Indian Child Welfare Act.
1979	Creation of the Office of Federal Acknowledgment, which regulates and administers the federal recognition process.
1980	*Passamaquoddy, Maliseet Penobscot Land Claims v. the State of Maine.*
	The Houlton Band of Maliseet Indians is federally recognized.
1981	Federal recognition of the Gay Head Indians (Aquinnahs) on Martha's Vineyard.
1983	Federal Recognition of the Narragansetts.

1984	Federal Recognition of the Mashantucket Pequots.
1988	Indian Gaming Regulatory Act.
1990	Native American Grave Protection and Repatriation Act.
1991	Federal recognition of the Aroostook Band of Micmacs.
1992	Mashantucket Pequots open the Foxwoods Resort Casino in Connecticut.
1994	The Mohegan Nation gains federal recognition.
1996	The Mohegan Sun Gaming Resort opens.
2002	The secretary of the interior recognizes the Eastern Pequot Nation.
2004	The secretary of the interior recognizes the Schagticoke Tribal Nation.
	The Golden Hill Paugusetts Indian Nation is denied federal recognition.
	The Nipmuc Nation is denied federal recognition.
2005	In an unprecedented decision, the Bureau of Indian Affairs revokes federal recognition of the Eastern Pequot and Schagticoke Tribal Nations in Connecticut after lobbying of state officials, Connecticut's members of Congress, and private landowners.
2007	The Mashpee Wampanoag tribe gains federal recognition.
2011	Hassanamesit is included on the National Register of Historic Places.

Bibliography

Published Primary Sources and Document Collections

Anonymous. "Extract from an Indian History." In *Collections of the Massachusetts Historical Society,* Vol. 9, 99–102. Boston: Hall and Hiller, 1804.

Apess, William. *Indian Nullification of the Unconstitutional Laws of Massachusetts: Relative to the Mashpee Tribe; Or, the Pretended Riot Explained.* Boston: Press of J. Howe, 1835.

Apess, William. *A Son of the Forest and Other Writings.* Edited by Barry O'Connell. Amherst: University of Massachusetts Press, 1997.

Axtell, James, ed. *The Indian Peoples of Eastern America: A Documentary History of Sexes.* New York: Oxford University Press, 1981.

Bradford, William. *History of Plymouth Plantation, 1606–1646.* Edited by Samuel E. Morrison. New York: Knopf, 1962.

Calloway, Colin, ed. *Dawnland Encounters: Indians and Europeans in Northern New England.* Hanover, NH: University Press of New England, 1991.

Calloway, Colin G., ed. *The World Turned Upside Down: Indian Voices from Early America.* Boston: Bedford/St. Martin's, 1994.

Champlain, Samuel de. *Voyages of Samuel de Champlain, 1604–1616.* New York: Barnes and Noble, 1946.

Church, Benjamin. *Entertaining Passages Relating to King Philip's War, Which Began in the Month of June, 1675: As Also Expedition, More Laterly Made against the Common Enemy, and Indians in the Eastern Part of New England.* Boston: B. Green, 1716.

Day, Gordon. *Western Abenaki Dictionary,* Vol. 2, *English-Abenaki.* Quebec: Canadian Museum of Civilization, 1995.

Denys, Nicholas. *The Description & Natural History of the Coasts of North America.* Edited and translated by William F. Ganong. Toronto: Champlain Society, 1908. [Originally published in 1672.]

Earle, John M. *Report to the Governor and Council Concerning the Indians of the Commonwealth.* Boston: William White, 1821.

Eliot, John. *The Holy Bible: Containing the Old Testament and New Translated into the Indian Language by John Eliot.* Cambridge, MA: Samuel Green and Marmaduke Johnson, 1685. [Originally published in 1663.]

Eliot, John. *Indian Grammar Begun; Or, an Essay to Bring the Indian Language into Rules for the Help of Such as Desire to Learn the Same for the Furtherance of the Gospel among Them.* Cambridge, MA: Marmaduke Johnson, 1666.

Eliot, John, and Thomas Mayhew. "*Tears of Repentance: Or, a Further Narrative of the Progress of the Gospel amongst the Indians in New England.*" London: Peter Cole, 1653.

Force, Peter, ed. *Tract and Other Papers Relating Principally to the Origin, Settlement, and Progress of the Colonies in North America from the Discovery of the Country to the Year 1776.* 4 vols. Reprint ed. Gloucester, MA: Peter Smith, 1947.

Goddard, Ives, and Kathleen J Bragdon. *Native Writings in Massachusetts.* Philadelphia: American Philosophical Society, 1988.

Gookin, Daniel. "An Historical Account of the Doing and Sufferings of the Christian Indians in New England in the Years 1675, 1676, 1677." In *Transactions and Collections of the American Antiquarian Society,* Vol. 2, 425–534. Cambridge, MA: Printed for the Society at the University Press, 1836.

Gookin, Daniel. "Historical Collections of the Indians in New England." In *Collections of the Massachusetts Historical Society.* Boston: Massachusetts Historical Society, 1792.

Gookin, Daniel. *Historical Collections of the Indians of New England: Of their Several Nations, Numbers, Customs, Manners, Religion, and Government before the English Planted There.* Boston: Belknap and Hall, 1674.

Josselyn, John. *John Josselyn, Colonial Traveler: A Critical Edition of Two Voyages to New England.* Edited by Paul J. Linddholt. Hanover, NH: University Press of New England, 1988.

Karr, Ronald Dale, ed. *Indian New England, 1524–1674: A Compendium of Eyewitness Accounts of Native American Life.* Pepperell, MA: Branch Line Press, 1999.

Lederer, John. *The Discoveries of John Lederer, with Unpublished Letters by and about Lederer to Governor John Winthrop, Jr., and an Essay on the Indians of Lederer's Discoveries by Douglas L. Rights and William P. Cumming.* Charlottesville: University of Virginia Press, 1958.

Lescarbot, Marc. *Nova Francia, a Description of Acadia.* New York: Harper and Row, 1928. [Originally published in 1609.]

Maine Indian Tribal State Commission Task Force on Tribal State Relations. "At Loggerheads: The State of Maine and the Wabanaki; Final Report of the Task Force on Tribal-State Relations." Hallowell: Maine Indian Tribal-State Commission, 1974.

Mather, Increase. *A Brief History of the Warr with the Indians in New England.* Boston: John Foster, 1676.

Moondancer and Strong Woman. *A Cultural History of the Native Peoples of Southern New England: Voices from the Past and Present.* Newport, RI: Aquidneck Indian Council, 1999.

Morton, Thomas. *New English Canaan of Thomas Morton.* Edited by Charles Francis Adams Jr. Boston: Prince Society, 1883. [Originally published in 1637.]

Newell, Darrell (Passamaquoddy). "A Man of the Dawn." In *Indian Voices: Listening to Native Americans,* ed. Alison Ownings, 3–17. New Brunswick, NJ: Rutgers University Press, 2017.

Nicolar, Joseph. *The Life and Traditions of the Red Man.* Edited by Annette Kolodny. Durham, NC: Duke University Press, 2007.

Occom, Samson. *The Collected Writings of Samson Occom, Mohegan: Leadership and Literature in Eighteenth-Century Native America.* Edited by Joanna Brooks. New York: Oxford University Press, 2006.

"Patooket Graunted Indian Graunt" (May 18, 1653). In *Records of the Governor and Company of the Massachusetts Bay in New England,* Vol. 3, *1644–1657,* ed. Nathaniel B. Shurtleff. Boston: Printer of the Commonwealth, 1854.

Peters, Russell M. *Clambake, a Wampanoag Tradition.* New York: Lehrer Publications, 1992.

Quinn, David, and Allison M. Quinn, eds. *The English New England Voyages, 1602–1608.* London: Hakluyt Society, 1983.

Rosier, James. *The Voyage of Archangel: James Rosier's Account of the Waymouth Voyage of 1605: A True Relation.* Edited and Annotated by David C. Morey. Gardiner, ME: Tilbury House Publisher, 2005. [Originally published in 1605.]

Rowlandson, Mary. *The Sovereignty and Goodness of God.* Edited by Neal Salisbury. Boston: Bedford/St. Martin's, 1997. [Originally published in 1682.]

Runningwolf, Michael B., and Patricia Clark Smith. *On the Trail of Elder Brother: Glous'gap Stories of the Micmac Indians.* New York: Persea, 2000.

Shoemaker, Nancy. *Living with Whales: Documents and Oral Histories of Native New England Whaling History.* Amherst: University of Massachusetts Press, 2014.

Smith, Captain John. *Writings with Other Narratives of Roanoke, Jamestown, and the First English Settlement of America.* New York: Library of America, 2007. [Originally published in 1624.]

Thwaites, Reuben G., ed. *The Jesuite Relations and Allied Documents: Travel and Explorations of the Jesuit Missionaries in New France, 1610–1791: The Original French, Latin, and Italian Texts with English Translations and Notes.* 73 vols. Cleveland, OH: Burrows Brothers, 1896.

Trumbull, James Hammond, Edward Everett Hale, and Robert D. Madison, eds. *Natick Dictionary: A New England Indian Lexicon.* Lincoln: University of Nebraska Press, 2009.

U.S. Senate, Select Committee on Indian Affairs. *Federal Recognition Administrative Procedures Act: Hearing before the Committee on Indian Affairs, United States Senate, One Hundred Fourth Congress, First Session, on S.479, to Provide for Administrative Procedures to Extend Federal Recognition to Certain Indian Groups, July 13, 1995.* Washington, DC: U.S. Government Printing Office, 1995.

Vaughan, Alden T., and Edward Clark, eds. *Puritans among the Indians: Accounts of Captivity and Redemption, 1676–1724.* Cambridge, MA: Belknap, 1981.

Williams, Roger. *The Complete Writings of Roger Williams,* Vol. 1, *Introduction: Key into the Language of America, Letters Regarding John Cotton.* Eugene, OR: Wipf and Stock Publishers, 2007.

Williams, Roger. *A Key into the Language of America.* Edited by John J. Teunissen and Evelyn J. Hinz. Detroit: Wayne State University Press, 1973.

Williams, Stephen. *What Befell Stephen Williams in His Captivity.* Edited by George Sheldon. Deerfield, MA: Pocumtuck Valley Memorial Association, 1889.

Winslow, Edward. "Winslow's Relation." In *Chronicles of the Pilgrim Fathers,* 2nd ed. Edited by Alexander Young. Boston: Charles C. Little and James Brown, 1844.

Winthrop, John. *The Journal of John Winthrop, 1630–1649.* Abridged ed. Edited by Richard S. Dunn and Laetitia Yeandle. Cambridge, MA: Harvard University Press, 1996.

Wood, William. *New England's Prospect.* Edited by Alden T. Vaughan. Amherst: University of Massachusetts Press, 1977. [Originally published in 1634.]

Secondary Literature

Anderson David G. "Paleoindian Interaction Networks in the Eastern Woodlands." In *Native American Interaction: Multiscalar Analysis and Interpretations in the Eastern Woodlands,* ed. Michael S. Nassaney and Kenneth E. Sassaman, 1–26. Knoxville: University of Tennessee Press, 1995.

Anderson, David G. "Pleistocene Settlement in the East." In *The Oxford Handbook of North American Archaeology,* ed. Timothy R. Pauketat, 96–107. New York: Oxford University Press, 2012.

Anderson, Karen Lee. *The Subjugation of Women in Seventeenth Century New France.* New York: Routledge, 1990.

Anderson, Terry L., ed. *Property Rights and Indian Economies.* Lanham, MD: Rowman and Littlefield, 1992.

Anderson, Virginia DeJohn. *New England's Generation: The Great Migration and the Formation of Society and Culture in the Seventeenth Century.* New York: Cambridge University Press, 1991.

Andrews, Edward E. *Native Apostles: Black and Indian Missionaries in the British Atlantic World.* Cambridge, MA: Harvard University Press, 2013.

Arnold, Laura K. "Crossing Cultures: Algonquian Indians and the Invention of New England." PhD diss., University of California Los Angeles, 1995.

Atkinson, Jay. *Massacre on the Merrimack: Hannah Duston's Captivity and Revenge in Colonial America.* Lanham, MD: Lyon, 2015.

Aubin, George. "A Historical Phonology of Narragansett." PhD diss., Brown University, 1972.

Axelrod, Alan. *Chronicle of the Indian War: From Colonial Times to Wounded Knee.* New York: Prentice Hall, 1993.

Axtell, James. "Ethnohistory: A Historians Viewpoint." *Ethnohistory* 26 (Winter 1979): 1–13.

Axtell, James. *The European and the Indian: Essays in the Ethnohistory of Colonial North America.* New York: Oxford University Press, 1981.

Axtell, James. *The Invasion Within: The Contest of Cultures in Colonial North America.* New York: Oxford University Press, 1985.

Bahar, Matthew R. *Storm of the Seas: Indians Empires in the Atlantic's Age of Sail.* New York: Oxford University Press, 2019.

Baker, Brenda. "Pilgrim's Progress and Praying Indians: The Biological Consequences of Contact in Southern New England." In *The Wake of Contact: Biological Responses to Conquest,* ed. Clark Spencer Larsen and George R. Milner, 35–45. New York: Wiley-Liss, 1994.

Baker, Emerson W., Edwin A. Churchill, Richard S. D'Abate, Kristine L. Jones, Victor A. Konrad, and Harald E. L. Prins, eds. *American Beginnings: Exploration, Culture, and Cartography in the Land of Norumbega.* Lincoln: University of Nebraska Press, 1994.

Bakker, Peter. "The Language of the Coast Tribes Is Half Basque: A Basque-American Indian Pidgin in Use between Europeans and Native Americans in North America, ca. 1540–ca. 1640." *Anthropological Linguistics* 1, nos. 3–4 (1989): 117–147.

Baron, Donna Keith, J. Edward Howd, and Holly V. Izard. "They Were Here All Along: The Native American Presence in Lower Central New England in the Eighteenth and Nineteenth Centuries." *William and Mary Quarterly* 53, no. 3 (1996): 561–586.

Bataille, Gretchen Mueller. *Native American Women: A Biographical Dictionary.* New York: Garland, 1993.

Bataille, Gretchen Mueller, and Kathleen Mullen Sands. *American Indian Women: A Guide to Research.* New York: Garland, 1991.

Beck Kehoe, Alice. *The Land of Prehistory: A Critical History of American Archaeology.* New York: Routledge, 1998.

Benison, Chris. "Horticulture and the Maintenance of Social Complexity in Late Woodland Southeastern New England." *North American Archaeologist* 18, no. 1 (1997): 1–17.

Bennett, M. K. "The Food Economy of the New England Indians." *Journal of Political Economy* 63 (1955): 360–396.

Blansett, Kent. *A Journey to Freedom: Richard Oakes, Alcatraz, and the Red Power Movement.* New Haven, CT: Yale University Press, 2018.

Bolotin, Norman, and Christine Laing. *The World's Columbian Exposition: The Chicago's World Fair of 1893.* Champagne: University of Illinois Press, 2002.

Bonfanti, Leo. *Biographies and Legends of the New England Indians,* Vol. 1. Burlington, MA: Pride Publications, 1993.

Bourne, Russell. *The Red King's Rebellion: Racial Politics in New England, 1675–1678.* New York: Oxford University Press, 1990.

Bourque, Bruce J. "Aboriginal Settlement and Subsistence on the Maine Coast." *Man in the Northeast* 6 (1973): 3–20.

Bourque, Bruce J. *Twelve Thousand Years: American Indians in Maine.* Lincoln: University of Nebraska Press, 2001.

Bourque, Bruce J., and Ruth H. Whitehead. "Tarrantiens and the Introduction of European Trade Goods in the Gulf of Maine." *Ethnohistory* 32 (1985): 327–341.

Bradley, James W. "Native Exchange and European Trade: Cross Cultural Dynamics in the Sixteenth Century." *Man in the Northeast* 33 (1987): 31–46.

Bradley, James W. *Origins and Ancestors: Investigating New England's Paleo Indians.* Andover, MA: Robert S. Peabody Museum of Archaeology, 1998.

Bragdon, Kathleen J. *The Columbia Guide to American Indians of the Northeast.* New York: Columbia University Press, 2001.

Bragdon, Kathleen J. "Gender as a Social Category in Native Southern New England." *Ethnohistory* 43, no. 4 (1996): 573–592.

Bragdon, Kathleen J. *Native People of Southern New England, 1500–1650.* Norman: University of Oklahoma Press, 1996.

Bragdon, Kathleen J. *Native People of Southern New England, 1650–1775.* Norman: University of Oklahoma Press, 2009.

Brodeur, Paul. *Restitution: The Land Claims of the Mashpee, Passamaquoddy, and Penobscot Indians of New England.* Boston: Northeastern University Press, 1985.

Brooks, Lisa. *The Common Pot: The Recovery of Native Space in the Northeast.* Minneapolis: University of Minnesota Press, 2009.

Brooks, Lisa. *Our Beloved Kin: A New History of King Philip's War.* New Haven, CT: Yale University Press, 2018.

Bross, Kristina, and Hilary E. Wyss, eds. *Early Native Literacies in New England: A Documentary and Critical Anthology.* Amherst: University of Massachusetts Press, 2008.

Bruchac, Margaret M. "Historical Erasure and Cultural Recovery: Indigenous People in the Connecticut River Valley." PhD diss., University of Massachusetts, 2007.

Brumwell, Stephen. *White Devil: A True Story of War, Savagery, and Vengeance in Colonial America.* Cambridge, MA: Da Capo, 2005.

Byrne, James P. *The Black Death.* Westport, CT: Greenwood, 2004.

Caduto, Michael J. *A Time before New Hampshire: The Story of a Land and Native Peoples.* Hanover, NH: University Press of New England, 2003.

Calloway, Colin G., ed. *After King Philip's War: Presence and Persistence in Indian New England.* Hanover, NH: University Press of New England, 1997.

Calloway, Colin G. *The American Revolution in Indian Country: Crisis and Diversity in Native American Communities.* New York: Cambridge University Press, 1995.

Calloway, Colin. *The Indian History of an American Institution: Native Americans and Dartmouth.* Hannover, NH: Dartmouth College Press, 2010.

Calloway, Colin G. "New England Algonkians in the American Revolution." *Annual Proceedings (Dublin Seminar for New England Folklife)* 16 (1991): 51–62.

Calloway, Colin G. *New Worlds for All: Indians, Europeans, and the Remaking of Early America.* Baltimore: John Hopkins University Press, 1997.

Calloway, Colin G. "Sentinels of the Revolution: Bedel's New Hampshire Rangers and the Abenaki Indians on the Upper Connecticut." *Historical New Hampshire* 45, no. 4 (1990): 270–295.

Calloway, Colin G. *The Western Abenakis of Vermont, 1600–1800: War, Migration, and the Survival of an Indian People.* Norman: University of Oklahoma Press, 1990.

Calloway, Colin G., and Neal Salisbury, eds. *Reinterpreting New England Indians and the Colonial Experience.* Boston: Colonial Society of Massachusetts, 2003.

Cameron, Catherine M., Paul Kelton, and Alan C. Swedlund, eds. *Beyond Germs: Native Depopulation in North America.* Tucson: University of Arizona Press, 2015.

Campisi, Jack. *The Mashpee Indians: Tribe on Trial.* Syracuse, NY: Syracuse University Press, 1991.

Cave, Alfred A. *The Pequot War.* Amherst: University of Massachusetts Press, 1996.

Ceci, Lynn. "Fish Fertilizer: A Native North American Practice?" *Science* 188 (1975): 26–30.

Chet, Guy. *Conquering the American Wilderness: The Triumph of European Warfare in the Colonial Northeast.* Amherst: University of Massachusetts Press, 2003.

Chilton, Elizabeth S. "Farming and Social Complexity in the Northeast." In *North American Archaeology*, ed. Timothy R. Pauketat and Diana DiPaolo Loren, 138–160. Malden, MA: Blackwell, 2005.

Chilton, Elizabeth S. "New England Algonquians: Navigating 'Backwaters' and Typological Boundaries." In *The Oxford Handbook of North American Archaeology*, ed. Timothy R. Pauketat, 262–272. New York: Oxford University Press, 2012.

Chilton, Elizabeth S. "The Origin and the Spread of Maize (Zea Mayz) in New England." In *Histories of Maize: Multidisciplinary Approaches to the Prehistory, Biogeography, Domestication, and Evolution of Maize*, ed. John Staller, Robert Tykot, and Bruce Benz, 539–547. New York: Routledge, 2006.

Clifford, James. "Identity in Mashpee." In *The Predicament of Culture: Twentieth-Century Ethnography, Literature, and Art*, ed. James Clifford, 277–346. Cambridge, MA: Harvard University Press, 1988.

Cobb, Daniel. *Native Activism in Cold War America: The Struggle for Sovereignty.* Lawrence: University Press of Kansas, 2008.

Cogley, Richard. *John Eliot's Mission to the Indians before King Philip's War.* Cambridge, MA: Harvard University Press, 1984.

Colwell, Chip. *Plundered Skulls and Stolen Spirits: Inside the Fight to Reclaim Native America's Culture.* Chicago: University of Chicago Press, 2017.

Cohen, Russ, with Stephanie Lettendre. *Wild Plants I Have Known . . . and Eaten.* Essex, MA: Essex Greenbelt Association, 2004.

Coleman, Emma Lewis. *New England Captives Carried to Canada: Between 1677 to 1760 during the French Indian Wars.* 2 vols. Westminster, MD: Heritage Books, 2008.

Cook, S. F. *The Indian Population of New England in the Seventeenth Century.* Berkeley: University of California Publications in Anthropology, 1976.

Cook, S. F. "Interracial Warfare and Population Decline among the New England Indians. *Ethnohistory* 20, no. 1 (1973): 1–24.

Cook, S. F. "The Significance of Disease in the Extinction of the New England Indians." *Human Biology* 45, no. 3 (1973): 485–508.

Cowley, Charles. *Memories of the Indians and Pioneers of the Region of Lowell.* Lowell, MA: Stone and Huse, 1862.

Cronon, William. *Changes in the Land: Indians, Colonists, and the Ecology of New England.* New York: Hill and Wang, 1983.

Crosby, Alfred W. *The Columbian Exchange: Biological and Cultural Consequences of 1492.* Westport, CT: Greenwood, 1973.

Crosby, Alfred W. *Ecological Imperialism: The Biological Expansion of Europe, 900–1900.* New York: Cambridge University Press, 1986.

Curran, M. L., and Dena Ferran Dincauze. "Paleoindian and Paleo-Lakes: New Data from the Connecticut Drainage." *Annals of the New York Academy of Science* 288, no. 1 (1977): 333–348.

Damm, Charlotte. "Archaeology, Ethnohistory, and Oral Traditions: Approaches to the Indigenous Past," *Norwegian Archaeological Review* 38, no. 2 (2005): 73–87.

Day, Gordon. "The Eastern Boundary of Iroquoia: Abenaki Evidence." *Man in the Northeast* 1 (1971): 7–13.

Day, Gordon. "English Indian Contacts in New England." *Ethnohistory* 9, no. 1 (1962): 24–40.

Day, Gordon. "The Indian as Ecological Factor in the Northeastern Forest," *Ecology* 34, no. 2 (1953): 329–346.

Day, Gordon. *The Mots Loups of Father Mathevet.* Ottawa: National Museum of Canada, 1975.

Day, Gordon. *In Search of New England's Native Past: Selected Essays by Gordon M. Day.* Edited by Michael K. Foster and William Cowan. Amherst: University of Massachusetts Press, 1998.

DeLucia, Christine M. "The Memory Frontier: Uncommon Pursuits of Past and Pace in the Northeast after King Philip's War." *Journal of American History* 98, no. 4 (2012): 975–997.

DeLucia, Christine M. *Memory Lands: King Philip's War and the Place of Violence in the Northeast.* New Haven, CT: Yale University Press, 2018.

Demos, John. *The Unredeemed Captive: A Family Story from Early America.* New York: Knopf, 1994.

Den Ouden, Amy E. *Beyond Conquest: Native Peoples and the Struggle for History in New England*. Lincoln: University of Nebraska Press, 2005.

Diamond, Jared. *Guns, Germs, and Steel: The Fates of Human Societies*. New York: Norton, 1997.

Dimmick, Frederica R. "Creative Farmers of the Northeast: A New View of the Indian Maize Horticulture." *North American Archaeologist* 15, no. 3 (1994): 235–252.

Dincauze, Dena Ferran. "An Archaic Sequence for Southern New England." *American Antiquity* 36, no. 2 (1971): 194–198.

Dincauze, Dena Ferran. *Cremation Cemeteries in Eastern Massachusetts*. Cambridge, MA: Peabody Museum Press, 1968.

Dincauze, Dena Ferran. "An Introduction to Archaeology in the greater Boston Area." *Archaeology of Eastern North America* 2 (1974): 39–66.

Dincauze, Dena Ferran. "A Late Archaic Culture in Massachusetts." *Man in the Northeast* 4 (1972): 40–61.

Dincauze, Dena Ferran. "The Late Archaic Period in Southern New England." *Arctic Anthropology* 12, no. 2 (1975): 23–24.

Dincauze, Dena Ferran. *The Neville Site: 8,000 Years at Amoskeag Manchester, New Hampshire*. Cambridge, MA: Peabody Museum Press, 1976.

Dincauze, Dena Ferran, and Victoria Jacobson. "The Birds of Summer: Lakeside Routes into Late Pleistocene New England." *Canadian Journal of Archaeology* 25 (2001): 121–126.

Dobyns, Henry F. *Their Number Become Thinned: Native American Population Dynamics in Eastern North America*. Knoxville: University of Tennessee Press, 1983.

Doughton, Thomas. "Unseen Neighbors: Native Americans of Central Massachusetts, a People Who Had 'Vanished.'" In *After King Philip's War: Presence and Persistence in Indian New England*, ed. Colin Calloway, 207–230. Hanover, NH: University Press of New England, 1997.

Drinnon, Richard. *Facing West: The Metaphysics of Indian-Hating and Empire Building*. Minneapolis: University of Minnesota Press, 1980.

Dunbar-Ortiz, Roxanne. *An Indigenous Peoples' History of the United States*. Boston: Beacon, 2014.

Duranleau, Deena L. "Subsistence and Settlement Patterns of the Late Archaic and Late Woodland Periods for Coastal New England and New York: A Regional Survey." PhD diss., Harvard University, 2009.

Eckstorm, Fannie Hardy. *The Penobscot Man*. Boston: Houghton Mifflin, 1904.

Fagan, Brian M. *Ancient North America: The Archaeology of a Continent*. 4th ed. London: Thames and Hudson, 2005.

Fisher, David Hackett. *Champlain's Dream: The European Founding of North America*. New York: Simon and Schuster, 2008.

Fisher, Julie A., and David J. Silverman. *Ninigret, Sachem of the Niantics and Narragansetts: Diplomacy, War, and the Balance of Power in Seventeenth-Century New England and Indian Country*. Ithaca, NY: Cornell University Press, 2014.

Fisher, Linford D. *The Indian Great Awakening: Religion and the Shaping of Native Cultures in Early America.* New York: Oxford University Press, 2012.

Fisher, Marvin. "Seeing New Englandly: Anthropology, Ecology, and Theology in Thoreau's *Week on the Concord and the Merrimack Rivers.*" *Centennial Review* 34, no. 3 (1990): 381–394.

Fitzhugh, William W, ed. *Cultures in Contact: The European Impact on Native Cultural Institutions in Eastern North America.* Washington, DC: U.S. Government Printing Office, 1985.

Fixico, Donald. *Daily Life of Native Americans in the Twentieth Century.* Westport, CT: Greenwood, 2006.

Fowler, William S. "Ceremonial and Domestic Products of Aboriginal New England." *Massachusetts Archaeological Society Bulletin* 27, nos. 3–4 (1966): 33–68.

Frazier, Patrick. *The Mohicans of Stockbridge.* Lincoln: University of Nebraska Press, 1992.

Ghere, David L. "Abenaki Factionalism, Emigration and Social Continuity: Indian Society in Northern New England, 1725–1765." PhD diss., University of Maine, 1985.

Ghere, David L. "The 'Disappearance' of the Abenaki in Western Maine: Political Organization and Ethnocentric Assumptions." *American Indian Quarterly* 17, no. 2 (1993): 193–207.

Ghere, David L. "Myths and Methods in Abenaki Demography: Abenaki Population Recovery, 1725–1750." *Ethnohistory* 44, no. 3 (1997): 511–534.

Goddard, Ives. "Early Pidgins and Creoles." In *Language Encounter in the Americas,* ed. Edward Gray and Norman Fiering, 61–80. Providence, RI: John Carter Brown Library, 1999.

Goddard, Ives. "Massachusett Phonology: A Preliminary Look." In *Papers of the Twelfth Algonquian Conference,* ed. William Cowan, 57–105. Ottawa: Carlton University Press, 1981.

Goode, Richard C. "The Only and Principal End: Propagating the Gospel in Early Puritan New England." PhD diss., Vanderbilt University, 1995.

Grandjean, Katherine. *American Passage: The Communications Frontier in Early New England.* Cambridge, MA: Harvard University, 2015.

Grayson, Donald K., and David J. Meltzer. "Clovis Hunting and Large Mammal Extinction: A Critical Review of Evidence." *Journal of World Prehistory* 16 (2002): 313–359.

Green, Monica, ed. *Pandemic Disease in the Medieval World: Rethinking the Black Death.* Amsterdam: ARC Medieval Press, 2015.

Grumet, Robert S. *Historical Contact: Indian People and Colonists in Today's Northeastern United States in the Sixteenth through the Eighteenth Centuries.* Norman: University of Oklahoma Press, 1995.

Grumet, Robert S., ed. *Northeastern Indian Lives, 1632–1816.* Amherst: University of Massachusetts Press, 1996.

Grumet, Robert S. "Sunksquaws, Shamans, and Tradeswomen: Middle Atlantic Coastal Algonkian Women during the Seventeenth and Eighteenth Centuries." In *Women and Colonization: Anthropological Perspectives*, ed. Mona Etienne and Eleanor Burke Leacock, 43–62. New York: Praeger, 1980.

Guillemin, Jeanne. *Urban Renegades: The Cultural Strategies of American Indians.* New York: Columbia University Press, 1975.

Gura, Philip. *The Life of William Apess, Pequot.* Chapel Hill: University of North Carolina Press, 2015.

Haefli, Evan, and Kevin Sweeney. *Captors and Captives: The 1704 French and Indian Raid on Deerfield.* Amherst University of Massachusetts Press, 2003.

Haefli, Evan, and Kevin Sweeney. "Wattanummon's World: Personal and Tribal Identity in the Algonquian Diaspora." In *Actes du Vingt-Cinquieme Congres des Algonquinistes*, ed. William Cowan, 212–224. Ottawa: Carlton University Press, 1994.

Hall, Mary Emery. *Roger Williams.* Boston: Pilgrim, 1917.

Hammell, George R. "Mythical Realities and European Contact in the Northeast during the Sixteenth and Seventeenth Centuries," *Man in the Northeast* 33 (1987): 63–87.

Hankins, Jean Fittz. "Bringing the Good News: Protestant Missionaries to the Indians of New England and New York, 1700–1775." PhD diss., University of Connecticut, 1993.

Hanzeli, Victor. *Missionary Linguistics in New France: A Study of Seventeenth and Eighteenth Century Descriptions of American Indian Languages.* The Hague: Mouton, 1969.

Harrington, Faith. "Sea Tenure in Seventeenth Century New Hampshire: Native Americans and Englishmen in the Sphere of Coastal Resources." *Historical New Hampshire* 40, nos. 1–2 (1985): 18–33.

Hauptman, Laurence M., and James D. Wherry, eds. *The Pequots in Southern New England: The Fall and Rise of an American Indian Nation.* Norman: University of Oklahoma Press, 1990.

Haviland, William, and Marjory W. Power. *The Original Vermonters: Native Inhabitants, Past and Present.* Revised and expanded ed. Hanover, NH: University Press of New England, 1994.

Haynes, Gary. *The Early Settlement of North America: The Clovis Era.* New York: Cambridge University Press, 2002.

Heard, J. Norman. *Handbook of the American Frontier: Four Centuries of Indian-White Relationships,* Vol. 2, *The Northeastern Woodlands.* Lanham, MD: Scarecrow, 1990.

Hine, Robert V., and John Mack Faragher. *The American West: A New Interpretive History.* New Haven, CT: Yale University Press, 2000.

Huden, John C. *Indian Place Names of New England.* New York: Heye Foundation, 1962.

Hunter, Douglas. *The Place of Stone: Drighton Rock and the Erasure of America's Indigenous Past.* Chapel Hill: University of North Carolina Press, 2017.

Hutchins, Francis. *Mashpee: The Story of Cape Cod's Indian Town.* West Franklin, NH: Amarta, 1979.

Iverson, Peter. *"We Are Still Here": American Indians in the Twentieth Century.* Wheeling, IL: Harlan Davidson, 1998.

Jacobs, Margaret D. *A Generation Removed: The Fostering and Adoption of Indigenous Children in the Postwar World.* Lincoln: University of Nebraska Press, 2014.

Jacobs, Margaret D. *White Mother to a Dark Race: Settler Colonialism, Maternalism, and the Removal of Indigenous Children in the American West and Australia, 1880–1940.* Lincoln: University of Nebraska Press, 2009.

Jennings, Francis. *The Invasion of America: Indians, Colonialism, and the Cant of Conquest.* Chapel Hill: University of North Carolina Press, 1975.

Jones, David S. "The Persistence of American Indian Health Disparities." *American Journal of Public Health* 96, no. 12 (2006): 2122–2134.

Jones, David S. *Rationalizing Epidemics: Meanings and Uses of American Indian Mortality since 1600.* Cambridge, MA: Harvard University Press, 2004.

Jones, David S. "Virgin Soils Revisited." *William and Mary Quarterly* 60, no. 4 (2003): 703–742.

Kelly, Marc A., Paul S. Sledzik, and Sean P. Murphey. "Health, Demographics, and Physical Constitution in Seventeenth-Century Rhode Island Indians." *Man in the Northeast* 34 (1987): 1–25.

Kelly, Robert L., and Lawrence C. Todd. "Coming into the Country: Early Paleoindian Hunting and Mobility." *American Antiquity* 53, no. 2 (1988): 231–244.

Kent, Jeanne Morningstar. *The Visual Language of Wabanaki Art.* Charleston, SC: History Press, 2014.

Kidwell, Clara Sue. "Indian Women as Cultural Mediators." *Ethnohistory* 39, no. 2 (1992): 97–107.

Knapp, Henry M. "The Character of Puritan Missions: The Motivation, Methodology, and Effectiveness of the Puritan Evangelization of the Native Americans in New England." *Journal of Presbyterian History* 76, no. 2 (1998): 111–126.

Knowles, Nathaniel. "The Torture of Captives by the Indians of Eastern North America." *Proceedings of the American Philosophical Society* 82 (1940): 151–225.

Kowtko, Stacy. *Nature and Environment in Pre-Columbian American Life.* Westport, CT: Greenwood, 2006.

Kreech, Shephard. *The Ecological Indian: Myth and History.* New York: Norton, 2000.

Kupperman, Karen. *Indians and English: Facing Off in Early America.* Ithaca, NY: Cornell University Press, 2000.

Kupperman, Karen. "'Nature's Rude Garden': English and Indians as Producers and Consumers of Food in Early New England." *Comparative Civilization Review* 1 (1979): 64–78.

Kupperman, Karen. *Settling with the Indians: The Meeting of English and Indian Cultures in America, 1548–1640.* Totowa, NJ: Rowman and Littlefield, 1980.

Lane, Ambrose I. *Return of the Buffalo: The Story behind America's Indian Gaming Explosion*. Westport, CT: Bergin and Garvey, 1995.

Lapmarda, Vincent A. "The Jesuit Missions of Colonial New England." *Essex Institute Historical Collections* 126, no. 2 (1990): 91–109.

Larsen, Clark Spencer, and George R. Milner. *In the Wake of Contact: Biological Responses to Conquest*. New York: Wiley-Liss, 1994.

Lavin, Lucianne. *Connecticut's Indigenous Peoples: What Archaeology, History, and Oral Traditions Teach Us about Their Communities and Cultures*. New Haven, CT: Yale University Press, 2013.

Leach, Douglas. *Flintlock and Tomahawk: New England in King Philip's War*. New York: Macmillan, 1958.

Leavenworth, Peter. "'The Best Title That Indians Can Claime': Native American Agency and Consent in the Transferal of Penacook-Pawucket Land in the Seventeenth Century." *New England Quarterly* 72, no. 2 (1999): 275–300.

Lepore, Jill. *The Name of War: King Philip's War and the Origins of American Identity*. New York: Knopf, 1998.

Lepper, Bradley T., and Robert E. Funk. "Paleo-Indian: East." In *Handbook of North American Indians*, Vol. 3, *Environment, Origins, and Population*, ed. Douglas H. Ubelaker, 171–193. Washington, DC: Smithsonian Institution, 2006.

Levine, Mary Ann, Kenneth E. Sassaman, and Michael S. Nassaney. *The Archaeological Northeast*. Westport, CT: Bergin & Garvey, 1999.

Lipman, Andrew. *The Saltwater Frontier: Indians and the Contest for the American Coast*. New Haven, CT: Yale University Press, 2015.

Lopenzina, Drew. *Through an Indian's Looking Glass: A Cultural Biography of William Apess, Pequot*. Amherst: University of Massachusetts Press, 2017.

MacDougall, Pauleena. *The Penobscot Dance of Resistance: Tradition in the History of a People*. Hannover, NH: University Press of New England, 2004.

Malone, Patrick M. *The Skulking Way of War: Technology and Tactics among the New England Indians*. Lanham, MD: Madison Books, 2000.

Mancall, Peter C. *Deadly Medicine: Indians and Alcohol in Early America*. Ithaca, NY: Cornell University Press, 1995.

Mandell, Daniel R. *Behind the Frontier: Indians in Eighteenth Century Eastern Massachusetts*. Lincoln: University of Nebraska Press, 1996.

Mandell, Daniel R. *King Philip's War: Colonial Expansion, Native Resistance, and the End of Indian Sovereignty*. Baltimore: Johns Hopkins University Press, 2010.

Mandell, Daniel R. "Shifting Boundaries of Race and Ethnicity: Indian-Black Intermarriage in Southern New England, 1760–1880." *Journal of American History* 85, no. 2 (1998): 466–501.

Mandell, Daniel R. *Tribe, Race, History: Native Americans in Southern New England, 1780–1880*. Baltimore: Johns Hopkins University Press, 2007.

Mann, Charles. *1491: New Revelations of the Americas before Columbus*. New York: Vintage, 2006.

Mann, Charles. *1493: Uncovering the New World Columbus Created.* New York: Knopf, 2011.

Marr, John S., and John T. Cathey. "New Hypothesis for Cause of Epidemic among Native Americans, New England, 1616–1619." *Emerging Infectious Diseases* 16, no. 2 (2010): 281–286.

Martino, Gina M. "'As Potent a Prince as Any Round about Her': Rethinking Weetamoo of the Pocasset and Native Female Leadership in Early America." *Journal of Women's History* 27, no. 3 (2015): 37–60.

Martino, Gina M. *Women at War in the Borderlands of the Early American Northeast.* Chapel Hill: University of North Carolina Press, 2018.

Mavor, James W., Jr., and Bryon E. Dix. *Manitou: The Sacred Landscape New England's Native Civilization.* Rochester, VT: Inner Traditions, 1989.

McBride, Bunny. *Women of the Dawn.* Lincoln: University of Nebraska Press, 1999.

McBride, Bunny M., and Harald Prins. *Indians in Eden: Wabanakis and Rusticators on Mount Desert Island, 1840–1920.* Camden, ME: Down East Books, 2007.

McBride, Kevin A. "Archaic Subsistence in the Lower Connecticut River Valley: Evidence from Woodchuck Knoll." *Man in the Northeast* 15–16 (1978): 124–132.

McBride, Kevin A., Nanepashemet, Neal Salisbury, Neal McMullen, and Ann McMullen, comps. "Selected Bibliography of Algonkian Peoples in New England." *Annual Proceedings of the Dublin Seminar for New England Folklife* 16 (1991): 144–151.

McMullen, Ann. "Culture by Design: Native Identity, Historiography, and the Reclamation of Tradition in Twentieth Century Southeastern New England." PhD diss., Brown University, 1996.

McMullen, Ann. "Soapbox Discourse: Tribal Historiography, Indian-White Relations, and Southeastern New England Powwows." *Public Historian* 18, no. 4 (1996): 53–74.

Meltzer, David J. *First Peoples in a New World: Colonizing Ice Age America.* Berkeley: University of California Press, 2009.

Merchant, Carolyn. *Ecological Revolutions: Nature, Gender, and Science in New England.* 2nd ed. Chapel Hill: University of North Carolina Press, 2010.

Miller, Robert J. *Reservation "Capitalism": Economic Development in Indian Country.* Santa Barbara, CA: Praeger, 2012.

Miller, Virginia P. "Aboriginal Micmac Population: A Review of the Evidence." *Ethnohistory* 23(20) (1976): 117–127.

Moore, Cynthia Marie. "'Rent and Ragged Relation[s]': Puritans, Indians, and the Management of Congregations in New England, 1647–1776." PhD diss., State University of New York at Stony Brook, 1999.

Moorehead, Waren King. *The Merrimack Archaeological Survey: A Preliminary Paper.* Salem, MA: Peabody Museum, 1931.

Morrison, Dane. *A Praying People: Massachusetts Acculturation and the Failure of Puritan Mission, 1600–1690.* New York: Peter Lang Publishing, 1995.

Morrison, Kenneth M. *The Embattled Northeast: The Elusive Ideal of Alliance in Abenaki-Euramerican Relations.* Berkeley: University of California Press, 1984.

Nanepashemet. "It Smells Fishy to Me: An Argument Supporting the Use of Fish Fertilizer by the Native People of Southern New England." *Annual Proceedings of the Dublin Seminar for New England Folklife* 16 (1991): 42–50.

Nash, Alice N. "The Abiding Frontier: Family, Gender, and Religion in Wabanaki History, 1600–1763." PhD diss., Columbia University, 1997.

Nash, Alice N. "'None of the Women Were Abused': Indigenous Contexts for the Treatment of Women Captives in the Northeast." In *Sex without Consent: Rape and Sexual Coercion in America*, ed. Merrill Smith, 10–26. New York: New York University Press, 2001.

Nash, Alice, and Christoph Strobel. *Daily Life of Native Americans from Post-Columbian through Nineteenth-Century America.* Westport, CT: Greenwood, 2006.

Nash, Gary B. *Red White and Black: The Peoples of Early North America.* 3rd ed. Englewood Cliffs, NJ: Prentice Hall, 1992.

Newell, Margret Ellen. *Brethren by Nature: Indian Slavery in Colonial New England.* Ithaca, NY: Cornell University Press, 2015.

Nielsen, Donald M. "The Mashpee Indian Revolt of 1833." *New England Quarterly* 58 (1985): 400–420.

Oberg, Michael Leroy. *Uncas First of the Mohegans.* Ithaca, NY: Cornell University Press, 2003.

O'Brien, Jean M. *Dispossession by Degrees: Indian Land and Identity in Natick, Massachusetts, 1650–1790.* Cambridge: Cambridge University Press, 1997.

O'Brien, Jean M. *Firsting and Lasting: Writing Indians Out of Existence in New England.* Minneapolis: University of Minnesota Press, 2010.

Parkman, Francis. *France and New England in North America,* Vol 2. Edited by David Levin. New York: Library of America, 1983.

Pauketat, Timothy R. *Cahokia: Ancient America's Great City on the Mississippi.* New York: Viking, 2009.

Pauketat, Timothy R., ed. *The Oxford Handbook of North American Archaeology.* New York: Oxford University Press, 2012.

Pendergast, John. *The Bend in the River: A Prehistory and Contact History of Lowell, Chelmsford, Dracut, Tyngsborough, and Dunstable (Nashua, NH), Massachusetts.* Tyngsborough, MA: Merrimac River Press, 1991.

Philbrick, Nathaniel. *The Mayflower: A Story of Courage, Community, and War.* New York: Viking, 2006.

Pilling, James Constantine. *Bibliography of the Algonquian Languages.* Smithsonian Institution, Bureau of Ethnology, Bulletin no. 13. Washington, DC: U.S. Government Printing Office, 1891.

Piotrowski, Thaddeus, ed. *The Indian Heritage of New Hampshire and Northern New England.* Jefferson, NC: McFarland, 2002.

Plane, Anne. "The Examination of Sarah Ahaton: The Politics of Adultery in an Indian Town of Seventeenth-Century Massachusetts." In *Major Problems in American Women's History: Documents and Essays*, 2nd ed., ed. Mary B. Norton and Ruth Alexander, 14–25. Lexington, MA: D. C. Heath, 1995.

Porter, Frank, III, ed. *Strategies for Survival: American Indians in the Eastern United States.* New York: Greenwood, 1987.

Prashad, Vijay. *The Darker Nations: A People's History of the Third World.* New York: New Press, 2008.

Prins, Harald E. *The Mi'kmaq: Resistance, Accommodation, and Cultural Survival.* Fort Worth, TX: Harcourt Brace College Publishers, 1996.

Prins, Harald E. "New England's Algonquian Cultures." *American Indian Quarterly* 14, no. 3 (1990): 289–291.

Prins, Harald E. L., and Bruce Bourque. "Norridgewock: Village Translocation on the New England-Acadian Frontier." *Man in the Northeast* 33 (1987): 137–158.

Proctor, Mary A. *The Indians of the Winnipesaukee and Pemigewasset Valley.* Franklin, NH: Towne and Robie Publishers, 1930.

Pulsipher, Jenny Hale. *Subjects unto the Same King: Indians, English and the Contest for Authority in Colonial New England.* Philadelphia: University of Pennsylvania Press, 2005.

Pulsipher, Jenny Halle. *Swindler Sachem: The American Indian Who Sold His Birthright, Dropped Out of Harvard, and Conned the King of England.* New Haven, CT: Yale University Press, 2018.

Ranta, Judith A. *The Life and Writings of Betsey Chamberlain: Native American Mill Worker.* Boston: Northeastern University Press, 2003.

Rees-Miller, Jamie. "Stages in the Obsolescence of Certain Eastern Algonquian Languages." *Anthropological Linguistics* 40, no. 4 (1998): 535–569.

Rhodes, Richard A. "Language Shift in Algonquian." In *Language Obsolescence, Shift, and Death in Several Native American Communities*, ed. Allan R. Taylor, 87–92. New York: Mouton de Gruyter, 1992.

Richter, Daniel K. *Before the Revolution: America's Ancient Pasts.* Cambridge, MA: Harvard University Press, 2011.

Richter, Daniel K. *Facing East from Indian Country: A Native History of Early America.* Cambridge, MA: Harvard University Press, 2001.

Richter, Daniel. *The Ordeal of the Longhouse: The Peoples of the Iroquois League in the Era of European Colonization.* Chapel Hill: University of North Carolina Press, 1992.

Ritchie, William A. *The Archaeology of Martha's Vineyard.* Garden City, NY: Natural History Press, 1969.

Robbins, Maurice. *An Archaic Ceremonial Complex at Assawompsett.* Attleboro: Massachusetts Archaeological Society, 1968.

Robbins, Maurice, and George A. Agogino. "The Wapanucket No. 8 Site: A Clovis-Archaic Site in Massachusetts." *American Antiquity* 29, no. 4 (1964): 509–513.

Roeber, A. G., ed. *Ethnographies and Exchanges: Native Americans, Moravians, and Catholics in Early North America.* University Park: Penn State University Press, 2008.

Rolde, Neil. *Unsettled Past, Unsettled Future: The Story of Maine Indians.* Gardiner, ME: Tilbury House Publishers, 2004.

Romero, R. Todd. *Making War and Minting Christians: Masculinity, Religion, and Colonialism in Early New England.* Amherst: University of Massachusetts Press, 2011.

Rubertone, Patricia. *Grave Undertakings: An Archaeology of Roger Williams and the Narragansett Indians.* Washington, DC: Smithsonian Institution Press, 2001.

Rushforth, Brett. *Bonds of Alliance: Indigenous & Atlantic Slaveries in New France.* Chapel Hill: University of North Carolina Press, 2012.

Russell, Howard S. *Indian New England before the Mayflower.* Hanover, NH: University Press of New England, 1980.

Salisbury, Neal. "The Atlantic Northeast." In *The Oxford Handbook of American Indian History*, ed. Frederick E. Hoxie, 335–358. New York: Oxford University Press, 2016.

Salisbury, Neal. "Embracing Ambiguity: Native Peoples and Christianity in Seventeenth Century Massachusetts." *Ethnohistory* 50, no. 2 (2003): 247–259.

Salisbury, Neal. *The Indians of New England: A Critical Bibliography.* Bloomington: Indiana University Press, 1982.

Salisbury, Neal. "The Indians' Old World: Native Americans and the Coming of Europeans." *William and Mary Quarterly* 53, no. 3 (1996): 435–458.

Salisbury, Neal. *Manitou and Providence: Indians, Europeans, and the Making of New England, 1500–1643.* New York: Oxford University Press, 1981.

Salisbury, Neal. "'Red Puritans': The Praying Indians of Massachusetts Bay and John Eliot." *William and Mary Quarterly* 31, no. 1 (1974): 27–54.

Salisbury, Neal. "Religious Encounters in a Colonial Context: New England and New France in the Seventeenth Century." *American Indian Quarterly* 16, no. 4 (1992): 501–509.

Salisbury, Neal. "Squanto: Last of the Patuxets." *Struggle and Surivival in Colonial America.* Edited by David Sweet and Gary Nash. Berkeley: University of California Press, 1981.

Salisbury, Neal. "Toward the Covenant Chain: Iroquois and Southern New England Algonquians, 1637–1684." In *Beyond the Covenant Chain: The Iroquois and Their Neighbors in Indian North America, 1600–1800*, ed. Daniel K. Richter and James M. Merrell, 61–73. Syracuse, NY: Syracuse University Press, 1987.

Salwen, Bert. "Sea Levels and the Archaic Archaeology of the Northeast Coast of the United States." PhD diss., Columbia University, 1965.

Sanger, David. *Discovering Maine's Archaeological Heritage.* Augusta: Maine Historic Preservation Commission, 1979.

Sassaman, Kenneth E. *The Eastern Archaic, Historicized.* Lanham, MD: AltaMira, 2010.

Saunt, Claudio. *West of the Revolution: An Uncommon History of 1776.* New York: Norton, 2015.

Saxine, Ian. *Properties of Empire: Indians, Colonists, and Land Speculators on the New England Frontier.* New York: New York University Press, 2019.

Schmidt, Ethan A. *Native Americans in the American Revolution: How the War Divided, Devastated, and Transformed the Early American Indian World.* Santa Barbara, CA: Praeger, 2014.

Shaffer, Lynda Norene. *Native Americans before 1492: The Moundbuilding Centers of the Eastern Woodlands.* Armonk, NY: M. E. Sharpe, 1992.

Shoemaker, Nancy. *Native American Whalemen and the World: Indigenous Encounters and the Contingency of Race.* Chapel Hill: University of North Carolina
Press, 2015.

Shryock, Andrew, and Daniel Lord Smail, eds. *Deep History: The Architecture of
Past and Present.* Berkeley: University of California Press, 2011.

Silliman, Stephen. "Change and Continuity, Practice and Memory: Native American Persistence in Colonial New England." *American Antiquity* 74, no. 2
(2009): 211–230.

Silverman, David J. *Faith and Boundaries: Colonists, Christianity, and Community
among the Wampanoag Indians of Martha's Vineyard, 1600–1871.* New York:
Cambridge University Press, 2003.

Silverman, David J. *Red Brethren: The Brothertown and Stockbridge Indians and the
Problem of Race in Early America.* Ithaca, NY: Cornell University Press,
2010.

Silverman, David J. *Thundersticks: Firearms and the Violent Transformation of Native
America.* Cambridge, MA: Belknap, 2016.

Simmons, William S. *Spirit of the New England Tribes: Indian History and Folklore,
1620–1984.* Hanover, NH: University Press of New England, 1986.

Simmons, William S., and George F. Aubin. "Narragansett Kinship." *Man in the
Northeast* 9 (1975): 21–31.

Singerman, Robert. *Indigenous Languages of the Americas: A Bibliography of Disser-
tations and Theses.* Lanham, MD: Scarecrow, 1996.

Sleeper-Smith, Susan, ed. *Contesting Knowledge: Museums and Indigenous Perspectives.* Lincoln: University of Nebraska Press, 2009.

Sleeper-Smith, Susan, ed. *Rethinking the Fur Trade: Cultures of Exchange in an Atlantic World.* Lincoln: University of Nebraska Press, 2009.

Sleeper-Smith, Susan, Juliana Barr, Jean M. O'Brien, Nancy Shoemaker, and Scott
Manning Stevens, eds. *Why You Can't Teach United States History without
Native Americans.* Chapel Hill: University of North Carolina Press, 2015.

Slotkin, Richard. *Regeneration through Violence: The Mythology of the American
Frontier, 1600–1800.* Middletown, CT: Wesleyan University Press, 1973.

Smith, Bruce D. *Rivers of Change: Essays on Early Agriculture in Eastern North America.* Washington, DC: Smithsonian Institution, 1992.

Snow, Dean R. *The Archaeology of New England.* New York: Academic Press, 1980.

Snow, Dean R., and Kim Lanphear. "European Contact and Indian Depopulation
in the Northeast: The Timing of the First Epidemics." *Ethnohistory* 35(1)
(1988): 15–33.

Spady, James. "As If in Great Darkness: Native American Refugees of the Middle
Connecticut River Valley in the Aftermath of King Philip's War, 1677–
1697." *Historical Journal of Massachusetts* 23, no. 2 (1995): 183–197.

Speck, Frank G. *Penobscot Man: The Life History of a Forest Tribe in Maine.* Philadelphia: University of Pennsylvania Press, 1940.

Squire, Mariella Rose. "The Contemporary Western Abenakis: Maintenance,
Reclamation, and Reconfiguration of an American Indian Ethnic Identity." PhD diss., State University of New York at Albany, 1996.

Stannard, David E. *American Holocaust: The Conquest of the New World*. New York: Oxford University Press, 1992.

Starkey, Armstrong. *European and Native American Warfare, 1675–1815*. Norman: University of Oklahoma Press, 1998.

Starna, William A. "The Biological Encounter: Disease and the Ideological Domain." *American Indian Quarterly* 6, no. 4 (1992): 511–519.

Stewart-Smith, David. "The Pennacook Indians and the New England Frontier, Circa 1604–1733." PhD diss., Union Institute, 1998.

Strobel, Christoph. "Conquest and Colonization." In *The Routledge Handbook to the History and Society of the Americas*, ed. Olaf Kaltmeier et al., 75–83. New York: Routledge, 2019.

Strobel, Christoph. *The Global Atlantic, 1400–1900*. New York: Routledge, 2015.

Strobel, Christoph. "Indigenous Peoples of the Merrimack River Valley in the Early Seventeenth Century: An Atlantic Perspective on Northeastern America." *World History Connected* 16, no. 1 (2019), https://worldhistoryconnected .press.uillinois.edu/16.1/forum_strobel.html. Accessed June 4, 2019.

Strobel, Christoph. "Pawtucket and Wamesit: The Challenges of [Reconstructing the History of] Two New England Native Communities." In *Ethnicity in Lowell: Ethnographic Overview and Assessment*, ed. Robert Forrant and Christoph Strobel, 9–24. Boston: Northeast Region Ethnography Program, National Park Service, U.S. Department of the Interior, 2011.

Strobel, Christoph, and Robert Forrant. "'Into a New Canoe': Thinking and Teaching Locally and Globally about Native Americans on the Confluence of the Merrimack and the Concord Rivers." *New England Journal of History* 72, no. 2 (2016): 62–75.

Strong, John. "Shinnecock and Montauk Whalemen." *Long Island Historical Journal* 2, no. 1 (1989): 29–40.

Swedlund, Alan C. "Contagion, Conflict, and Captivity in Interior New England: Native American and European Contacts in the Middle Connecticut River Valley of Massachusetts, 1616–2004." In *Beyond Germs: Native Depopulation in North America,* ed. Catherine Cameron, Paul Kelton, and Alan Swedlund, 146–173. Tucson: University of Arizona Press, 2015.

Szasz, Margaret Connell. *Indian Education in the American Colonies, 1607–1783*. Albuquerque: University of New Mexico Press, 1988.

Tantaquidgeon, Gladys. *Folk Medicine of the Delaware and Related Algonkian Indians*. Harrisburg: Pennsylvania Historical Museum Commission, 1977.

Temin, Peter, ed. *Engines of Enterprise: An Economic History of New England*. Cambridge, MA: Harvard University Press, 2000.

Thomas, David H. *Exploring Ancient Native America*. New York: Routledge, 1999.

Thomas, G. E. "Puritans, Indians, and the Concept of Race." *New England Quarterly* 48, no. 1 (1975): 3–27.

Thomas, Peter A. "Contrastive Subsistence Strategies and Land Use as Factors for Understanding Indian-White Relations in New England." *Ethnohistory* 23, no. 1 (1976): 1–18.

Thomas, Peter A. "In the Maelstrom of Change: The Indian Trade and Cultural Process in the Middle Connecticut River Valley, 1635–1665." PhD diss., University of Massachusetts Amherst, 1979.

Thornton, Russell. *American Indian Holocaust and Survival: A Population History since 1492*. Norman: University of Oklahoma Press, 1987.

Tooker, Elisabeth. *The Indians of the Northeast: A Critical Bibliography*. Bloomington: Indiana University Press, 1978.

Tooker, Elisabeth. *Native North American Spirituality of the Eastern Woodlands*. New York: Paulist Press, 1979.

Trigger, Bruce G., ed. *Handbook of North American Indians: Northeast,* Vol. 15. Washington, DC: U.S. Government Printing Office, 1978.

Ubelaker, Douglas H. "North American Indian Population Size: Changing Perspectives." In *Disease and Demography in the Americas*, ed. John W. Verano and Douglas H. Ubelaker, 169–176. Washington, DC: Smithsonian, 1992.

Van Lonkhuyzen, Harold W. "A Reappraisal of the Praying Indians: Acculturation, Conversion, and Identity at Natick, Massachusetts 1646–1730." *New England Quarterly* 63, no. 3 (1990): 396–428.

Vaughan, Alden T. *New England Frontier: Puritans and Indians, 1620–1675*. 3rd ed. Norman: University of Oklahoma Press, 1995.

Vaughan, Alden T. *Transatlantic Encounter: American Indians in Britain, 1500–1776*. New York: Cambridge University Press, 2006.

Waldman, Carl, and Molly Braun. *Atlas of the North American Indian*. Revised ed. New York: Checkmark Books, 2000.

Waldman, Carl, and Molly Braun. *Word Dance: The Language of Native American Culture*. New York: Facts on File, 1994.

Warren, Wendy. *New England Bound: Slavery and Colonization in Early America*. New York: Liveright Publishing, 2016.

Waters, Wilson. *History of Chelmsford, Massachusetts*. Lowell: Courier Citizen Company, 1917.

Weaver, Jace. *The Red Atlantic: American Indigenes and the Making of the Modern World, 1000–1927*. Chapel Hill: University of North Carolina Press, 2014.

Weaver, John C. *The Great Land Rush and the Making of the Modern World, 1600–1900*. Montreal: McGill University Press, 2006.

Weinstein, Laurie, ed. *Enduring Traditions: The Native Peoples of New England*. Westport, CT: Bergin & Garvey, 1994.

Weinstein, Laurie. "We're Still Living on Our Traditional Homeland: The Wampanoag Legacy in New England." In *Strategies for Survival: American Indians in the Eastern United States,* ed. Frank W. Porter III, 85–112. Westport: CT: Greenwood, 1986.

Wheeler, Rachel. *To Live upon Hope: Mohicans and Missionaries in the Eighteenth-Century Northeast*. Ithaca, NY: Cornell University Press, 2008.

White, Richard. *The Middle Ground: Indians, Empires and Republics in the Great Lakes Region, 1650–1815*. New York: Cambridge University Press, 1991.

Wilbur, Keith C. *The New England Indians*. Old Saybrook, CT: Globe Pequot, 1996.

Williams, Robert A., Jr. *The American Indian in Western Legal Thought: The Discourses of Conquest*. New York: Oxford University Press, 1992.

Wiseman, Frederick Matthew. *Reclaiming the Ancestors: Decolonizing a Taken Prehistory of the Far Northwest*. Hanover, NH: University Press of New England, 2005.

Wiseman, Frederick Matthew. *The Voice of the Dawn: An Autohistory of the Abenaki Nation*. Hanover, NH: University Press of New England, 2001.

Wolf, Eric R. *Europe and the People without History*. Berkeley: University of California Press, 1982.

Wroth, Lawrence C. *The Voyages of Giovanni da Verrazzano, 1524–1528*. New Haven, CT: Yale University Press, 1970.

Wyss, Hilary. *Writing Indians: Literacy, Christianity, and Native American Community in Early America*. Amherst: University of Massachusetts Press, 2000.

Websites of Indigenous Communities of New England

Aroostook Band of Micmacs, http://www.micmac-nsn.gov/html/history.html.

Cowasuck Band of the Pennacook Abenaki People, http://www.cowasuck.org.

Eastern Pequot Reservation, http://www.easternpequottribalnation.com.

Houlton Band of Maliseet Indian, http://www.maliseets.com/index.htm.

Indian Township Passamaquoddy Tribe, https://www.passamaquoddy.com.

Mashantucket Pequot Museum and Research Center, https://www.mptn-nsn.gov/default.aspx.

Mashpee Wampanoag Tribe, http://www.mashpeewampanoagtribe-nsn.gov.

Mohegan Tribe, https://www.mohegan.nsn.us.

Narragansett Nation, http://narragansettindiannation.org.

Nipmuc Nation, http://www.nipmucnation.org.

Passamaquoddy at Sipayik (Pleasant Point), https://www.wabanaki.com.

Penobscot Nation, https://www.penobscotnation.org/r-home.

Schaghticoke Tribal Nation, http://schaghticoke.com.

Wampanoag Tribe of Gay Head/Aquinnah, http://www.wampanoagtribe.net/.

Newspapers and Documentaries

Administrator. "The Penobscot Indian Nation Now Molds High-Tech Parts For Aviation." *Plastics Today*, December 21, 1998, https://www.plasticstoday.com/content/penobscot-indian-nation-now-molds-high-tech-parts-aviation/9891179041045. Accessed May 2, 2019.

Cook, Robert M. "Tribal Works: Defense Contracts Position Penobscots for Long-Awaited Prosperity." *Mainebiz*, August 23, 2010, https://www.mainebiz.biz/article/tribal-works-defense-contracts-position-penobscots-for-long-awaited-prosperity. Accessed May 2, 2019.

Flisiuk, Francis. "'Maine Has Its Own Standing Rock'—The Penobscot River Fight Explained." *Conway Daily Sun*, October 1, 2017, https://www.conwaydaily sun.com/portland_phoenix/news/maine-has-its-own-standing-rock ---the-penobscot/article_5a1679fa-a800-5f89-9e71-c5a7b63222c2.html. Accessed April 18, 2019.

Kim, E. Tammy. "The Passamaquoddy Reclaim Their Culture through Digital Repatriation." *New Yorker*, January 30, 2019, https://www.newyorker.com /culture/culture-desk/the-passamaquoddy-reclaim-their-culture -through-digital-repatriation. Accessed January 31, 2019.

Mazo, Adam, and Ben Pender Cudlip, dirs. *Dawnland: Documentary*. PBS: Independent Lens, 2018.

Reidy, Chris, and Janette Neuwahl. "Legislature Votes to Repeal 1675 Hub Ban on Indians." *Boston Globe*, May 20, 2005.

Spector, Zeke. "A Native American Tribe Is Using Traditional Culture to Fight Addiction." VICE News, March 15, 2018, https://news.vice.com/en_ca /article/59knjz/a-native-american-tribe-is-using-traditional-culture-to -fight-addiction. Accessed August 13, 2018.

Stening, Tanner. "Mashpee and Tribe Officials Hold Rare Joint Meeting." *Cape Cod Times*, March 5, 2018, http://capecodtimes.com/news/20180305 /mashpee-and-tribe-officials-hold-rare-joint-meeting. Accessed April 24, 2019.

Villeneuve, Marina. "Maine Tribe Pushes in Court to Retain Strict Water Quality Standards." centralmaine.com, December 7, 2018, https://www.central maine.com/2018/10/30/maine-tribes-are-skeptical-of-federal-move-to -revisit-river-water-standards/?rel=related. Accessed December 13, 2018.

Wurmfeld, Becka. "Neighbourhood: At Conscience Point." BBC World Service, August 15, 2018, https://www.bbc.co.uk/programmes/w3csxh4h. Accessed August 27, 2018.

Index

About the Author

Christoph Strobel is professor of history at the University of Massachusetts Lowell. He is author of *The Global Atlantic: 1400–1900* and *The Testing Grounds of Modern Empire* and coauthor, with Alice Nash, of *Daily Life of Native Americans from Post-Columbian through Nineteenth-Century America*. Strobel has published three books on immigration, and his scholarly essays appear in many academic journals and in various edited collections.